Quantum Psychology

QUANTUM
PSYCHOLOGY

Steps to a Postmodern Ecology of Being

STEPHEN T. DeBERRY

 PRAEGER

Westport, Connecticut
London

Library of Congress Cataloging-in-Publication Data

DeBerry, Stephen.
    Quantum psychology : steps to a postmodern ecology of being /
Stephen T. DeBerry.
      p. cm.
    Includes bibliographical references and index.
    ISBN 0–275–94171–X (alk. paper)
    1. Psychology—Philosophy.   2. Clinical psychology—Philosophy.
3. Quantum theory. I. Title.
    BF38.D42   1993
    150′.1—dc20   92–28474

British Library Cataloguing in Publication Data is available.

Library of Congress Catalog Card Number: 92–28474
ISBN: 0–275–94171–X

First published in 1993

Praeger Publishers, 88 Post Road West, Westport, CT 06881
An imprint of Greenwood Publishing Group, Inc.

Printed in the United States of America

The paper used in this book complies with the
Permanent Paper Standard issued by the National
Information Standards Organization (Z39.48–1984).

10 9 8 7 6 5 4 3 2 1

This book is dedicated to Jed and Nicole,
who after an infinity,
have reentered my life in a quantum way

Contents

Preface

I suppose, then, that all the things that I see are false...

Descartes

This book represents the culmination of ideas I have been cultivating for the past three decades. It is written mainly for scientist-philosophers or, dependent on one's intellectual persuasion, philosopher-scientists. Since my audience represents an educated and critically thinking population, I feel it would be appropriate to present my intentions in writing such a volume.

Twenty or so years ago, when I first wanted to write about my impressions of American culture and self-development, I discovered, much to my regret, that because I could not financially support my family or myself, such an endeavor was practically impossible. Even then, I became angry at what I perceived as the unacknowledged inverse correlation between pragmatic social philosophy and money—an association that, if anything, has since multiplied. The resolution of this predicament resulted in my obtaining a PhD in clinical psychology, a profession that, to my estimate, represented a very marketable commodity. Indeed, 12 years following my doctorate and on earning Diplomate status, this youthful perception has more than proven to be true. Professional success as a clinical psychologist has, however, led me to some depressing conclusions about the specialty's current condition. I have discovered that my effort to cultivate both a bankable and thinking profession has, paradoxically, resulted in my no longer being expected to think—that is, at least, to think, in a broader, more pragmatic sense about what is occurring in the Nation.

All that is really expected of me is the application of specific clinical "techniques," grounded within precise and accepted paradigms of an all too exclusive practitioner's club. Essentially, I am expected, even by the people who willingly choose to consult with me, to "fix them," or, to phrase it in the contemporary vernacular, get them to "function." In the depths of my being, I find these circumstances both reprehensible and morally corrupt, a condition that, I must confess, is my principal reason for writing this book. As clinical psychology becomes increasingly commercialized, so too does general education and eventually, unless something is done, we might all be functioning like workers in an ant colony. Instead of immersing ourselves in pecuniary arguments over the scientist-practitioner versus the clinical-practitioner models and devoting time to the American Psychological Association's policy of "marketing psychology," the profession could devote more thought to a social or philosophical-practitioner approach.

Two primary groups that I am addressing in the text are new students in clinical psychology and mental health who, hopefully, will see that to be truly alive and healthy, more than formula, technique and functioning are necessary. The second group represents my colleagues, and I do employ this term in the most general of ways. I would like to provoke a cross disciplinary dialogue, similar to what Heinz Pagels (1989) termed the horizontal integration of different disciplines. With this in mind, it is not my intention to be "methodologically or logically" correct, but rather, to provoke thought and discussion. As separate disciplines converge, we can initially expect the waters to be somewhat muddied. As time goes on and the epistemological integration of different disciplines proceeds, new clarity can be achieved.

Clinical psychology, psychiatry and the entire "mental health establishment" desperately require the synthesis of alternative perspectives, particularly those of anthropology, politics, sociology and the creative and liberal arts. Since the book is written from the perspective of a clinical psychologist, in all likelihood it will be in the above areas that the reader finds the text most deficient. Undoubtedly, there is a rather large portion of this literature that I will have failed to notice. To those authors whom I have forgotten to mention, or, who in the past have espoused similar perspectives, I offer my apologies and desire for future dialogue. As science becomes more specialized, we all become increasingly fragmented and alienated from each other's work. This isolation is, I believe, a serious deterrent to practical progress and forces us to inquire why the alienation the social sciences were designed to remedy has become a malady of the profession itself.

Having seduced the reader into reading at least this much of the book, my next hope is that the material will be approached with an open mind. Since the text concerns itself with consciousness, it becomes fairly obvious that my perspective will be a personal one. The openness that I request of the reader has to do with two factors: (1) the awareness that one's conception of the world is a socially constructed reality (SCR) and (2) the acceptance that numerous SCRs are possible (Cushman, 1991; Gergen, 1973; Smedslund, 1985). The acceptance of these basic premises changes the evaluation of ideas from deciding whether they are right or wrong to testing their "goodness of fit." By goodness of fit I refer to the degree to which axioms can construct "optimal" conditions for the development of individual and community consciousness (Bergin, 1991; DeBerry, 1991).

In order to improve readability, I have deliberately omitted most direct references from the main chapters of the text and instead have used substantive footnotes, concentrating references within the preface and initial chapters. Likewise for the sake of smooth reading, I have limited myself to the use of masculine pronouns. When referring to abstract persons, the consistent use of the masculine pronouns should not be interpreted as exclusionary because no implications with respect to gender are intended.

Finally, I have deliberately ignored a rather large body of Eastern philosophy that many would consider especially germane to this book. I have done this for several reasons, the most prominent being that many others, in a more scholarly and eloquent manner, have already accomplished this.

On this note, let us begin our introduction into quantum psychology.

Acknowledgments

I would like to express my appreciation to the following people whose welcome presence contributed to the book's completion. My thanks to Linda who graciously accepted my submersion in thought and resulting refusal to go the movies; to Julian, for napping and getting in the sandbox with me; to Brian, for knowing *resonance*, constantly validating my ideas and helping me resolve my anger; to Scott, for being the first new friend in 10 years who is *responsive* and to Dr. Marjorie Miller for being a patient philosopher who helped clarify my thoughts. Recognition is also extended to my editor, Paul Macirowski, and Praeger Publishers for their willingness to present new ideas. Finally, I would like to thank and acknowledge all the people I have ever *connected* with whose *interactions* make this book possible. Hopefully, this book will place both past and future involvement within a perspective that makes some sense.

Quantum Psychology

Introduction

Once again, human perception of things seems out of step with reality.
Nick Herbert

Within the science of physics, the past 60 years have witnessed a quiet and consistent, yet radical, revolution. The theories of Dirac, Bohm, Schrödinger, Heisenberg and Bohr have supplanted Newton, Descartes, Galileo and even, to an extent, Einstein. The revolution, called quantum mechanics, is now the accepted theory of the physical universe. Yet, despite the enormous philosophical and scientific implications of quantum mechanics, very little of it has found its way into psychology. Psychology still remains a science steeped in the classical Cartesian dualism and Newtonian mechanics of the nineteenth century. The present work may be considered a beginning attempt to integrate quantum theory into psychological thought.

As a way of introducing quantum psychology I would like to start with consciousness. Quantum psychology is a psychology of consciousness and, as such, is reflective of the entire process of being. Because consciousness is involved, quantum psychology must also be considered a psychology of experience. Because quantum psychology concerns itself with experience, it is an empirical psychology.

Admittedly, the topic of consciousness could be considered too vast an arena for the introduction of a new psychology. However, because consciousness is regarded as one of the more salient features of living organisms, I feel it is a good place to start. The book, therefore, can be classified as a general introduction to quantum psychology that provides basic formulations that may be used as a springboard for future development.

For many reasons consciousness is considered an unscientific subject, and with few exceptions, clinical psychology does not really concern itself with the subject.[1] This is, of course, rather odd considering that (1) most people would consider themselves conscious and (2) physics is moving closer to embracing consciousness as a necessary and, perhaps most essential, element of the universe itself. Physicists consider consciousness not only an integral part of the universe but also a builder of the cosmos, a process that in part *constructs* the world (Davies, 1983; Pagels, 1982, 1989; Penrose, 1989).

Because quantum psychology represents a significant departure from traditional psychology, the development of a suitable format in which to present my ideas entailed a rather peculiar struggle. On one hand, my intention was to present a new *psychology* while avoiding the pitfalls of classical psychology. The problem with this approach is that psychology has become far too large and fragmented a discipline in which new ideas can easily be introduced (Bevan, 1991). The American Psychological Association now lists 48 divisions of supposedly separate subspecialties. Thus, psychology, like many other sciences in the postmodern age, is becoming increasingly overspecialized. Changes or discoveries in one division often go unrecognized in other divisions that could benefit from the new knowledge. Although my perspective and concerns are those of a clinically trained psychologist, I nevertheless feel that the ideas presented here can be of interest not only to psychologists but also to all critical thinkers.

My intention is not to formulate only a new clinical perspective, but to formulate one that can be utilized to better understand the bewildering complexities of postmodern life. I am in agreement with the evolutionary scientist Erich Jantsch (1980) who believes that "false paradigms" and expectations are becoming an increasingly serious threat to our existence. The contemporary social sciences, especially clinical psychology, often unknowingly operate under false paradigms. The mistaken nature of paradigms can be identified by certain pragmatic liabilities the paradigm maintains. One liability of classical clinical psychology is its overreliance on constructing linear explanatory models.

LINEAR FACTORS

Linear factors are causal and presuppose a direct relationship between events. Direct relationships, like serial electronic circuits, are usually simple and fairly straightforward. Ilya Prigogine (1976), a pioneer researcher in the non-linear aspects of dissipative structures claims that most classical science concerns itself with the equilibrium of linearity.[2]

Essentially, quantum psychology is an indirect, non-linear approach that is rather complex and hardly straightforward at all. Yet, quantum psychology also incorporates direct relationships and may, therefore, be considered a more general and inclusive clinical psychology. Because it incorporates both linear and non-linear phenomena, quantum psychology encompasses and extends the classical clinical model.

Normally, direct relationships are obvious and require simple causative explanations. Such causative explanations typically are of a linear—A causes B causes C—nature. For explaining certain situations, linear direct explanations work very well. For the intricate and often exasperating daily predicaments of the late twentieth century they are barely adequate. Far too often, we have been satiated and satisfied by the pablum of linear simplicity. As Maruyama states, "We have been misguided, by the traditional mainstream 'scientific' logic of unidirectional causality and by the model of classical physics, into believing that (these rules) are not only the rules of the universe but also the desirable goals of our society" (1976, p. 202).

Overreliance on linear thought affects all levels of social interaction. The general perception of the relationship between drugs and crime provides an excellent cultural example. Politically, the relationship is perceived directly as drugs (A) causing crime (B) causing the need for increased law enforcement (C), as a means of resolving the drug problem. Thus, an appealing, simple linear A–B–C model is erroneously employed as a solution to increasingly complex and systemic social issues. The formalization, or simplistic reduction, of social factors to a few linear indicators does not represent a step toward either understanding or amelioration. As Vega and Murphy (1990) state:

In more sociological terms, social indicators do not necessarily supply any insight into the causes of behavior. A does not strictly lead to B, because these or other social factors are complex processes that do not exist in a vacuum. Variables such as these are mediated by human presence, because human action cannot be separated neatly from knowledge. However, when the attempt is made to conceptualize social life dualistically, roles, norms, and laws gain a sense of autonomy. These structural factors are not only thought to cause behavior, but serve as *a referent for judging normativeness*. (my emphasis) (p. 25)

In contrast, a quantum psychological approach employs non-linear as well as linear models of description. Non-linear explanatory paradigms are common in quantum physics, artificial intelligence or chaos theory but are relatively absent in psychology. For purposes of this introduction, linearity may be associated with logical and rational thought and non-linearity with intuitive and irrational thought. In most cases, psychological models, especially those of a clinical or developmental nature, have been skewed in a linear direction. This bias has resulted in a significant paucity of research and theory concerning consciousness, a phenomenon that by nature can be intrinsically non-linear.

We have been fooled into thinking that in order for consciousness to be legitimate it has to be rational, when in actuality, it has identifiable irrational components. This is a fundamental misconception of our Western materialistic bias, a bias firmly rooted in our sociopolitical-economic traditions, which neither accepts nor understands the irrational. By eliminating the irrational from our mode of experience we have constructed a lopsided existence that directly affects the quality of our lives. Crime, drug abuse, violence, suicide, greed, exploitation, racism and sexism are all by-products of our one-sided consciousness. Because the irrational is an intrinsic dimension of the operation of consciousness, a unidimensional consciousness is not conducive to the development of a healthy state of being. Quite clearly, what the U.S. culture perceives as irrational is the emotional or affective dimension of reality processing. The very notion of a phrase like "reality processing" denotes quantum psychology's affinity with the constructivist model.

EXPLANATORY MODELS

Linear causative models are created as explanatory vehicles. Because such models purport to explain things, they tend to persist and predominate. A more accurate statement would be to say that linear models *appear* to explain things. Because very few things are as satisfying as a good explanation, the objectivist bias of a real and consistent external reality with predictable and rational explanations endures. Objectivists, who believe in a discoverable and explainable external world existing independent of the consciousness of the observer, offer a perspective that traditional *clinical and applied* psychology is still distorted toward. There are times, of course, when explanations are quite useful, but explanations can be used for the wrong reasons and, at times, are spoon-fed to us to assuage anxiety and alleviate fear. Although helpful, they can also be red herrings that limit perspective and hide realistic, and usually more painful, revelations and questions. If a model adequately explains something, very often further exploration is inhibited. Numerous scientists have proposed that such models can either inhibit or dictate the direction of scientific inquiry, providing the illusion of answers to questions that really have no *definite* answers or even represent the wrong questions (Kuhn, 1970; Lakatos, 1974; Popper, 1959, 1972; Weimer, 1982; Youngdale, 1988). Very often, psychologists accumulate volumes of the correct answers to irrelevant questions. This type of explanatory model has been the hallmark of official institutions as well as the plethora of pop psychological theories that flood our sensibilities with euphemistic nonsense. As the eminent physicist/mathematician Roger Penrose (1989) notes, most theories can barely pass the muster of authentic scrutiny.

In place of developing linear causative models, constructing theories or creating explanatory paradigms, I would like to substitute a more empirical approach. I employ the term empirical very much in the classical sense of the word: a word that denotes pristine sensory observation. Empiricism is the key foundation for a quantum understanding of experience. It is, of course, impossible to develop new ideas without constructing some sort of new theoretical structure. As much as is possible, I will constrain myself to observation and limit excess theoretical baggage. Essentially, observations, especially as related to consciousness, will be explored from a quantum—non-linear, intuitive—perspective.

Such a perspective must include the factors most essential to the understanding of conscious experience. Therefore, connected to the general theme of consciousness will be the subjects of relationships, community and culture. It is within relationships, with ourselves, others (animals included) or the material world that consciousness expresses itself. Consciousness is always *in relation to something*. Communities, from families to larger groups, are the context within which relationships occur. Culture is almost always the substructure in which the values of any given family or community originate. A complex reciprocal relationship exits between consciousness, community and culture. In part, it is culture that forms our consciousness and consciousness that modifies our culture. Communities are the vehicles by which these transactions take place. No adequate discussion of quantum psychology and consciousness could exist without an exploration of modern community and culture.

PSYCHOLOGY AND CONSCIOUSNESS

Theologians, philosophers and scientists, especially in earlier centuries, have been fascinated with *consciousness*. Its nature, operation, structure and reason for being have always been areas of curious inquiry. Is consciousness a property of being human or do all creatures have it? Is the universe conscious? Is God representative of a supreme consciousness? These are just a few of the questions that can be raised, and although they are important questions, the topic of consciousness has all but been ignored by contemporary psychology. Most of the recent work on consciousness has been the offspring of physicists and mathematicians. Some of these writings are brilliant, whereas others remain vague metaphysical speculation.

CONSCIOUSNESS AND THE SELF

One of my principal interests concerns the relationship of consciousness to what we call our present identity, or the process of Self-development. A lot of confusion remains as to exactly what the Self is. The development of the personal identity structure we call our *Self* is a central theme of this book. The genesis and development of the Self is an incredibly complex process, a miracle and mystery of evolution and individual development. Yet, psychology and the mental health profession deal with issues of human development in a curiously linear and limited manner. Within psychology, the traditional answer to the question of human development revolves around issues of "developmental stages."

In that it is assumed that people undergo internal developmental transformations, developmental stages are always discussed as occurring within the individual. Paradoxically, however, these hypothetical *internal* changes are always measured against *external* standards. People are placed within a developmental framework in which individual development is compared with the progress of others. Again paradoxically, we consider the external standards static and internal development fluid. Basically, we expect internal dynamics to conform to specific and fixed external standards of development. Certain markers are established for "normalcy," whereas other signs are decided on as representing "psychopathology." To quote William Vega and John Murphy:

As Michael Foucalt writes, clients are approached as ideal persons, who do not have a unique biography. In this sense, health and illness are conceptualized as if these ideas do not have any relationship to social existence. . . . That is, technical procedures are used to collect information and render decisions. The problem is that an extremely sterile image of social life is preferred. . . . Key to success in this endeavor is technical competence, whereby value-free procedures are invoked to generate valid evidence. (1990, pp. 24–25)

Under these technical conditions, maturation becomes both comparative and competitive, relying on normative comparisons similar to being in school. There are unfailing rules or laws of development that everyone follows and receives grades for. Perhaps the example of my son can be an illustration.

When Julian was five months old he was taken to see his pediatrician. The doctor inquired as to whether or not Julian was mimicking our facial expressions. We replied that he had yet to behave in such a way and asked the pediatrician why she had questioned this. She stated that comparatively, at five months old, it was developmentally normal for infants to mimic facial expressions. The doctor then went on to say that she was "concerned" and inquired if we wished a referral to a pediatric neurologist. Feeling that Julian was otherwise healthy, we decided that he seemed to be meeting the world according to his own schedule and thus declined the referral.

At approximately 15 months, Julian began to exuberantly mimic us. When he returned to the pediatrician for an examination, she noticed his behavior and inquired as to when it started. On hearing our answer, with a concerned look she nervously asked if we had second thoughts about that neurological referral. Such idiosyncratic behavior was "clearly off the developmental timetable."

This illustration is, I believe, fairly common experience for parents. Because not everyone has the luxury of being well informed, such "expert" warnings are often quite alarming. We are constantly being graded, measured and compared in terms of how we "fit in." Grades may be disguised as wealth, social status, power or the material acquisitions that have become symbols of success, progress, normalcy and accepted development. Because these symbols are embraced by what seems to be a majority of people in our culture, they are often called the *establishment* or *traditional* success symbols of our society. Within this value system, a system currently dominant in both psychology and psychiatry, little attention is paid to a very important phenomenon; the ecological implications of consciousness.

ECOLOGY AND CONSCIOUSNESS

Traditionally, ecology is perceived as an environmental discipline. This is partially true but does not completely represent the way I am using the word. The term ecology can also refer to the human environment, the kaleidoscopic and incredibly complex series of interpersonal and intrapersonal variables that influence and, in essence, determine our identity and development. An ecology of the self, so to speak.

Ecology is basically a systems approach, an orientation especially suited to quantum psychology. A systems discipline like ecology maintains an evolutionary, holistic perspective that describes an interconnected universe in which everything that occurs in some way affects everything else.[3] Nothing is isolated and no one is an individual. What happens to the individual affects and influences the community, just as what occurs in one's community must have impact on the individual. According to Erich Jantsch:

Evolution, or order of process, is more than just a paradigm for the biological domain; it is a view of how a *totality* that hangs together in all of its interactive processes moves. This dynamic totality spans a vast spectrum from subatomic processes to social and further on to noetic (mental and psychic) processes. (1976, p. 9)

This statement may sound rather odd coming as it does at the height of the "me" decade and the worship of the independent and separate individual, but it is nevertheless, at least for now, worth considering. After all, no one has yet claimed excessive happiness from too much individuality. In fact, numerous signs indicate that a new era is coming and that we are leaving the individualistic excesses of the "me" decade. Essentially, we are more interconnected than is realized. This is true not only on the level of individual relationships but also in terms of the growing global economy and community of nations. In essence, we are all an integral part of a very vast and complex system. This perspective is similar to what Jantsch terms "process teleology," a position that views "human existence at all levels simultaneously by virtue of homologous relations across all levels. Social relations, cultural values and mankind paradigms all result from processes expressing themselves through the individual" (1976, p. 62).

QUANTUM PHYSICS

Actually, if I may stretch this comparison, the system I am talking about is nothing short of the entire universe itself. People are more than just an isolated part of the universe, we are an interconnected part. In a sense, we are the universe or, to put it more succinctly, we are part of the universe looking at itself. The classic anthropometric cosmic view is that the universe is the way it is because from our unique position of time and space we see it as such. In the words of a classic oriental aphorism, "we are that in which the Earth comes to appreciate itself" (Lockwood, 1989).

The title of this book owes a debt to quantum physics because quantum science has ushered in a slowly growing revolution of philosophy and thought that is only barely beginning to touch the psychological sciences. The Latin word *quantum* is translated as "as much," but, in the manner in which physicists employ it, quantum means an "indivisible lump or package." It turns out that the practical implications of quantum physics are closely related to ecology, a discipline that stresses the indivisible and holistic aspects of our environment. The conditions that determine the development of consciousness also include all aspects of the environment and must be considered a total package.

The difference between quantum psychology and traditional or classical psychology is briefly described in the Quantum Model.

QUANTUM FACTORS	CLASSICAL FACTORS
non-linear	linear
holistic	reductionistic
normal	abnormal
dynamic	fixed
non-local	local
synergistic	mechanistic
irrational	rational

Written in lowercase letters, *quantum and classical factors* emphasize the postulated divergence between the two models, whereas the capitalized *Quantum Model* indicates that both classical and quantum factors are subsumed within the Quantum Model. Quantum psychology does not *replace* but rather augments the classical model.

Another crucial point concerning quantum psychology is that it is based on the principle of *emergent interactionism*. The term, which originated from the work of Roger Walcot Sperry (1987) on consciousness and the mind/body problem, has a solid philosophical basis in the science of complex systems. Emergent interactionism is also related to the concepts of existential and functional emergence, which state respectively that

1. in the course of the complex evolution of systems certain properties and processes may arise that previously never existed and that knowledge of such existents, or emergents, cannot be understood based on the knowledge that previously existed; and

2. the functioning of emergent systems cannot be reduced to a single theory but depends on the often novel interaction of different organizational systems.

Quantum psychology represents an emergent system of understanding consciousness that has been exposed to the complex and *accelerating* effects of a *postmodern* culture. It is a step toward augmenting the singularity of traditional psychological theories with the plurality of a quantum perspective. A statement from Richard L. Gregory in reference to the phenomenon of emergence is most applicable here:

(It) implies that the biological and medical sciences are essentially outside the kinds of explanation by reductive analyses that have proved so powerful in the natural sciences. If this is so, biology (*and psychology even more so*) [my emphasis] would seem to be essentially different in kind from physics. (1987, p. 217)

The similarities and differences of the classical and quantum models are explained in detail in subsequent chapters.

Physicists and mathematicians have written numerous books on quantum physics and consciousness. After reading many of these books, a nagging uneasiness plagued me. Although it seemed clear that physicists and mathematicians understood a great deal about the mathematics and theory of quantum mechanics, they were rather perplexed concerning its pragmatic philosophical and psychological implications. Everyone agrees that consciousness is an integral part of quantum theory, but there is little agreement as to what consciousness is. Not only is no one really certain *what* consciousness is, but there is little agreement concerning *who* has it. No one seems at all certain what quantum theory has to do with the psychology of our daily lives. In contrast, consciousness is the cornerstone of a quantum psychological approach that comprehends it as an evolving and dynamic process. Throughout its abundant transformations, consciousness has always represented a true mirror of experience, and hence of existence itself. Consciousness should never be ignored, because in its inclusion and exclusion of information and experiences it conveys a unique picture of what it is like to be human.

In an earlier book on consciousness I asked the question, Why is it that what my "patients" are conscious of I am sometimes also conscious of? Why are they the patients and I the doctor? What is it about their consciousness that has caused them to be labeled as mentally ill? If their consciousness is "sick," then why does it share some common elements with mine? Is it that I am also sick? Hopefully, some answers to these questions will begin with this book. As in my previous work, I expect to produce more questions than answers. But, because I consider questions to be a sign of intelligence, I firmly believe that asking the *right* questions will begin to lead to answers.

NOTES

1. There are, of course, exceptions to this statement, the most notable being the recent *Consciousness Explained* by Daniel C. Dennett (1991). I picked up this excellent volume only a week ago and have the distinct feeling that Daniel Dennett, the Director of Cognitive Studies and a distinguished Arts and Sciences Professor at Tufts University, is not a clinical psychologist.

2. The term dissipative refers to the fact that in order to exist, such structures must constantly dissipate entropy so that equilibrium cannot be reached.

3. Although ecological psychology and clinical ecology have become important disciplines, their emphasis is on the relationship of the environment to the individual, whereas my approach focuses on the ecological relationship of the person to culture. Refer to S. Stokols (1992).

One

The Classical Model

Nothing is proved, all is permitted.

Theodore Dreiser

Why should quantum psychology exist? Is there really a need for yet another form of psychology? The answer, with three principle qualifications, is yes. The main stipulation is that the topic itself must be understood as new and in its early stages of both conceptualization and development. In this sense, it must be accepted as *a work or perspective in progress*.

It is not my intention to either proselytize or pretentiously develop *the* new psychological theory of existence, nor do I intend to offer a new theory of human consciousness. There now exists a rather abundant garden of consciousness theories. The last thing we need is another untestable cognitive map. Rather, I would like to extend a new way of looking at our *being in this world*—in short, the same data observed from another perspective. My desire to do so stems in part from the inadequacies of contemporary psychological models of human development. Currently, the predominant model in clinical psychology and psychiatry is a biological-cognitive-behavioral or biopsychosocial paradigm. This is the standard model that "experts" in human behavior use to decide who is, and who is not, a well-adjusted member of society. Because models partially determine how we behave on this planet, the ones we use are matters of ultraimportance.

The current models are no longer working, and it is time to admit that without a shift of perspective we are all in trouble. The United States has one of the highest rates of homicide and suicide in the world. The numbers of homeless and so-called "underclass" citizens are increasing. Politicians are becoming wealthier while the actuality of true system change becomes increasingly difficult. Children are dying in our streets, innocent victims of mindless and rageful drug wars. The gap between an ever increasing underclass and the wealthier section of our population is growing, as is the divorce rate, as is the teenage pregnancy rate, as are the vulgar and rageful acts of violence against women and minority groups. The infrastructure of what it is like to be human in this country is falling apart. We urgently need a new way of understanding what is happening to us. This is one of the reasons behind my writing. As a psychologist, I feel there is a lot more we could be doing to help each other.

At this point in time, quantum psychology can be perceived as a fresh way of envisioning the psychology of the *self* or *person*. Specifically, quantum psychology is a clinical psychology that concerns itself with a holistic understanding of experience and consciousness. In this sense, it represents a type of peculiar hybrid derived from both personality and clinical psychology. Yet, quantum psychology is more than a simple combination of original clinical and personality concepts. Quantum psychology's crossbred complexity enlarges the scope of its questioning and understanding. History, sociology, anthropology, theology, the political and communication sciences and everyday affairs must likewise be considered part of its structure.

The choice of the word quantum is neither accidental nor a capricious attempt at inventing a "catchy new phrase." As mentioned in the introduction, quantum is borrowed from the science of physics. Its new application is meant to convey to psychology the same dramatic revolution in thought that occurred in physics. The birth of quantum physics ushered in a dramatic revolution concerning how physicists conceptualize the structure of the universe. According to the physicist Fritjof Capra,

The concepts of quantum theory were not easy to accept even after their mathematical formulation had been completed. Their effect on the physicists' imagination was shattering . . . quantum theory has thus demolished the classical concepts of solid objects and of strictly deterministic laws of nature. At the sub-atomic level, the solid material objects of classical physics dissolve into wavelike patterns of probabilities, and these patterns ultimately do not represent probabilities of things, but, probabilities of interconnections. (1977, pp. 58–59)

Quantum physics has shifted our perspective of the universe from an isolated arena of fragmented and separate objects to an ecological network of interconnected possibilities. For clinical psychology and psychiatry, quantum psychology necessitates a shift from understanding people as a collection of separate symptoms or abnormal behaviors to a more holistic conception of what it means to be alive. Basically, quantum psychology represents an attempt to expand the understanding of what it is like to be alive beyond the confines of the present clinical model.

This brings us to another qualification. Quantum psychology connects the experience of what it is like to be yourself, not to any ideal theoretical structure but rather to the daily aspects of contemporary culture—the nitty-gritty stuff of life. In other words, it is a constructionist psychology that explores the relationship between the self and society (Erikson, 1963). Quantum psychology is an empirical psychology in that it first considers observations of *ordinary* life and then attempts to comprehend them within the context of a general theory.

Now this may seem like a minor point, but in fact, it is crucial to the understanding of a quantum approach. Many theories of human development are constructed in reverse. First, as a means of explaining ordinary behavior, abnormal or *extraordinary* behavior is examined, and based on these observations, a theoretical structure is constructed. Individual experiences, especially those of an *ordinary* type are then modified to fit the theory. In the early days of the theory's development, especially if the theory is a good one, there is usually a "fit" between the theoretical structure and the observed phenomenon. However, if the theory becomes a success, as was the case when psychoanalysis was first developed, then a rather peculiar transformation ensues. Instead of the theory being modified to fit the observed event or person, the event or person is modified to fit the theory. The following passage from Werner Heisenberg is relevant to this process:

Even in antiquity, Aristotle, as an empiricist had raised the objection—I cite more or less his own words—that the Pythagoreans (among whom Plato must be included) did not seek for explanations and theories to fit the facts, but distorted the facts to fit certain theories and favored opinions and set themselves up, one might say, as coarrangers of the universe. (1984, pp. 39–40)

In order to accomplish this magical manipulation, at least two processes must occur: (1) a great deal of relevant information must be discarded or ignored and (2) the people who are observing, whether they be clinicians, scientists or the lay public must wear observational blinders. In that they determine both what is noticed and explained, such blinders are both perceptual and conceptual. I am firmly in agreement with D. R. Griffin who, in discussing animal awareness, states that

It is very easy for scientists to slip into the passive assumption that phenomena with which their customary methods cannot deal effectively are unimportant or even nonexistent. To quote Fouts (1973): "All one needs to do is to look around and not see something and then conclude that the thing that was not seen in a particular species is totally absent in that species." Here I should also like to follow the example of Holloway (1974) in quoting Daniel Yankelovich (Smith, 1972): "The first step is to measure whatever can be easily measured. This is ok as far as it goes. The second step is to disregard that which can't be measured or give it an arbitrary quantitive value. This is artificial and misleading. The third step is to presume that what can't be measured easily isn't very important. This is blindness. The fourth

step is to say that what can't be easily measured really doesn't exist. This is suicide."
(1981/1990, p. 96)

In taking a quantum approach I am doing my best to avoid such limitations. In essence, it is experience, not theory, that is most meaningful and must come first. A major portion of this book is devoted to exploring the relationship between experience, consciousness and culture.

THE PRESENT CLINICAL MODEL

The term "clinical model" refers to the way in which psychologists and other mental health professionals think about people. A clinical model represents the manner in which psychological problems are understood. In that it provides clinicians with guidelines for diagnosis and treatment, a model is like a map. Within psychiatry, models represent rather unusual maps. Let me explain.

A map is a representation of something, and although we tend to think of maps as predominantly geographic, in essence, a map of just about anything can be constructed. Now, in the real world no one really confuses a map of Arizona with the territory itself. The map of Arizona is simply viewed as a glove compartment aid to getting there and finding one's way about. The map is not confused with the area.

Maps of the clinical sciences are often called models or paradigms. These models represent the basic diagnostic framework and treatment philosophies employed in understanding and assisting "people in distress." In clinical psychiatry and psychology, a rather unusual metamorphosis occurs—*the map is substituted for the person*. The maps, or paradigms, tend to mold or fit the person being observed into the structure of the map itself. As I have already pointed out, this is a very selective process that requires the loss of a great deal of important information. In other words, the observed data, in this case a person or a person's problems, have to be modified to fit the existing model or theory. This is like someone going to China with a map of Kansas.

This type of theoretical approach to clinical work encourages the development of meta-theory, a process that in turn leads to meta–meta-theory and so on ad infinitum. The original theory's need to maintain internal consistency becomes the chief driving force. In order to explain observations that do not mesh with the original theoretical structure, meta-explanatory structures are created, and tenaciously, the theory persists. No one within the theoretical paradigm bothers to question the theory, instead, ingeniously, meta-structures that incorporate the discrepant observations are developed, and magically within the theoretical framework, the observations are maintained. For clinical and theoretical zealots, the clarion call "at all costs preserve the theory" echoes loudly. In preserving theoretical consistency, psychology has somehow managed to lose the person (remember the person, the original object of study?). With few exceptions, this pattern reflects the last 50 years of psychological and psychiatric theory building. A vivid example comes to mind. Recently, while attending clinical rounds at a major psychiatric hospital, I witnessed an intense and passionate debate concerning whether the depressed and tearful patient being interviewed was "vertically splitting" or "protectively identifying." In addition, because the patient's dexamethasone suppression test (an endocrinological test associated with depression) was negative, several clinicians were arguing that the patient could not possibly be depressed; after all, an important biological marker was negative. Clearly, the theoretical formulation became more important than the person.

With few exceptions, our current clinical models are based on three assumptions: linearity, reductionism and abnormality.

Linearity

Linearity describes cause-and-effect type phenomena in which condition A causes condition B. If you are sexually molested in your childhood (condition A), then you will either sexually molest others or have an enduring conflict regarding sex (condition B). If your parents or, at one time yourself, abuse drugs and/or alcohol (condition A), then you will either abuse, or have a struggle with, drugs and alcohol in the future. F. A. Wolfe states that the psychological tendency to think linearly

Arises from classical mechanics, which in turn is based on the assumption that events occur without our consciousness. These events are natural sequences following a temporal order. . . . Abnormal behavior or inappropriate behavior is a considered result of error, often attributed to an *unconscious* set of initial conditions. Since these hidden initial conditions are thought to be causatively operating, they will produce a predictable outcome. (1984, p. 189)

As a result of this tendency to think in a linear A-causes-B fashion, certain clinical syndromes or clusters of symptoms and behaviors are specifically assigned to certain groups. Children of incest, holocaust survivors, children of alcoholics, the offspring of schizophrenics, victims of rape and drug abuse and siblings of compulsives all describe syndromes in which identified negative events are directly associated with psychological difficulties. A linear psychological model suggests that the conditions of your early life (doing drugs, dropping out of school, not doing your homework or having alcoholic parents) will cause you difficulty later on. Mihaly Csikszentmihalyi, a psychologist who writes about peak or what he calls "flow" experiences, comments on this tendency, stating that

Ever since Freud, psychologists have been interested in explaining how early child-hood trauma leads to adult public dysfunction. This line of causation is fairly easy to understand. More difficult to explain, and more interesting, is the opposite outcome: the instances when suffering gives a person the incentive to become a great artist, a wise statesman, or a scientist. If one assumes that external events must determine psychic outcomes, then it makes sense to see the neurotic response to suffering as normal and the constructive response as defense or sublimation. (1990, p. 234)

This passage suggests that things do not always turn out the way we would expect them to. When it comes to complex phenomena like people, A does not always cause B. Nevertheless, linearity is so deeply embedded in scientific thought that it is extremely difficult to change. Speaking of linearity and evolution, the eminent paleontologist Stephen Jay Gould states:

I strongly reject any conceptual scheme that places our options on a line, and holds that the only alternative to a pair of extreme positions lies somewhere between them . . . the diversity of possible itineraries does demonstrate that eventual results cannot be predicted at the outset. Each step proceeds for a cause, but no finale can be specified at the start, and none would ever occur a second time in the same way, *because any pathway proceeds through thousands of improbable stages.* (my emphasis) (1989, p. 51)

I emphasize Gould's last remarks because they are reflective of a quantum approach. A quantum approach entails a system of probability in which all possible outcomes are considered. This does not mean that clusters or patterns do not develop from the experiences of one's upbringing. But, patterns are very different from symptoms or syndromes. Patterns reflect general possibilities or tendencies of behavior, whereas symptoms reflect specific events. Patterns are dynamic and interactive, whereas symptoms are static and discreet. Psychological patterns, like waves and particles in the physical universe are interactive; they do not manifest themselves unless certain conditions exist. Interestingly enough, these conditions depend on what we are looking for as well as the methods we employ.

The Construction of Reality

As an illustration, let us examine an earlier problem of physics: the wave/particle paradox. Prior to the development of quantum theory, physicists were faced with the dilemma of explaining how certain phenomena, light for instance, could sometimes be a particle and sometimes a wave. This did not seem to make sense and, in fact, violated the notion of classical reality. In our "real world," things are either particles or waves, they cannot be both. A grain of sand is a particle and an ocean wave is just that, a wave. Neither can exchange its substantial nature with the other. Once we reach the subatomic level, this solid dichotomy becomes meaningless. Matter may be either a wave or a particle depending on the reasons and methods of our search. In essence, physicists have discovered that the interaction of our conscious searching affects the results of what we eventually discover. If we look for a wave with instruments that detect waves, then, indeed, it will be waves that we discover. On the other hand, if we employ a particle-detecting apparatus as a means of measuring particles, then it will be particles that we will find. One of the possible conclusions physicists have come to as a way of explaining this phenomenon is that consciousness plays a role in constructing reality.

Now this illustration applies not only to the physical world but to the world of human relationships as well. In fact, it especially applies to both interpersonal and intrapersonal experiences. These are important points and we will return to their implications later. For now, however, let us continue to understand psychology's traditional linear way of conceptualizing problems.

When appropriate, as in situations where the number of variables involved is limited or predictable, linear thinking can be quite useful. In fact, linear thought is also called *logical* thinking. Obviously, it is often quite beneficial and even important that we think in a logical fashion. Proper medical diagnosis, mechanical repair or even certain decisions are dependent on a logical/linear mode of thought. Problems begin, however, when we overly rely on this mode of thought or when we attempt to apply it to complex and highly variable phenomena like human development, relationships or politics. This type of misplaced linear thinking is especially prevalent in both the current war on drugs and our beliefs and attitudes concerning the sexual abuse of children.

The United States recently witnessed the California McMartin trial, a legal battle in which the owners of a nursery school were charged with sexually molesting school children. During the trial it was discovered that a great deal of the testimony was biased and distorted. Apparently, the counselor who was assigned to interview the supposedly sexually mistreated children was (A) so convinced that sexual misconduct took place that she was looking for sexual misconduct and (B) employed methods of inter-rogation that were bound to uncover or transform events into appearing to be sexual misconduct, so (C) sexual misconduct was found.

A similar pattern of simplistic linear thinking was evident in the rejection of Ronald Reagan's *conservative* Supreme Court nominee Judge Douglas Ginsberg because he once smoked marijuana in college. When clear-cut linear forms of logic are applied to complex issues, the solutions become not only simplistic but reductionistic as well.

Reductionism

Reductionism refers to a method of analysis in which matters are separated and reduced into their elementary components and is one of science's basic methods. In biology, for example, organisms are understood as the combined function of their constituent systems—the heart, the liver, brains, lungs—which in turn are understood in terms of cells and chemical hormones and then molecules and atoms. Chevrolets and Hondas are understood in terms of carburetors, radiators, valves and electrical systems, which are then understood in terms of the laws of chemistry and physics. Commenting on the early scientific beginnings of reductionism, Alfred North Whitehead states that

It is the defect of the eighteenth century scientific scheme that it provides none of the elements which compose the immediate psychological experience of mankind. Nor does it provide any elementary trace of the organic unity of a whole, from which the organic unities of electrons, protons molecules and living bodies emerge. (1925/1990, p. 54)

We are faced with the dilemma that when reductionistic thinking is applied to complex phenomena, the results are often simplistic, inappropriate or even dangerous. We can use marriage as an illustration. There is no way to reduce the elements of marriage into its component parts. If one were to offer, as is often the case, a reductionistic solution to a marital problem, not only will the attempt not really help the situation but it will actually prevent comprehension of the total problem and delay the discovery of an adequate and lasting resolution. That is, in order to offer what is nothing more than a falsely reassuring statement of comfort and hope, certain aspects of the marriage would have to be ignored. Situations involving the interactions of people who are either family, lovers or friends are so difficult to understand that unless they reach obviously violent proportions and have a damaging effect on society we tend to ignore them. If you have had the experience of trying to break up an argument between people, you know what I am talking about. If the people happen to be a married couple, the results of the intervention can be disastrous. As a rule, even the police have learned to avoid such situations.

In my early days as a counselor with the family court system, I learned how disastrous and ineffective reductionistic solutions are. A reductionistic solution, at the expense of the total number of factors involved, concentrates instead on one or two factors and attempts to ameliorate the dilemma by changing these isolated factors. To continue with the example of marriage, the state of any marriage, at any given point in time, depends on a complex set of interacting factors and forces. A partial list would include the following:

1. Age
2. Attitude toward marriage
3. Culture

4. Ability to communicate

5. Ethnicity

6. Presence of family problems

7. Income

8. Number of siblings

9. Relationships among the siblings

10. Relationships among the siblings and one parent

11. Relations between the siblings and both parents and so on . . .

Each partner constructs a story or personal narrative of the marriage, combining the above elements in combinations based on his or her unique and individual history. Very often, however, the personal narratives are contradictory. The situation can be compared to a play with two directors, multiple scripts and numerous casts. If the relationship is good, the play works and the action stays in sync. Inevitably, however, the directors are going to clash.

Now, obviously not all of the possible factors have equal impact; some are more important than others. The point is that it is essential that all factors be considered. Norman Cousins (1992) takes the same position in relation to illness. The course and prognosis of an illness depends on a multitude of variables. One of the most important, as Cousins points out, is a sense of humor and the ability to laugh. In a diagnosis of either marital or organic illness that is only linear and reductionistic, the relation of humor to either the patient or situation is inconsequential. A variable such as humor is not even considered. Yet, not only in Norman Cousins's case but for many others as well, humor along with factors such as support systems, a loving family, financial security and attitude toward illness have all proven to be critical elements of recovery. Too often, when dealing with psychological anomalies, reductionism obfuscates the problem, complicates the treatment and oversimplifies the solution. Our present mental health system deals with people in a linear and reductionistic fashion that focuses on deviance—only those who do not outwardly conform or who fail to meet cultural expectations are noticed. People who are internally deviant but outwardly appropriate, or politically correct, may not be noticed at all and, in our present cultural climate, may actually flourish. Such people may, or may not, present with identifiable symptoms, but even when the symptoms are distinct, they are always rooted in a cultural context. It is this context that the current psychiatric establishment myopically ignores.

Two of the most common psychiatric diagnoses of our time are borderline and narcissistic personality disorders. These conditions, phenomena that encompass the whole personality, are being diagnosed in a narrow and increasingly reductionistic fashion. In order to establish a definitive diagnosis, especially one of personality disorder, numerous ingredients concerning the person have to be ignored. These ingredients are neglected because, within the framework of the diagnosis, they are considered unimportant. For example, factors such as environment, cultural background, race, gender, ethnicity, religion, income, political-economic status, level and flexibility of consciousness, or degree of awareness, are considered superfluous to an accurate diagnosis of personality disorder. I have termed these seemingly indirect elements *quantum factors*.

Quantum factors represent influences that are non-linear, non-local and seemingly tangential to the problem at hand. Although presumably extraneous, quantum factors are extremely important, a matter that brings us to one of the central paradoxes of contemporary psychiatric diagnoses. Quite often, very essential elements of a person's life are ignored so that an explainable diagnosis can be made. Because they do not fit the linear/reductionistic model of psychiatry and psychology, crucial elements that might have brought someone in for a consultation are disregarded.

Reductive diagnoses, a key earmark of modern technological medicine, is often misapplied in psychiatry. In medicine, reductionistic approaches are more frequently necessary.[1] For example, if you have stomach cramps, leg pains or a bad cough, quantum factors may not be as relevant as the need for a basic etiological diagnosis, such as, a bacterial infection, a sprained muscle or a pulmonary virus. When it comes to quandaries of a psychological nature such as personality disorders, depression or "problems in living," reductive approaches do not work very well. As a clinical psychologist, it is becoming more apparent to me that many people, from all walks of life, are experiencing a vague sense of uneasiness. Certainly, I am not the first person to make such a statement, so the question becomes How long are we going to let this line of development continue? In order to change our evolutionary direction, a new perspective is required. As part of this new perspective, values are going to have to be reintegrated within psychology.

Values

The uneasiness that I refer to stems in part from the values on which our daily lives are based. These values are firmly rooted in a distorted cultural consciousness that affects our entire existence. I further postulate that the reason the linear/reductive/abnormal model is dominant and quantum factors are ignored has little to do with scientific efficacy or clinical success, but rather with *external reasons of a sociopolitical-economic nature*. A large portion of this book is spent exploring these external issues. As matters now stand within clinical psychology, sociocultural factors are virtually ignored. Perhaps it is no surprise that the system that purports to "heal" people is in itself ailing.

Yet, when cultural ignorance is endemic to American society, it becomes difficult to find fault only with the behavioral sciences. In reference to a multiethnic, pluralistic culture like the United States this statement might seem a bit farfetched if not totally wrong. It is my contention, however, that our culture provides only the *appearance* of a melting pot, culturally aware society. Beneath the surface, the reality is a bit more disheartening. Our appearance of cultural acceptance is a media illusion, and like so many postmodern illusions, it is an effective and well-orchestrated one. To a large part, the continuation of cultural illusions depends on the neglect of quantum factors. The methods of the behavioral sciences must be enlarged to include both linear and quantum factors. In other words, the entire system of a person's life must be examined. The possibility that *external* reasons influence people (*the internal*) to act a certain way must be considered more seriously.

In a quantum model, we do not have separate external and internal factors, rather we have a contextual unity, a holistic system in which each subsystem or part affects the other. This, of course, makes each system or person wonderfully unique. Although certain generalizations between systems can be made, such universalizing must remain secondary to understanding each system (person) as a totally unique entity with different causes, effects and contents. The quantum factors of a white, upper-middle-class doctor will not always construct the same internal reality of the person being diagnosed. In fact, under different cultural conditions the doctor could also be diagnosed as having a psychiatric disorder.

This does not mean that the biopsychosocial model should be replaced by the quantum model, but rather that it should be augmented by it. The noted psychiatrist/philosopher Richard Chessick (1985) believes that the biopsychosocial model is really the biological model in disguise. He points out that the psychiatric/psychological establishment gives only "lip service" to factors of psychological and sociological importance. To make the model sound inclusive, such factors are simply appended to the biological model as a rather hasty afterthought.

I would like to consider this a brief introduction to a few of the implications of linear and reductionistic thinking. We deal with these issues throughout the book. For now, let us turn our attention to the effects the *abnormal model* of development has had on psychology.

The Abnormal Model and the Tyranny of the Ordinary

The psychology of the ordinary has been constructed on the extraordinary. Doesn't this seem a bit odd? As early as 1938, Ruth Benedict stated that

The confusion is present in practically all discussions of abnormal psychology, and it can be clarified chiefly by adequate consideration of the character of the culture, not of the constitution of the abnormal individual. . . . It is clear that statistical methods of defining normality, so long as they are based on studies in a selected civilization, only involve us, unless they are checked against the cultural configuration, in deeper and deeper provincialism. *The recent tendency in abnormal psychology to take the laboratory mode as normal and to define abnormalities as they depart from the average has value in so far as it indicates that the aberrants in any culture are those individuals who are liable to serious disturbances because their habits are culturally unsupported.* (p. 76)

A psychology of the usual based on the unusual is bound to be a biased psychology; a discipline that is distorted in terms of the abnormal. For example, if condition A is decided on as the definition of normal, then conditions B, C or G will by definition be abnormal. With the exception of humanistic scientists who have intensely studied so-called "normal children," most models of both development and psychopathology are based on studies of abnormal behavior, or clinical psychopathology. Although the biopsychosocial model may be appropriate for certain psychological problems, it is clearly not enough for all difficulties.

How do we decide what is accepted and ordinary and what is deviant? Why is it so important for certain groups, like teenagers or politicians for example, to feel that they fit in or belong? In order to answer these questions we are going to have to understand a little about the psychology of the ordinary. In fact, we will see that being ordinary has a great deal to do with the concept of conformity.

We do not notice the child who has successfully negotiated a developmental phase, but rather the child who has not. The person who appears normal is hardly ever noticed. It is only when the veneer of "normality" or ordinariness is missing that we begin to pay attention to a person. We compare unusual events with usual examples and arrive at a series of normative developmental data. These data are usually based on the investigation of thousands of subjects, an approach that in psychology is termed nomothetic and represents the principal manner by which we decide who fits in. The problem with this technique is that although it tells us a lot about individuals or groups as *compared* with other individuals or groups, it tells us very little about any one person within any of the groups. The frightening fact is that the tendency to make decisions about individuals based on their position in comparison to "legitimate" groups is increasing. As we shift to a global society individual/group comparisons proliferate and their impact on individuals multiplies. Moreover, this tendency is no longer limited to psychometric psychology but applies to our entire political structure. The relationship of group/individual comparisons to economics is discussed by L. C. Thurow who states that

Individuals have to be judged based on group data, yet all systems of grouping will result in the unfair treatment of some individuals. . . . Ideally, group data could only be used for making economic decisions where all members of the group had the same characteristics. Fair treatment of the group would be a fair treatment of each individual member of the group. *Unfortunately, this situation almost never exists. . . .* What this illustrates, however, is that every society has to have a theory of legitimate and illegitimate groups and a theory of when individuals can be judged on group data. (1980, p. 182)

The reason this *loss of the individual* occurs has to do with the process of measurement as well as with what it is that we decide to measure. The process of measurement is mathematically based on the statistical concept of normality in which normal refers to a particular point on a particular kind of curve. In terms of behavior, normality is simply the location on the curve with the greatest concentration. To quote F. A. Wolfe, "The 'great desire' for normality—the squeeze towards the middle—is reinforced as each person learns the acquired characteristic. As it is with nations, so it goes with neurons" (1984, p. 91).

Historically, the science of psychology has always measured deviance. Psychologists have constructed scores of tests and scales that measure traits in terms of comparative deviance. Comparative deviance means that your score on a certain measure will be compared to the scores of a large number of other people. But to whom are you being compared? Where do these people come from?

The comparative sample is selected from the general population of the predominant culture. In the United States this population is basically a white, middle-class sample with white, middle-class values. This sample selection places a definite bias in terms of what is considered "normal" and places anyone who is not from the above group at a comparative disadvantage. This partiality does not extend just to minority groups but to anyone who is very sensitive, creative or unusual. Thus, not only is the individual lost, but anyone who deviates from the white, middle-class sample bias as well.

Once again we seem to be confronted with a scientific problem that should be quite obvious. The problem is that in developing postulates of human development, psychology has excluded numerous dimensions of our daily lives. In the section on reductionism, for example, I began to briefly describe the multitude of variables involved in a case of potential marital therapy. It has often seemed, as it does, perhaps, to the intelligent reader, that such omissions should be quite obvious. After all, aren't psychologists and psychiatrists scientists who are trained in the scientific method, a method that includes the thorough analysis of all variables connected to a particular study or person? Should it not be accepted that when someone is diagnosed as having a psychiatric disorder, we can assume everything personally relevant and important has been taken into account? Unfortunately, we cannot. Furthermore, this neglect has little to do with clinical precision or optimal treatment. Clinical diagnosis has become a value-laden process highly correlated with the dominant sociopolitical economic factors of our culture.

Very often, psychiatric diagnoses are strongly influenced by time, money and value judgments (Szasz, 1987). Fortunately, when working with people, "good" clinicians take these cultural test prejudices into account. Not everyone, however, it a "good" clinician. The state, bureaucratic agencies, schools or the police use developmental normative data to diagnose, label, judge, coerce and medicate people. The steadily increasing diagnoses of the hyperactive, developmentally disabled, antisocial or learning disabled child are often results of this misplaced emphasis on normative conformity.

Commenting on society's tendency to label non-conforming behavior, the psychologist Richard Coan makes the following point:

The disease concept . . . has come to be applied to many conditions that bear far less resemblance to physical illness as psychiatry has embraced an expanding sphere of behavior. Thus criminal behavior, juvenile delinquency, and behaviors regarded by teachers as disruptive of the classroom routine have come to be regarded as medical problems and are often *subject to labeling in terms of disease categories. Such terms as "moral amentia" and "constitutional psychopathic inferior," which suggest an inherent deficiency in the individual, have been applied to people whose behavior might have proved more understandable if its social context had been taken into account. There has been an unfortunate tendency for the disease label to be applied in a way that simply legitimizes society's condemnation of the individual whose behavior is not currently deemed socially acceptable.* [my emphasis] (1987, p. 69)

The process of psychiatric labeling is much more pervasive than the profession is willing to admit. Numerous people, already with an attached psychiatric label such as depression, schizophrenia or hyperactivity have been referred to me. In only a small percentage of my caseload have I found the preexisting diagnosis to be either accurate or inclusive of all the crucial factors that, in my judgment, are necessary in making a proper diagnosis and developing an effective treatment plan.

SUMMARY

This chapter provided a discussion of the limitations of the classical model as well as a brief introduction to the quantum approach. Overreliance on linear thinking, reductionism and abnormal phenomena precludes a comprehensive and helpful understanding of clinical and cultural issues. Certainly, it encourages the loss of both autonomous individuality and healthy viable community. In that these limitations determine the structure and content of inquiry and understanding, they may be considered philosophical or paradigm limitations. Such limitations act as underlying suppositions that restrict understanding of ourselves and others. In this sense, they act as powerful presumptions that, in essence, severely limit the full understanding of consciousness, and likewise, divorce both doctor and patient not only from each other but from the feeling of being *truly alive* as well.

In chapter 2 the text begins to explore how the inclusion of quantum factors can constructively alter the situation.

NOTE

1. Actually, many physicians object to rampant reductionism in medicine as well; see R. Chessick (1985) and R. Mendelsohn (1990).

Two

The Quantum Model

Anyone who is not shocked by quantum theory doesn't understand it.
                                                                Niels Bohr

Bohr's statement always reminds me of babies. Perhaps this association has to do with the fact that I live with one. I could easily modify Bohr's remark to: anyone who thinks he knows what having a baby will be like does not understand babies.

What does having a baby have to do with quantum physics? Anyone who has a baby knows you never really know what it's like until you actually have one. You may think you know what it's like, you may have plans or hopes, expectations and preconceptions, but I am afraid that quantum psychology and having a baby are very similar to John Lennon's suggestion that life is something that happens to you while you're busy making other plans. Like *real* babies, quantum psychology is dynamic, unpredictable and often irrational.

What makes quantum psychology different? In essence, a quantum approach is not new. What is unique is the verification that a quantum approach in physics extends to a systems approach in psychology. As already stated, the term itself translates as "indivisible package," a meaning that implies a holistic, systems orientation. A quantum psychological mode represents an evolving, dynamic, supraordinate hierarchical systems approach that is not novel to psychology but has definitely been ignored.

A systems orientation was inherent to the philosophy of John Dewey (1991) and Williams James (1890/1950) as well as the clinical formulations of a varied number of people including Gordon Allport (1955), Erik Fromm (1976), Kurt Goldstein (1939), Kurt Lewin (1936), Alfred Maslow (1962), Rollo May (1986) and Gardner Murphy (1947). In the late 1960s and early

1970s, an orientation very similar to systems thinking known as "field theory" became very popular. Contemporary clinicians know very little concerning these points of view. Graduate training does not include them, nor do the plethora of technique-oriented postdoctoral seminars even remotely begin to address them. As discussed in chapter 1, the suppression of systems thinking exists for several reasons. In ensuing sections, we discuss these reasons in greater depth. For now, we should at least be cognizant that changes within the physical sciences, especially the development of quantum physics, render such suppression extremely problematic. From this discussion, one would think as far as physics is concerned that quantum mechanics represents a fairly recent development. Actually, the quantum revolution began occurring in the early part of the twentieth century. The early beginnings of quantum thinking are evidence for how astoundingly long it often takes scientists to alter the way in which they think. If psychology continues to ignore the systems implications of quantum physics, it has a strong potential for becoming a dead-end science.

Quantum theory represents a new way of understanding that basically leads to a more holistic perception. As Michael Lockwood states,

But quantum mechanics is not to be regarded as just another scientific theory. To the extent that it is correct, it demands a complete revolution in our way of looking at the world, more profound than was required by any previous scientific breakthrough: this is what makes it so exciting philosophically. Moreover, it embodies within itself, as no other scientific theory does, a radically new conception of the relationship *between observer and reality* . . . quantum mechanics, in effect, incorporates a physics of observation or measurement as an integral part of the theory itself: *one that strikes at the heart of our common sense conception of what happens when one observes or measures something.* (my emphasis) (1989, p. 178)

What is especially fascinating about quantum theory is that its origins lie in abstract mathematical theory and esoteric subatomic experimentation. The laws of quantum mechanics apply to a subatomic universe that bears scant resemblance to our macroscopic world of trees and boulevards, people and skyscrapers. The everyday world in which we live clearly follows a Newtonian, classical cause and effect paradigm that is implicated in one of the central paradoxes that quantum psychology inspires. The paradox is that the commonsense, organized causal world we inhabit is built on a startlingly mysterious, subatomic, quantum world. In some clandestine manner, it is the interaction of these levels of reality that results in our world being.

Although quantum theory is based on highly refined, non-ordinary and abstract mathematical models, all quantum experiments consist of ordinary, concrete events. The fact that people only directly experience classical reality has been termed the Cinderella effect (Herbert, 1987). No one directly experiences the quantum world, somehow and someway it transforms itself into the "real world." The interaction of different levels of reality is a difficult concept to comprehend scientifically. Readers more interested in the theoretical science of these interactions should consult the works of David Bohm (1980), Erich Jantsch (1980) and Ilya Prigogine (1980).

Although our experience of the world is confined to the classical level, the world itself seems composed of at least two separate dimensions: the quantum and the classical. Yet, as applied physics demonstrates, events on the quantum level in an unknown, but very direct manner, affect our everyday lives. The philosopher Michael Lockwood feels that it is misleading to think of separate levels of reality and essentially calls for a more quantum way of conceptualizing the world. He states that

There is a widespread belief about quantum mechanics, as also about relativity, that it is something that one is entitled to ignore for most ordinary philosophical and scientific purposes, since it only seriously applies at the micro level of reality: where "micro" means something far smaller than would show up in any conventional microscope. What sits on top of this micro level, so the assumption runs, is a sufficiently good approximation of the old classical Newtonian picture to justify our continuing, as philosophers, to think about the world in essentially classical terms. *I believe this to be a fundamental mistake. What I shall be urging . . . is that the world is quantum-mechanical through and through; and that the classical picture of reality is, even at the macroscopic level, deeply inadequate.* (my emphasis) (1989, p. 178)

I am in fundamental agreement with Michael Lockwood. We must always be aware that our comprehension, even at the sensory level, of what appears to be may not be what actually is. Such understanding must, likewise, be tempered by the tenets of epistemic dualism, a method of reasoning that distinguishes between what in principle must be true and what in reality can be accomplished. In terms of practice, these issues will be explored further as the text proceeds. Many of the recent technological advances of our modern world are based on the insights of quantum mathematical theory. In other words, quantum mechanics, despite its obscure nature, works. As the physicist Nick Herbert states,

Heaping success upon success, quantum theory boldly exposes itself to potential falsification on a thousand different fronts. Its record is impressive: quantum theory passes every test we can devise. After sixty years of play, the theory is still batting a thousand. (1987, p. 94)

I am not prepared to explain quantum mechanics. Actually, after 5 years of study I am still perplexed, shocked and confused by it. I suppose this is what Neils Bohr would consider a "normal" response. The important point, I would imagine, is that 5 years after discovering quantum physics I remain even more intrigued and fascinated with a theory that has been creatively heuristic, improving both my clinical and personal life. Nevertheless, be-

cause of a series of unwaveringly incompetent and often sadistic elementary
and secondary school mathematics teachers, I still retain what could only
be described as a mathematical learning disability. Needless to say, this
disability has severely hindered my ability to comprehend theoretical physics. Fortunately, for myself and the reader, there exists an abundance of
general and excellent texts on quantum physics, most of which are included
in the reference section. What I hope to accomplish in this chapter is to
begin to develop a transitional bridge between the *philosophical* implications
of quantum physics and the psychology of experience. As previously stated,
this bridge needs to be cross disciplinary and based not on *formal scientific
proof but rather on observation and experience.* Therefore, at this point let me
introduce the theoretical concepts of quantum mechanics that bear directly
on quantum psychology. These are

1. Complementarity
2. The role of consciousness in observation and measurement
3. The interaction of systems
4. Non-linearity and Non-locality.[1]

COMPLEMENTARITY

The concept of complementarity, first introduced by Neils Bohr, states
that the universe can never be described in a singular, unitary manner, but
rather, must be understood through multiple, overlapping reality perspectives. Such layers of reality sometimes complement one another, but often,
they are paradoxical. Like the quantum world, humans rarely directly experience other levels of reality. Such perception remains beyond the capacities of our sensory apparatus. The human brain constructs its representation
of the physical universe from an extremely narrow range of the energy
spectrum. We can, however, be aware of the paradoxical aspects of existence, and often, indirectly, the mysterious complexity of the universe calls
to us. Glimpses into the enormity, the sheer and utter convoluted vastness
of the world, the infinite imploding possibilities of the microscopic and
subatomic universe, enfolded within a multiverse so immense that it becomes inconceivable, is becoming a rare experience. Consciousness, for
most people, is becoming constricted, externalized and unidimensional.
Surmounting this constriction is a central tenet of quantum psychology, a
position that in many different ways is reiterated throughout the text. For
the present, let us return to the key principles of quantum physics.

CONSCIOUSNESS

In the formulations of quantum theory, the consciousness of the observer
is always taken into account. In essence, it becomes an integral factor in

any experiment. Nick Herbert (1987) states that it is not possible to formulate the laws of quantum mechanics in a fully consistent way without reference to consciousness. As the physicist E. P. Wigner (1972) suggests, if consciousness cannot affect matter, then it is the only scientific example where one system (matter) can affect another system (mind) without being affected itself.

In classical physics, the universe was divided into separate parts, and the observer was considered separate from the observed. The initial work of quantum theorists such as Werner Heisenberg and Erwin Schrödinger paved the way for consciousness to become an integral part of the picture. The inclusion of the observer's consciousness is a varying matter, depending on the type and nature of the experiment as well as the theoretical philosophy of the physicist. David Bohm (1980) is the best example of a physicist who thoroughly embraces consciousness as an essential part of being. For Bohm,

Both observer and observed appear from the same underlying indivisible process and flow into and out of each other like the stream through vortexes. The division between the observer and observed is a sometimes convenient abstraction which permits some deeper observation to take place. . . . The observer is not causing the observed. They are both in a sense causing each other and being caused by the whole underlying movement. (Briggs & Peat, 1984, p. 131)

Bohm's theories of holonomy and the implicate and explicate order of the universe are as startling as they are insightful and interesting. More than any other contemporary physicist, Bohm includes consciousness as an integral process in all physical interactions. The interested reader should definitely pursue his works more directly.

INTERACTION

The third quantum factor is interaction. The notion of interaction is implicit in both complementarity and the effect of the observer. Quantum mechanics is a physics of intricacy in which different systems are constantly interacting. If, as the principle of complementarity suggests, the universe is multilayered, then in some mysterious way it is the interaction of these layers that results in "being" and what our Selves perceive as reality. From these interactions, a world is constructed. Karl Popper and John Eccles (1977) describe our perception of a unitary world as the interaction of three worlds, whereas other physicists have suggested that the interaction of quantum and classical factors makes us who we are. According to Roger Penrose,

Perhaps, also, the phenomena of consciousness is something that cannot be understood in entirely classical terms. Perhaps our minds are qualities rooted in some strange and wonderful feature of those physical laws which *actually* govern the world we inhabit, rather than being just features of some algorithm acted out by the so-called "objects" of a classical physical structure. Perhaps, in some sense, this is "why" we as sentient beings, must live in a quantum world, rather than an entirely classical one, despite all the richness, and indeed mystery, that is already present in the classical universe. *Might a quantum world be "required" so that thinking, perceiving creatures, such as ourselves, can be constructed from its substance?* (my emphasis) (1989, p. 226)

This passage is, I believe, one of the most perceptive and sagacious statements by a physicist concerning the nature of the quantum dimension. But, then again, Roger Penrose is a virtual genius, a person very much like Stephen Hawkings, another prodigy whom Penrose has collaborated with. What is truly admirable about Doctor Penrose's statement is its tentativeness. When concerning quantum physics' implications for the classical world, provisional statements are de rigueur. It can be no other way. Quite plainly, at this point in evolution, humans do not yet have the perceptual or conceptual abilities to accurately comprehend the environment in which they exist. I employ the term environment in its widest and most cosmic sense as the multiverse that, at this point in time, we inhabit. Interestingly enough, my last sentence sounds like science fiction, a passage from a Robert Heinlein or Ursula LeGuin novel. But science fiction is rapidly becoming science, a transformation that definitely owes a debt to quantum physics. We must be wary, however, of falling into the metaphysical trap of using quantum physics to validate a mystical world view (Wilbur, 1984).

NON-LINEARITY

The concept of non-linearity was introduced in chapter 1. As stated, non-linear systems differ fundamentally from linear ones. Prior to the development of high-speed computers and twentieth-century mathematical analysis, physicists were mainly capable of analyzing linear equations. Because their methodology was linear, scientists tended to comprehend the world as a linear function. There is a certain neat, compartmentalized simplicity to linear systems; they tend to add up and, likewise, can easily be separated into a series of connected separate parts. Linear systems lend themselves to a reductionistic perception of a concrete and predictable universe that can, for the sake of analysis, be fragmented into identifiable sections. Such sections can be separated and labeled, and then almost magically, in the process of labeling and separation a certain definitive understanding can be reached.

As a species, we have a remarkable tendency to label and categorize. In this matter, our bias leans toward clean, organized and uncluttered classifications. Humans (I am not just picking on scientists, most people, myself included, have a pervasive tendency to think this way—in chapter 3 we discuss some of the neurological reasons behind this preference) abhor lack of closure and uncertainty. We detest the little hanging strings; the pieces that do not quite fit in our antiseptic boxes; the mold of uncertainty that, despite our most arduous efforts, constantly clings to consciousness. Chaos terrifies, and in many ways our response to the dynamic vitality and unpredictability of nature evokes this terror. The characters in Jean Paul Sartre's novel *Nausea* clearly reflect such sentiments.

We also have an uncommon proclivity to confuse labels of reality with reality itself. Again, quite subtly, the symbol is substituted for the designated object and the label misconstrued for the underlying reality. The tired rituals and worn out dogma of many religions are excellent examples of this virtually unconscious confusion. This notion becomes especially clear when one realizes that throughout human history, in comparison to evil, more harm has been done in the name of righteous good. That nearly one quarter of a million Iraqis perished in the brief Persian Gulf war has more to do with the good and noble intentions of America than it does with an evil intent to destroy Arab babies. My digression is an attempt to explain why linear explanations are so persistent. Linear concepts satisfy our almost innate desire for logical completeness. Perhaps of greater importance is that linear explanations promote predictability. Based on the initial state of the observed phenomena, changes in linear systems lead to predictable outcomes. If the interaction within the system is increased by a small amount, there will be a subsequent small change in the outcome. The rules within linear systems are unvariable. According to Briggs and Peat,

In linear systems, therefore, small changes produce small effects, determinism is everywhere apparent, and by reducing interactions to very small values the system can be considered to be composed of independent parts. . . . The linear world is a world without surprises. It is a clockwork world in which things can be taken apart and rebuilt again. (1984, pp. 174–175)

In contrast, non-linear phenomena represent non-symmetrical, paradoxical and unpredictable processes in which small initial changes can lead to large or non-apparent outcome stages. These features are connected to the development of chaos theory, a contemporary scientific perspective that concerns itself with non-linear phenomena. Chaos itself has no formal scientific definition and has been defined as follows:

1. The irregular, unpredictable behavior of deterministic, non-linear dynamical systems and 2. Dynamics freed at last from the shackles of order and predictability . . . systems liberated to randomly explore their every dynamical possibility . . . exciting variety, richness of choice, a cornucopia of opportunity. (Gleick, 1987, p. 306)

An interesting example of non-linear phenomena in the everyday world is what meteorologists refer to as the "butterfly effect," a concept meaning that it is possible for a butterfly moving its wings in China to eventually cause a violent storm in Kansas. In terms of quantum psychology, the important point to remember is that analysis must include non-linear as well as linear phenomena. Last, but certainly not least, we come to the mind-boggling concept of non-locality. Comprehending non-locality is a little bit like understanding the concept of a billion people, God or the idea that independent organisms live within our bodies. Intellectually, perhaps, many people can accept or imagine that these entities exist, but such things can never be fully grasped in the way, for example, that the existence of 10 people, a religious celebration or the ubiquitous presence of the nose on one's face can be perceived and understood. In the latter case, comprehension, in that it is directly perceived, is experiential and complete and understanding occurs within all aspects of being.

In reference to the other examples, such complete comprehension is virtually impossible to achieve. Aside from certain rare exceptions, no one can directly perceive or directly experience a billion, God or the host of swarming life that lurks within. These qualifications also apply to understanding non-locality. In discussing these limitations, I am not suggesting that such intangible ideas are worthless, because to the contrary, they are incredibly important to our lives. My digression is solely for the purpose of stressing the difficulty many people have in *integrating* such concepts. Integration requires processing within all levels of consciousness—thinking, feeling, sensing, imagining, behaving. In other words, we have to *really* experience what the implications of the existence of a billion microscopic creatures within a cubic foot of soil really implies. What are the ramifications of our belief in a God? Why am I not conscious of the multitude of organisms within the organism of myself? Most people do not think about these matters, or if one does happen to think about such things, the thoughts occur in an extremely limited way. Once again, our linear and reductionistic tendency to classify, dissect, organize and explain such phenomena rears its persistent head.

I would like to avoid the snare of reductionism. My wish to do so applies not only to the concept of nonlinearity but also to the entire range of quantum physics. What is required are more questions; the answers will come later. In fact, the answers are much less important than the questions. As Jacob Needleman says, "Questioning makes one open, makes one sensitive, makes one humble. We don't suffer from our questions, we suffer from our answers. Most of the mischief in the world comes from people with answers, not from people with questions" (1990, p. 166).

NON-LOCALITY

Few things can be as humbling as quantum physics, and within quantum physics it is the idea of non-locality that truly astounds. In terms of the other three important quantum factors, non-locality has the profoundest implications. From a personal perspective, my own consciousness was always apparent to me and definitely seemed to have an effect on the world—for example, I knew it influenced other people. Furthermore, it always seemed obvious that reality was interactive, and at a fairly early age I was aware of the absurdity of overextended linear thinking. Thus, the first three factors of quantum physics were fairly easy to accept. The concept of non-locality was a harder nut to swallow. Non-local effects were something that I could never directly perceive and always considered removed from a scientific domain. Non-locality always seemed to be a quasireligious or mystical concept, far removed from objective verification, closer in spirit to Jungian synchronicity or Buddhist and Zen doctrines.

Just what is non-locality and why is it so important? Basically, non-locality is just what the term implies—that events not physically near to one another in some way affect one another. In order to influence each other, these events, or objects, must somehow communicate with one another. As Heinz Pagels (1982) has pointed out, quantum non-locality is a theory of information transfer. Although it is somewhat easy to comprehend how objects in close physical proximity might communicate, as the objects move farther apart it becomes harder to accept the non-local view. Because non-locality is not limited by spatiotemporal factors, the distance can be virtually infinite and can exist within any dimension of reality ranging from the subatomic to the cosmic. Furthermore, in order for such communication to occur, the message must travel *faster than the speed of light*. Now this is where even Einstein began to reject quantum methodology. According to the theory of relativity travel beyond the speed of light is *theoretically* impossible, and thus far, physicists have yet to measure anything going beyond it. Yet, according to the mathematical proofs of non-locality, such faster than light communication must in some way exist. Could this proposition be wrong? Essentially, it is not, as Michael Lockwood states,

Now of course it could be that quantum mechanics is in error, in so far as it predicts a degree of correlation in excess of that which any non-local hidden variable theory could account for. *But that has now been tested, most notably by Alain Aspect et al. (1982) in the crucial case where the influence would have to propagate faster than light. And the predictions of quantum mechanics have been triumphantly confirmed.* (my emphasis) (1989, p. 204)

Nick Herbert (1987) points out that John von Neumann, the Hungarian-born mathematician who wrote *Die Grundlagen*, a work many consider to be the "quantum bible," has proved that if quantum theory is correct the world cannot be made of ordinary objects. The term "ordinary objects" denotes things, for example, like this book, that independent of interaction with consciousness have a real structural existence. The book is the book, case closed; it exists independent of observation. To assume this view of reality places one in the neorealist school, a fellowship that includes Albert Einstein as one of its principal members. For Einstein and neorealists there is no underlying quantum reality; the universe is exactly what it appears to be. Neorealism has had a great deal of difficulty substantiating itself theoretically and clearly does not represent the predominant perspective of most physicists. As stated, both non-locality and the underlying quantum nature of reality have been both theoretically and experimentally verified.

In some manner, on another level of reality, information is being transmitted at faster than light speeds. Non-locality implies that correlated systems can instantaneously influence each other. The theory further suggests that the act of observation (consciousness) correlates the observer to the observed—the observer *always* becomes part of the system. Non-locality intimates that in some way events occurring in a far distant part of the cosmos can potentially and instantly affect events occurring in another part. The next time you observe a star, think about this.

A non-local universe definitely changes the rules of the game and it does so in ways we have not even begun to understand. Years after von Neumann's mathematical postulates, the development of Bell's theorem and its subsequent experimental verification by John Clausner and later by Alaine Aspect and his colleagues proved that the universe is indeed non-local and therefore of a quantum nature.

QUANTUM PSYCHOLOGY

In the transition from physics to psychology we encounter some potential difficulties. Interestingly, like quantum theory these problems are paradoxical in nature. Perhaps the biggest potential dilemma is that although the implications of quantum theory are serious, we cannot take them too seriously. Nick Herbert (1987) has pointed out that quantum mechanics still leads to at least eight possible versions of what reality may be. What I am advocating is a middle of the road, Zen-like approach to the subject, namely, to know and understand that quantumness exists, but not to interpret its existence too literally. In fact, quantum theory, in that it is fluid and dynamic, should never be frozen through literal interpretation. As I have stated previously,

From the position of psychology, quantum theory means a lot and a little. Quantum theory means a lot in the sense that people should not take any one theory of human behavior as absolute law; it means a little in that they must continue to develop consistent and orderly laws of human behavior. Both meanings are necessary and important. In essence, quantum mechanics as it applies to human existence in this world strongly evokes the laws of epistemic dualism. Mathematically, theoretically and intuitively people can know and understand that the world is different from what it appears to be and yet, on another level, they must develop practical constructivist models as if the world were definitely what it seems to be—the reality most people are used to. For their continued personal and evolutionary success, people must do their utmost from both perspective to make the world and their lives on it as robust as possible. (DeBerry, 1991, pp. 34–35)

The problem is that it is too easy to begin a journey of untestable mystical speculations. As Ken Wilbur (1984) has pointed out, quantum theory can be used to justify the existence of all sorts of personal and meta-realities that can lead to additional new "New Age" mythology. Commenting on our cultural dilemmas and escapist tendencies, B. F. Skinner notes that "when thousands of millions of people in other parts of the world cannot do many of the things they want to do, hundreds of millions of people in the West do not want to do many of the things they can do. Human behavior in the West has grown weak" (1986, p. 568).

I am in agreement with Skinner that our behavior has indeed grown weak—weak in the sense that often, what we involve ourselves with does little to change the direction or quality of our lives. Instead of constructing practical personal realities, we are seduced into creating meta-realities. Channeling, satanism, witchery and crystal healing are but a minute sample of alternate and often misguided applications of scientific knowledge. They make a lot of money for a few people but basically leave those directly involved more impoverished than before.

Because individual and planetary problems sometimes seem overbearing, an unfortunate tendency to immerse oneself in the transpersonal dimension arises. The dilemma with the transpersonal dimension is that it is very difficult to locate. Just where is the transpersonal? What can be located and definitely can be modified is the here and now of existence—what I have termed the intrapersonal, interpersonal and impersonal dimensions of consciousness. This is where our work needs to begin. Not on Venus or some quasimystical other world, Shirley MacLaine dimension of reality but, right here, on the planet, between people, among families, friends and enemies. The transition from quantum physics to quantum psychology should be an empirical leap that improves the quality of life in the here and now.

The four principles of quantum physics that have been stressed:

1. The role of consciousness in observation and measurement
2. Interaction of systems
3. Non-linearity
4. Non-locality

alter the manner in which reality is understood. As a psychologist, I am particularly interested in how the existence of a quantum universe affects models we construct in order to comprehend human behavior. Essentially, what quantum mechanics does is corroborate a holistic, ecologically dynamic perspective, an outlook that is not new and is, perhaps, as old as the human race itself. Many American Indian tribes used to conceive and act as if the world were an undivided wholeness, in which earth spirits, for example, were accepted as a viable and integral part of the world itself. For certain tribes, rivers and clouds, animals and mountain streams all were perceived as being animate. Within classical psychology such beliefs are considered to be symptomatic of deeper ego problems.

Emergent Interactionism

Quantum psychology, however, understands such beliefs in context, as one subsystem out of a potentially infinite number of substructures subsumed within the total system. By approaching the entire system, we arrive at a holistic or ecological comprehension, an awareness that incorporates all polarities, for example, good and evil or mind and body. Quantum psychology understands these polarities as related but separate system levels, with each level necessitating a new perspective or understanding. This approach is based on the principle of emergent interactionism, which states that (1) new properties and processes can emanate from the evolving complexity of system development and (2) these properties and processes can *interact* in *unpredictable* ways that previously were never thought possible.

Thus, quantum psychology represents a new way of understanding the emerging consciousness of postmodern existence. Instead of *reducing* consciousness to a set of biological symptoms or ego problems, quantum psychology expands the comprehension of consciousness to include the myriad of multiple perspectives brought about by an ever increasing, complex existence. According to R. L. Gregory, "The converse of reduction is that when parts are combined, surprising or mysterious 'emergent' properties may appear mysterious because reduction descriptions are inadequate" (1987, p. 217).

Multiple perspectives represent different layers or substructures of the general system of consciousness. Emergent interactionism has been employed to explain, for example, how *mind* may represent a layer or system that originates from the brain. Again, to quote R. L. Gregory on this matter:

The Cambridge philosopher C. D. Broad argued (1929) that the universe is inherently "layered" to give emergences with increasing complexities that can never be predicted or explained from any knowledge of lower (generally simpler) "layers of reality." On this account, mind may remain beyond understanding despite knowledge of brain or other function—even though mind is causally given by physical functions. (1987, pp. 217–218)

Although the mind depends on the brain for existence, one does not necessarily have to understand the brain to comprehend the mind. Brain and mind interact but, at some point, a *causal decoupling* occurs and the system operation of mind becomes separate from the brain. One can, therefore, be extensively educated about the brain and yet know very little about the mind. This is an excellent analogy for comparing quantum psychology to the classical model. Classical psychology is concerned with a level of analysis that, although extremely important, neglects the emergent postmodern conditions of consciousness. Such conditions include types and levels of permutations, combinations and interactions, local and non-local, the previously did not exist and were never thought possible. Classical approaches are still concerned with *parts* of the system but neglect the *system* itself. R. L. Gregory provides a relevant machine analogy:

A machine is assembled from component parts, yet how it functions may be explained by more or less abstract general concepts rather than in terms of its parts. . . . We have to look beyond the parts of a mechanism to explain what the parts do. Moreover, there is no simple relation between a machine's structure and its function. A single part, such as the anchor of the clock's escapement, may have several functions, or several parts may combine to produce a single function. Similarly, there is no simple correspondence of parts to function in an organism. (1987, p. 217)

The substitution of the word "symptoms" for "parts" provides an excellent metaphor for comparing a classical to a quantum approach. Emergent interactionism is a central precept of quantum psychology because, as we see in later chapters and especially in the chapter on the deconstruction of the Self (chapter 5), the necessity of incorporating a quantum analysis is directly related to the complex and accelerated pace of postmodern life.

The changes within physics brought about by quantum theory have reached a point where they can be applied toward a fresh understanding of human behavior. What quantum physics implies for psychology is a modification of boundaries. Essentially, we must begin to perceive people and their problems as part of a total system. Once this perception is realized, the next task becomes understanding the *interaction* of the necessary component systems—for example, what factors are important and how they influence one another. This approach is in contrast to the typical thrust of classical psychology and contemporary psychiatry, whose aim is to dissect, label, categorize and normalize. The latter approach emphasizes the understanding of separate parts, whereas the former, quantum approach stresses wholeness.

Furthermore, because conventional psychiatric approaches accent the analysis of parts, the analysis itself can more easily assume a *political agenda*. Parts, in comparison to whole systems, are much easier to manipulate. Inevitably, treatment becomes subtly but inexorably entwined with politics. The political construction of psychiatric diagnosis and treatment is covered in subsequent chapters. For now, the transition to quantum psychology needs to continue.

QUANTUM BUTTONS AND QUANTUM EFFECTS

At this juncture, I would like to introduce two new terms, quantum buttons and quantum effects, concepts that, I believe, best explain the quantum nature of consciousness.

Quantum buttons and quantum effects represent two general processes necessary for understanding quantum psychology. Quantum buttons can be thought of as emotional triggers, whereas quantum effects can be thought of as ripples, or wave-like aftereffects of the triggered event. Both these concepts are based on the non-local theories of quantum mechanics. Yet, quantum buttons and quantum effects do not refer only to the non-physical realm of mind or consciousness; they are further validated by recent developments in neural research, which suggest that the brain itself is organized in a holistic manner. In chapter 3, we discuss the brain in greater depth. For now, I would like to continue with quantum buttons and quantum effects. To do so, I would like to return to the infant analogy with which this chapter began.

Looking at a newborn infant can be an incredible, almost inexplicable, *emotional* experience. People often report feeling choked up or flooded with intense emotions. Babies can evoke this type of response. If we ask, why this is so, some rather peculiar possibilities arise. I have heard infant/adult interactions described as:

1. They (infants) remind me of my childhood.
2. They just *need* me so much, I really feel wanted and loved.
3. They make me feel emotional about my mother.
4. They're just so wonderful, babies are totally there . . . their love is unconditional.

These descriptions happen to come from psychotherapists, but, my impression is that their responses are fairly representative of the general population. Babies, it seems, are receiving a lot of good press these days. Part of this "good press" has to do with how infants make us feel, that is, they induce an affective response. The affective reaction may be positive, negative or lie somewhere in between; the important point is that a reaction is present. In an age of ever increasing alienation, to many people, babies seem the only *real* objects around.

The emotional buttons that babies push could be termed *quantum buttons*. Quantum buttons represent sensitive configurations of consciousness that are often below our level of awareness. Usually, such configurations are prelinguistic or, as termed in the psychoanalytic literature, preoedipal. The phenomena of blushing or unprovoked anger are good examples of quantum buttons being activated. Quantum buttons resonate in and activate unconscious or split-off parts of early preverbal emotional memories. The concept of "split-off parts" is an important facet of object relations theory. It refers to a mental operation quite distinct from the classical concepts of repression, suppression or denial. Splitting is discussed more in the chapter on the schizoid self.

The notion of early, preverbal emotional memories is well established in the literature and such memories are labeled, for example, as global emotional responses, primary process and parataxic/protaxic reactions (Stern, 1988). Often, they lack a specific purpose, but nevertheless, global emotional reactions always *flavor* our interaction with the world. Pristine and sometimes primitive recollections of one's childhood can be triggered, often by seemingly unrelated stimuli. Such processes offer fuel for the speculation that consciousness can potentially contain everything that happened to us. The psychoanalytic notions of the unconscious or archetypal consciousness represents similar ideas. In terms of quantum buttons, it is important to remember that the response they evoke always has an emotional component. The stimuli may be neutral but the button is always emotional and triggers an emotional response.

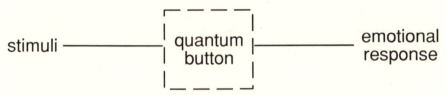

Popular language has a number of ways of describing quantum buttons. That is his "sore spot," or she is very "sensitive" to that topic or "don't act like that around him" are but a few examples. A fascinating related phenomenon is associated with drugs such as alcohol, marijuana and hallucinogens, which, in certain people, often evoke extreme and "uncharacteristic" reactions. To say these behaviors are drug induced is a bit misleading, because, in fact, they are drug released. The potential for these behaviors is already present, or as object-relations theory would submit, such behaviors reflect "split-off" parts of the person that *are denied access to consciousness.*

Artistic creations are definitely capable of pushing our quantum buttons; literature, theatre, music, painting, sculpture and movies have a dramatic tendency to both illustrate and induce quantum effects. A timeless masterpiece like the Mona Lisa or a controversial postmodern work like Andre Serrano's *Piss Christ* always evoke sudden, strong and unexpected emotional reactions. Music is likewise capable of evoking primitive and powerful affective responses. Throughout history tribal drumming has been ritualistically employed to induce altered states that provided access to buried levels of consciousness, whereas in the postmodern "men's movement," tribal drumming is often used to trigger suppressed feelings. I have seen people in advanced states of dementia who, in response to music, often reveal a flood of memories and feelings. Of all the arts having quantum effects, music is perhaps the most primitive and powerful.

Literature can also be powerful both as an elicitor and vivid example of quantum effects. The classic Greek story of Odysseus provides a brilliant example of an event in the present evoking long-forgotten images, memories and emotions. When, after 40 years of wandering, Odysseus finally returns home no one recognizes him. An old nurse who cared for him when he was a child is directed to bathe Odysseus's feet. On recognizing the telltale sign of an old boar wound, a scar that only she knew about, her consciousness becomes inundated with early emotional memories.

The affective response induced by the quantum button being activated is what produces the quantum effect. The quantum effect is non-linear, non-local and interacts within all levels of consciousness. What quantum effects imply is that the end results of behaviors may not necessarily have the predictive and causal relationship often ascribed to them. Some examples of quantum effects are

1. A married man, after having an encounter with a stunning and engaging woman, finds himself buying beautiful roses for his wife as he returns home.
2. A university professor, after delivering a well-received graduate seminar, finds herself getting intoxicated with one of her female students. She is absent from her next two classes of that course.
3. A young black child from a single parent family living in an impoverished area, after being berated in class, is rude toward the teacher and antagonistic toward classmates.

Within consciousness, everything is potentially connected and any connection is both probable and possible. The dilemma we often get into involves etiology. That is, the models employed to provide causal explanations to mental events are often misguided. In the preceding three illustrations, unless one understands the total historical and attending context, it is impossible to conceive a causal relationship. Yet, I am certain most readers did just that. Those trained in classical psychology must have found it impossible not to do so. Guilt, conflict, rationalization, reaction formation, repression, sublimation and displacement, concepts from the armamentarium of classical pschodynamics might all have been summoned as possible explanations.

Case 1 could have been a case of repressed lust and attraction toward one woman leading to guilt and either reaction formation or displacement in buying flowers for another woman. Case 2 might also have been interpreted as a conflict or repressed or sublimated sexual attraction, whereas the third example lends itself to formulation in terms of victimization. The child could be a victim of racial bias within an oppressive system. His behavior might be an expression of thinly concealed rage—an example of poor impulse control.

It is extraordinarily easy to think this way, in fact, among clinicians it can be almost reflexive. Our cultural paradigm makes it simple to jump to conclusions. The automatic tendency to respond according to the parameters of a particular paradigm induces a neglect of the systems context of the event. This very human limitation is not limited to psychodynamics; I easily could have substituted examples germane to the laws of Judaism, Catholicism, liberalism or politically correct behavior. It is, perhaps, also extraordinary to realize that as a matter of course, such fragmentary diagnoses have become an accepted part of daily psychiatric business. What I am saying does not imply that the initial impressions or primary diagnoses that are based on any specific model are always wrong. What I mean is that such judgments are matters of probability, and when considering matters of probability all parts of the system in question must be taken into account. As Vega and Murphy state,

The search for the causes of problems should not be limited to a particular realm. In fact, a pluralistic approach to treatment is supposed to be fostered. Instead of restricted, the knowledge base of practitioners should be flexible and permitted to expand as far as possible. (1990, p. 22)

In all three examples, the entire history and context of the behaviors involved must be understood; the entire story must be taken into account. From a quantum perspective, case 1 could mean an intensification of the man's love for his wife; case 2 could contain innumerable reasons as to why class was missed and for case 3, the question of a real organic impulse disorder cannot be dismissed. In a quantum analysis, these are all possibilities and probabilities that cannot be ruled out. A quantum approach reinforces the notion that it is bad science to jump to conclusions based on preexisting theoretical parameters. In chapter 8 on quantum diagnosis, the importance of understanding complete personal narratives is discussed in greater depth. Furthermore, diagnosis and treatment *are always a matter of judgments, and as such, values are always involved. The diagnostic process is a value judgment.* The established dictums of psychiatric wisdom do not take values into account. Psychotherapy, especially psychoanalysis or medical psychotherapy, is a science, and science, as we are all taught, is supposed to be value free. Commenting on the loss of language, culture and the full range of sociohistorical values in psychiatric diagnosis, Vega and Murphy state:

However, under the guise of value-freedom and science, these so-called subjective elements are often viewed by traditional mental health practitioners and researchers as impeding the development of sound intervention strategies. Precision, accordingly, has tended to be equated with methodological or procedural rigor. Yet, when rigor is pursued as a panacea, precise but socially insensitive clinical judgments are likely to follow. (1990, p. 22)

It is essential to assume a systems perspective in order to understand the quantum implications of an event. Perhaps the best way to illustrate this is with a clinical vignette.

The Case of Mr. T

Mr. T, a 32-year-old caucasian male, came into therapy because of problems of anxiety and guilt. The patient had recently married for the second time and was feeling both guilty and anxious because he was having thoughts and feelings involving his first wife. These symptoms affected his ability to work, interfered with his sleep and were putting a strain on his new marriage. Prior to his second marriage, Mr. T had been divorced for 4 years. Mr. T claims his first marriage was relatively unhappy and that he and his wife fought consistently. During the 4-year hiatus between marriages, the patient claimed that he never even gave his first wife a second thought. He reports being very happy in his second marriage and is extremely upset and puzzled over recollections of his former wife. Mr. T has not confided any of his problems to his present wife.

Let us examine the list in the introduction that compares the classical and the quantum psychological models.

QUANTUM FACTORS	CLASSICAL FACTORS
non-linear	linear
holistic	reductionistic
normal	abnormal
dynamic	fixed
non-local	local
synergistic	mechanistic
irrational	rational

The classical perspective would speculate that Mr. T has unconscious feelings toward his ex-spouse. These thoughts and feelings could represent wishes to be with his former wife. It might be postulated that Mr. T still loves her and that his statements are just examples of denial, repression or reaction formation. Classical psychology might postulate anxiety over unconscious wish fulfillment and guilt over hidden sexual desires. It would certainly hypothesize that there was conflict in the present marriage.

A quantum perspective would evaluate Mr. T's statements at their face value; it would accept that he loves his second wife and has little or no interest in his first one. Since quantum psychology conceptualizes both the mind and brain as being organized in a modular fashion, it would seem only natural that the new marriage would, on occasion, trigger thoughts or feelings concerning the old marriage. This would be an example of a quantum button, or non-local effect, where one event activates feelings or memories associated with another event. The association may be totally insignificant to the content of the memories. For example, if marriage 2 triggers feelings about marriage 1, the only common connection may be the variable of marriage. In some cases, there may be no common connection at all and the aroused memory may be totally random. *No direct causative processes are postulated. There may be no hidden reason for the memories, they may simply be just that—memories.* There may be no need to search for unconscious causes, hidden meanings or to explore what is often called the latent content. Events happen. The anxiety and guilt may simply be misplaced concern over what might be a perfectly ordinary, perhaps even random process.

If the case of Mr. T were encapsulated and summarized within the parameters of both models it might appear as follows.

Non-linear—Mr. T's being in love again in his second marriage was like a quantum button triggering old feelings and memories associated with past loves and former relationships. The evoked affect and memories would be the quantum effects. Such effects do not necessarily mean that Mr. T is still in love with his ex-wife. There is simply a correlation between two events. Mr. T's reactions were a matter of probability.

Linear—The correlation between Mr. T's two marriages would be given more of a causal explanation and interpreted as having hidden meaning. The second marriage could be analyzed as directly causing the release of unresolved feelings toward both his wives.

Holistic—Individual guilt and anxiety are appreciated as unavoidable emotions occurring within a cultural system that is both guilty and anxious. On a personal level, Mr. T's guilt and anxiety need to be understood within a contextual framework. Before any conclusions can be reached, his developmental history, life story, values and especially the quality of his present marital relationship must be understood.

Reductionistic—Guilt and anxiety are always symptomatic of underlying conflicts and difficulties.

Normal—guilt and anxiety are not conceived of as symptoms but as an ordinary, individual substructure of a guilty and anxious cultural suprastructure.

Abnormal—Guilt and anxiety are anomalous phenomena. Such feelings need to be corrected and removed. Guilt and anxiety represent unacceptable responses.

Dynamic—Life is paradoxical. Guilt and anxiety are part of being alive. To be alive and sensitive means that there will be times when one feels guilty and anxious. Because consciousness is fluid and evolving thoughts and feelings will change. At times, guilt and anxiety must be accepted.

Fixed—Guilt and anxiety are negative feelings and symptomatic of a failure to successfully adapt. In order to eliminate them, such emotions must be worked on and addressed with determination and vigor.

Non-local—The sudden appearance of uncomfortable feelings about Mr. T's first wife could be elicited by random factors in his second marriage. There might not even be a connection because a causal association is only a probability, one that seems fairly clear, but a probability nonetheless. There might be numerous intervening variables separating the two marriage events.

Local—A direct and obvious A causes B connection is postulated between the second and first marriages.

Synergistic—A combined and correlated complex interaction of different system levels of consciousness could have produced Mr. T's symptoms. In its implications, synergy is very close to non-locality in that the relationship of the two marriages may be just one possibility.

Mechanistic—This is also similar to locality. A direct causative relationship is hypothesized between two events.

Irrational—Mr. T may be experiencing feelings that are culturally judged as illogical, mad, crazy or foolish. What postmodern culture labels as irrational is, however, an integral substructure of consciousness. Irrational experiences must be accepted and reintegrated into ordinary experience.

Rational—Only logical, common sense, culturally sanctioned experiences are acceptable.

The quantum and classical models represent two poles of a greater whole. Together, the combination leads to a more questioning, accepting and less rigid method of understanding behavior. *Problems develop only when either model is used at the exclusion of the other model.* Every free and liberal approach has the danger of developing its own orthodoxy. Quantum comprehension seeks, at all costs, to avoid dogma and orthodoxy.

OCCAM'S RAZOR AND THE UNCONSCIOUS

A central principle of quantum psychology is that *it makes no inferences about unconscious processes.* Once the unconscious is conjured as an explanatory device, all sorts of meta-psychological mythologies are possible. This is exactly what occurs in psychoanalysis and, to an extent, in other psychotherapies as well. The patient has a problem that he does not understand; the problem manifests itself as symptoms that are understandable to the therapist; the therapist provides an explanatory framework that puts the patient's problem within a specific perspective, a procedure that, usually, is enormously reassuring to the patient. What was once painfully puzzling is now at least comprehendible. Reasons and causes, couched in the meta-language of whatever particular theory the therapist is using, comfort the patient with the knowledge that someone understands what is happening. What often occurs at this point is the insidious and subtle shift from the life of the patient to the life of the theory. For example,

Mr. G came into therapy following a 10-year break from a 7-year twice weekly psychoanalytic psychotherapy. The patient was articulate and sensitive but experienced overwhelming anxiety when relating to females. The anxiety was so debilitating that, despite wishes to start a family, he was, after 60 years, still a bachelor. Mr. G's presenting complaint was that he overidentified with his penis and, in fact, described himself as a walking penis. Mr. G also stated that he had extreme "oedipal rage" and never resolved his feelings toward his mother.

"Who told you this," I inquired.

"My analyst," Mr. G responded.

Apparently, Mr. G spent his 7-year stint of analytic therapy working on his penis identification and unresolved oedipal rage. In a remarkably convoluted and overly analytic manner, he could spend an entire session talking about "his conflict." During our second session, I explained to Mr. G that it would not be helpful to spend our time discussing such matters. Instead, I recommended a short-term cognitive/behavioral assertiveness and relaxation approach. Mr. G's psychotherapy lasted 6 months, after which he dated women on a regular basis.

This clinical vignette in no way implies that cognitive behavioral therapy is preferred over psychoanalytic therapy. It is provided as an illustration that *any* psychotherapeutic encounter faces the danger of transforming into a preoccupation with the viability of theory and meta-theory at the expense of the person. When, in order to comprehend a problem, a person is reduced to elements that fit a theory, the potential for a labyrinth-like meta-journey becomes all too possible. Psychotherapists often forget the principle of Occam's razor—that the simplest and least complicated of explanations is the most preferred. Unless the unconscious becomes manifest in the conscious, quantum psychology does not concern itself with it.

Now this may seem like a subtle distinction, but it is not. For many therapists, the latent and symbolic material of the unconscious is the preferred hunting ground; it is where one should look first. Like a huge vat of metaphorical, primordial soup, the unconscious awaits analytic consumption. A quantum approach entails looking for the unconscious as part of the total consciousness system. If an element of one's consciousness is unconscious it *always* manifests itself as behavior. Furthermore, if a person's problem has to do with unconscious factors there are *always* contradictions in subsystems of consciousness. Behavior, affect, sensations, images and cognition to not correspond. Incongruous phenomena manifested in any one of these spheres is the way to recognize unconscious components of consciousness. Recognition should always be a posteriori and rarely a priori. Humans analyze things too much, search for hidden meanings and probe too deeply. If you look for psychopathology, inevitably it will be found. It all depends on how we look, because as Freud is purported to have said, "sometimes a cigar is just a cigar."

SUMMARY

This chapter provided a very basic introduction to quantum physics. The implications that a quantum approach in physics has for psychology were discussed in depth. Four key principles of quantum physics that are directly relevant to quantum psychology were discussed. These are

1. The role of consciousness in observation and measurement
2. Interaction of systems
3. Non-linearity
4. Non-locality

These factors alter the manner in which reality is perceived and people are understood. It was stressed, however, that the concept of a quantum psychology is paradoxical and must be grasped within the limits of epistemic dualism.

As the chapter proceeded, it might have become evident that the text was shifting into a discussion of contemporary consciousness. Because quantum psychology is a systems approach, it is necessary to explore substructures of consciousness that are often ignored. It is my contention that human consciousness is shifting to a schizoid mode of being, and because this mode has profound implications for the evolution of the species, it would be useful to recognize and understand it. A distinct relationship exists between quantum psychology and schizoid phenomena. Chapter 3 begins to explore the schizoid state.

NOTE

1. In making this comparison, *I am in no way suggesting that what occurs in the subatomic universe parallels our intrapsychic and interpersonal dimensions*, because as Ken

Wilbur (1984) has stated, such analog laws are extremely vague and general. What I am proposing, however, is that similarities between the different system levels that the text discusses should counsel clinical and social scientists to make a "paradigm check." Vague correlations, although imprecise, are often pragmatically critical.

Three

The Schizoid Process

If I must be wrung through the paradox,
—broken into wholeness, wring me around the moon;
pelt me with particles, from the dark side.

                                        Avah Pevolor Johnson

In 1965, the distinguished English psychoanalyst, D. W. Winnicott wrote:

I suggest that in health there is a core to the personality that corresponds to the true self of the split personality; I suggest that this core never communicates with the world of perceived objects, and that the individual person knows that it must never be communicated with or be influenced by external reality. . . . Although healthy persons communicate and enjoy communicating, the other fact is equally true, that each individual is an isolate, permanently non-communicating, permanently unknown, in fact, unfound. (p. 187)

In 1985, the noted neuropsychologist Michael Gazzaniga wrote:

But what of the idea that the self is not a unified being, that there may exist within us several realms of consciousness? It is precisely the idea of the unity of conscious awareness, of SELF, as it is commonly understood, that comes under direct challenge from brain neurology. From these studies the new idea that emerges is that there are literally several selves in man, and they do not necessarily "converse" with each other internally. (p. 346)

   What is remarkable concerning these passages, aside from their implied similarity, is that they originate from two separate disciplines. Winnicott's statement concerning schizoid phenomena is rooted in psychoanalytic meta-psychology, whereas Michael Gazzaniga's conclusions derive from neurobiological brain studies. Yet, the two men, one 21 years later and quite separate from the other, have come to quite similar conclusions regarding the nature of man's psychological being.

Schizoid phenomena indicate a division or split within the mind, and therefore are, in a very general way, related to the problem of consciousness. The following quote from William James reflects psychology's earlier interest in the question of consciousness and the self:

It must be admitted, therefore, that in certain persons, at least, the total possible consciousness may be split into parts which coexist but mutually ignore each other, and share the objects of knowledge between them. More remarkable still, they are complementary. (1890/1950, p. 206)

Psychology's interest in William James's ideas seems to have waned. Yet, inevitably, consciousness remains and should be more precisely understood. I am in complete agreement with the preceding quotations, and considering contemporary cultural trends they are, in all likelihood, understatements. As consciousness becomes an increasingly schizoid system, the manner in which we think, feel, behave and, especially, relate is schizoid. The schizoid situation is pervasive and ubiquitous and affects every substructure of the cultural system. In a sense, most of humankind is now at the point where it becomes necessary to pause, take a deep breath, sit back and say "well, how did we get here?"

THE PSYCHOLOGY OF THE SCHIZOID PROCESS

> Sometimes all of our thoughts are misleading.
>
> Robert Plant

The schizoid nature of our world, as manifested by splits within systems, such as human consciousness and Self is ubiquitous. The schizoid split is reflective of the duality of our existence, a duality that for centuries has plagued and intrigued us. This duality can be found everywhere, from the basic distinction between matter and mind to the relative differentiation between animals and humans and the tragic discriminations among humans themselves. We notice difference before similarity.

The psychological dimensions that are affected by the schizoid condition are

1. Behavior
2. Emotions
3. Thoughts
4. Sensations
5. Imagery

Although space limitations preclude a thorough clinical exploration of how schizoid processes affect these dimensions, they might be briefly summarized in the following way.

Behavior—becomes inconsistent and situational; different self systems act in distinct ways.

Emotions—represent the primary psychological process affected by schizoid structure. Emotions are split off from awareness and tend to be the anathema of schizoid phenomena (Guidano, 1987; May, 1953).

Thoughts—as manifested through language, cognition represents the primary schizoid defense against emotions—that is, the "rationality" of thought is culturally selected over the "irrationality" of emotion. Thoughts and emotions are complementary and represent two different but necessary modes of processing information; each without the other produces a unidimensional and inevitably distorted world view.

Sensations—bodily sensations, especially erotic perceptions are either absent, or situationally determined within schizoid organizations. Symbolization supplants sensuality or, as the cultural philosopher Alan Watts observed, "Our pleasures are not material pleasures but symbols of pleasure, attractively packaged but inferior in content" (1972, p. 75).

Imagery—within schizoid structures the capacity for imagery is virtually nullified and imagery tends to fall beneath the shadow of a linguistically dominated consciousness (Huxley, 1953, 1990).

The condition of the psychological state is a relative affair that is determined by the degree of schizoid organization. Furthermore, splits that occur in consciousness manifest themselves both between and within each of these elements. The longer such splits are allowed to exist, the more unintegrated, unhealthy and one-sided the organism becomes. There also seems to be a magnification and generalization effect in that the longer the schizoid condition goes unrecognized the more pervasive and stronger it becomes. According to Alice Miller,

The more one-sided a society's observance of strict moral principles such as orderliness, cleanliness and hostility toward instinctual drives, and the more deep seated its fear of the other side of human nature—vitality, spontaneity, sensuality, critical judgment and inner independence—the more strenuous will be its efforts to isolate this hidden territory; to surround it with silence or institutionalize it. . . . Splitting of the human psyche into two parts, one that is good, meek, conforming and obedient and the other that is the diametrical opposite, is perhaps, as old as the human race, and one could simply say that it is part of "human nature." (1984, pp. 190–191)

Miller is correct, although she and her fellow psychoanalysts, including the traditional object-relationists tend to underestimate the situation. The split in human nature is more than the dichotomy between good and bad, spontaneity and rigidity, sensuality and detachment. Schizoid processes are not simply tidy black and white opposites. Between and within all subsystems of consciousness there are quantum permutations and combinations, splits within splits upon non-splits. The situation is much more complicated than anyone has yet realized.

We live in a twilight zone land characterized by vast difference between public and private behavior. Ours is a culture mediated and controlled by images and appearances, in which not what is, but what appears to be is seized as reality. Behind the closed doors of our well-attended and proper houses, no one really knows what is happening. In postmodern culture, people become aware of what they think they need to be aware of, which, more often than not, is what the predominant cultural media-technology exposes us to. An example of a common media distortion is the belief that blatant cases of psychopathology and secret behaviors are limited to alcoholics, drug addicts, sexual deviants, dysfunctional families and other assorted victims of psychological trauma. Our culture is accustomed to the unusual and abhorrent behavior that occurs as a result of alcohol and drug use. What we are not used to and refuse to admit is that similar behaviors occur in our living rooms.

AWARENESS, CONSCIOUSNESS AND GENERAL SYSTEMS THEORY

How can consciousness be schizoid? When consciousness is conceptualized in systems terms as a process or operation, the answer becomes clearer. We can only be *aware* of the substructures or parts of consciousness that we experience. At this juncture it is, perhaps, apparent that a rather archetypal tautology can develop as the statement "we can only be aware of what we are conscious of" leads us into a rather vicious circle. In order to avoid this tautological trap, the concepts of awareness and consciousness must be distinguished from one another.

Not everyone is in agreement with this position.[1] Historically, a loose precedent for interchanging the terms consciousness and awareness has been established. But, if consciousness is conceptualized within a general systems framework, awareness can be understood differently. General systems theory describes *systems* as complex regulatory structures with clear boundaries and identities that maintain an osmotic interdependence on surrounding systems. A paramecium, a person, a parliament and a proton can all be considered systems. Both the existence and quality of a system depends on the level of organization involved. One of the reasons general systems theory is so powerful an analytic tool is that all matter, within any level of reality—subatomic, microscopic, personal, international or cosmic—organizes itself.

Expanding organization is a general principle of evolution. In fact, the tendency for matter to organize itself in ever increasing complexity presents another outstanding paradox that physicists are well aware of. The paradox is due to the law of entropy, an established thermodynamic principle that states that over time, physical systems break down, energy is lost and chaos increases. Repeatedly, it has been mathematically and experimentally validated that entropy is increasing as the universe runs out of energy. Now, if on a physical or inorganic scale things seem to be winding down, why is it on a biotic scale that life is becoming increasingly complex? All one has to do is contrast the processes of organic and inorganic evolution to realize that two opposing processes are occurring on very different time scales. Speculation on these questions is well beyond the scope of the book; the issue is raised only to emphasize the complexity of the topic. For now, the important point to remember is that organization is ubiquitous.

If the propensity for matter to organize itself is universal, so too must be systems. Just about any organized entity or process can be conceptualized as a general system; what varies are the system's degree of

1. Complexity
2. Differentiation
3. Integration

Complexity, integration and differentiation are what distinguish one system from another. These three criteria separate people from mitochondria and squirrels and make each organism a unique being. Complexity refers to the variation and number of operations that a system can engage in. There are enormous variations of system complexity both within and between systems. The evaluation of system complexity is an immensely relative and arbitrary task, dependent on value judgments and teleological imperatives. Such analysis depends on a myriad of factors, including the beliefs and purposes of the investigation. In terms of animal research, for example, depending on the values and intended purposes of the investigation, a cat may either be considered a simple creature destined to serve human purposes or a complicated being with an ontological lifeline of its own.

Differentiation concerns the separateness or organizational autonomy of system operations or functions. A system may be complex and yet relatively undifferentiated. Single- or multiple-cell primitive organisms are relatively complex systems that maintain an impressive adaptation to their environment. The same could be said to be true for certain insects. Yet, within such organisms or systems there is relatively little differentiation of function. A single substructure, or part, is often capable of performing multiple operations—digestion, breathing and locomotion. As we move up the evolutionary ladder, these operations begin to be performed by independent structural systems. Differentiated systems have a greater number of substructures and parts. Differentiation does not preclude complexity, it simply provides the system with a better chance at survival. In an undifferentiated system, destruction of one operation usually leads to destruction of the entire system, whereas in a differentiated system, parts or substructures may be lost without endangering the entire system.

Integration pertains to the interdependence of the differentiated system. The human body is a highly differentiated and integrated system. Although the stomach and liver represent independent operations, they are nevertheless in functional communication with one another. Integration refers to the ecological relationship between parts and substructures of a system. In a sense, system integration alludes to the communication or exchange of information between differentiated parts or substructures. In an evolutionary sense, like differentiation, integration is a highly adaptive mechanism. In the event of substructure or part damage or loss, an integrated system is more capable of operational substitution. The brain, one of the most highly complex and differentiated of systems is also one of the most integrated of all organ systems. When a part of the brain is damaged, other systems or parts are often capable of functional replacement. Interestingly and unfortunately, integration of the brain structure does not generalize to the mind or consciousness. This ill-fated shortcoming is what the schizoid state is all about. Before we directly explore the schizoid condition a clearer understanding of general systems theory is necessary.

The existence and identity of a system depends on its difference from its surroundings. When the difference no longer exists, as in death for example, the system structure, as one knows it, no longer exists. That is, the identity of the system changes. Structures act as regulatory devices, governing processes so that the system maintains itself. The ongoing identity of a system depends on its substructures and parts. The substructures determine the nature and purpose of the system, whereas the parts determine its expression. System substructures are what maintain the system; parts may change but the system continues. Although the parts of a system may determine the system's quality, the system itself exists independent of its parts. For example, the human body can be thought of as a general system that persists independent of the removal or change of parts like the spleen, left arm or prefrontal lobe. Legislative bodies can also be thought of as systems that despite individual changes continue to exist.

The separate parts of a system exhibit numerous possibilities that the substructures organize. The brain and nervous system have, in principle, a large number of possibilities that are never realized. One could easily say the same for legislative bodies. Parts, therefore, may determine the flavor or content of what the structure regulates and expresses, but they do not alter the expression itself. As long as the substructures remain, the identity and purpose of the system continues. For example, a general system such as language that organizes and regulates expression will, regardless of changes in parts such as grammar or words, continue to serve its function. It should likewise be noted that systems are a property of *organization* and are not limited to biotic entities. Inorganic elements, whether on an atomic or galactic scale follow systems principles, but because life is continuously organizing itself, living matter provides the optimal example of systems theory.

The levels of organization involved in the processes or operation of consciousness allow it to be conceptualized as a system, with awareness representing a key subsystem. What I am suggesting is that consciousness be understood as a larger process that encompasses awareness. This position clarifies the earlier raised problem of the terms consciousness and awareness being used interchangeably. The question is resolved by utilizing a general systems perspective that conceptualizes consciousness and awareness as connected, but different, system levels. For purposes of illustration, awareness can be conceived of as a beam or flashlight that, depending on the situational context, illuminates specific subsystems of consciousness.

It is the *interaction*, then, of the situational context with consciousness that determines the level of awareness. People are usually only aware of what they have to be aware of, and more often than not, we settle for the lowest common denominator. To accept that awareness can be understood as an interactive process is a radical departure from conventional usage. It is commonly assumed that, once information is learned and becomes part of consciousness, awareness of such information exists independent of any particular situation. But, in reality, it is impossible to always be aware of everything. Awareness is selective; its discriminating nature to a large extent depends on contextual elements that are determined by values and embedded within the cultural system. The relationship of values to awareness and consciousness is a fascinating and integral part of this book and is discussed more in the ensuing chapters.[2]

Unlike awareness, consciousness is not circumspect but a universal aspect of organizational systems principles that, potentially, can include all aspects of experience. Sentient beings, at least as we are familiar with them, can never be simultaneously aware of all levels of consciousness but can, however, be potentially aware of other levels. When potential awareness is diminished, an organism can be said to be in a schizoid state.

A schizoid state is, however, not just a diminished state of awareness but, rather, a split-off or segregated condition. Consciousness may remain complex and the number of differentiated functions may remain intact and actually proliferate, but communication between these different functions or subsystems is impaired. Schizoid consciousness becomes, in essence, an unintegrated phenomenon. Figures 1 and 2 provide a rough schemata of integrated and schizoid consciousness. The terms within each boundary represent different possible subsystems of consciousness, the only difference is that in Figure 1, the subsystems are separated from each other, whereas in Figure 2, the subsystems are available to each other.

Figure 1
Schizoid Consciousness

| SCHOOL | | FEMALENESS | | WORK |

| SOCIAL | | CHILD | | FANTASY |

| SENSUALITY | | MALENESS | | EMOTION |

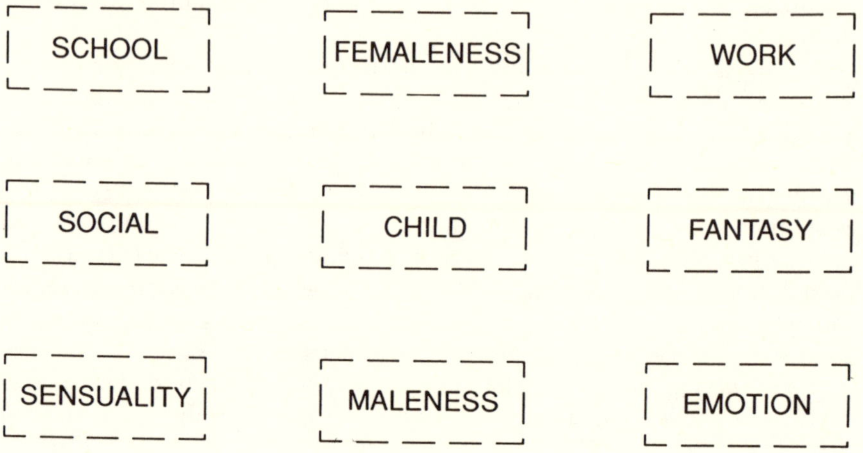

THE NATURE OF SEGREGATED CONSCIOUSNESS

If schizoid consciousness is a segregated consciousness, the question then arises as to the structural nature of this segregation. On both a cognitive and neurological level, this question has received ample experimental validation. In terms of mental models, the mind, or consciousness, may be conceived as being organized in a modular fashion. At first, there appears to be nothing radical about this idea. In fact, however, a modular model of the mind represents a profound departure from psychology's conventional notion of mental operations.

Thinking of the mind as organized in a modular fashion is a relatively recent development, an outgrowth of neuropsychological research that, oddly enough, is very much in accord with the early British object-relations school. The initial object-relations speculations of W.R.D. Fairbairn (1952), H. Guntript (1969) and D. W. Winnicott (1965, 1988) created a theoretical structure that described the existence of separate, *split-off* parts of consciousness coexisting with ordinary consciousness. *Ordinary* consciousness is usually appraised as the Self, a personal construct that represents an organism's predominant and accepted personal mode of being in the world. In other words, it is the Self that is presented to the world and the Self that most people see. As a precursor to self-psychology, the object-relationists began employing the organizational concept of the Self-system. As we shall see, there is much more to the Self than what is socially presented.

Figure 2
Integrated Consciousness

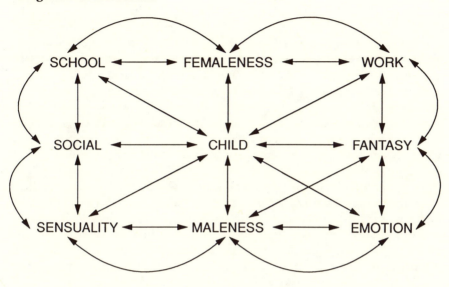

The understanding that in addition to component parts such as ego, id and super-ego that the human psyche could contain autonomous Self-systems was a bold leap. The critical difference between a Self and an ego is simply a systems matter of organizational inclusion. The Self is a larger system that includes the ego as one of its substructures. As a larger, more complex entity, the Self-system is a quantum construction, whereas the ego is a cause and effect holdover from Newtonian mechanics. Ego, id and super-ego represent, of course, the jargon of early Freudian psychoanalysis. What is not often discussed is that Freud's usage of these terms was firmly couched in the Cartesian dualism and Newtonian mechanics of late nineteenth and early twentieth century science. Old paradigms die slowly, and Freud was never really able to extricate his mental models from their effects. It is in comparing the ego and Self-systems that the radical nature of both the schizoid and modular models of the mind becomes apparent.

The Ego

The ego, or ego functions as they are usually called, is conceptualized as a higher level "executer" function of the personality. As such, the main purpose of the ego is adaption and the principal vehicle of adaption is logical thought and rationality. Within classical or mainstream psychoanalytic theory little emphasis, except in a psychopathological   nse, is placed on creative, unusual, emotional, intuitive or irrational thought processes. This is not to say that psychoanalytic theory does not address such phenomena, because clearly, the literature abounds with analytic explorations into artistic, mystical and extraordinary phenomena. But such inquiries are designed to do what psychoanalysis does best, which is, of course, the psychoanalytic investigation. This inquiry is, by nature, a reductionistic, interpretive process that could more aptly be termed the psychoanalytic dissection. In this interpretive/disective process, the patient's life is understood within a highly selective, value-laden, linear framework. Essentially, a life is taken apart, reduced to a particular set of theoretical components, then reassembled according to the value system of the psychoanalyst. In the majority of cases this value system is what I have already, following an historical precedent, termed the "establishment" cultural value system. Employing the basic canon of psychoanalysis, "where once was id, now shall be ego," most psychoanalysts concentrate on reinforcing ego functioning and ego boundaries. The ego is the defender of the faith, and the faith is, of course, a rational, linear, constrained, mechanistic mode of processing information. The following 12 ego functions reflect the predominance of our preoccupation with predictability, order and control:

1. Reality testing
2. Judgement
3. Sense of reality
4. Regulation and control of drives, affects and impulses
5. Object relations
6. Thought processes
7. Adaptive regression in the service of the ego
8. Defensive functioning
9. Stimulus barrier
10. Autonomous functioning
11. Synthetic-integrative functioning
12. Mastery-competence (Bellack & Hurvich, 1977)

An error indigenous to traditional psychology is the common assumption that these 12 functions are absolute and universal. Julian Jaynes (1976), in reference to early Greek civilizations, and Ruth Benedict (1938), in discussing modern cultural varieties, both elucidate the relativity of ego functions. What we consider natural and universal survival skills are historically and culturally relative. The ego depicted above, in addition to being a relatively recent historical development, is the ego of the modern industrial age and represents an entity whose purpose and function is restraint of the id. Now, just what is the id? In classical psychoanalysis the id was originally conceived of as primitive, impulsive, self-serving and destructive, its primary raison d'être being sexual and aggressive. The id needed to be contained, and the ego was to set the boundaries. Firm boundaries are a very important concept in psychoanalysis and are usually perceived as a sign of health. The ego, therefore, is the gatekeeper of civilization, the guardian of rationality and the defender of linearity; in short, the protector of the predominant cultural value system.

A final point before we leave the ego—in an historical sense, it is interesting to note that when comparing the two original giants of psychoanalysis, Sigmund Freud and Carl Jung, it is Freud's work that has remained prominent and popular. With the exception of major metropolitan Jungian enclaves and a few esoteric academic journals, Jungian thought seems to have been designated as a footnote of psychoanalytic history. Although Jung was, at times, a bit erratic and prone to mystical speculation, if one really stops to think about it so was Freud. Over the past decade, Freudian meta-theory has come under accurate and virulent attack, not only by feminists and anthropologists but also by ego, self and object-relations psychoanalysts. Nevertheless, Freud rather than Jung endured, and one of the reasons for the tenacity of Freudian thought is its adherence to the linear party line. In many ways, Carl Jung was a person ahead of his time. His concepts of synchronicity, archetypal and collective consciousness, persona and anima/animus are in accord with a quantum approach.

In describing the ego, I have taken the reader on a bit of a side trip. This divergence, although important, will be discussed in greater depth in the chapter on quantum diagnosis. For present purposes, the primary point is that the language of classical psychoanalytic thinking is firmly couched in the mechanical Newtonian paradigm. Concepts comparing the ego to a steam engine or boiler room and expressions like safety valve, discharge, libidinal energy, repression, displacement and sublimation are but a few examples of such language. Such language is reflective of a linear causal model where parts of one system distinctly act on the parts of another system.

The Self

Ahh, the Self. In contemporary culture the Self has achieved a preeminence bordering on preoccupation and, perhaps, obsession. At this juncture, however, it is not my intention to express cynicism, but rather to describe the self in general system terms. What has come to be known as the Self is a composition of modular self subsystems that, potentially, can operate in tandem. By potentially, I refer to the fact that under certain conditions such subsystems act disjunctively. Thus, the components of the general Self-system may not always act collectively or be in agreement.

Disjunction may be caused by organic violation, such as neurological, structural or endocrinological damage, or may be related to psychological factors. In the complex and often contradictory postmodern civilized world, conflicting Self-subsystems of a psychological origin are increasingly becoming the norm.

For present purposes, the essential point is that the Self is a *multiple* rather than solely a unitary system. Some of the parts and substructures within the various Self-systems represent key instinctual drives, such as sex, maternal nurturance, aggression, territoriality and emotion, that are partially biologically determined. The expression of the biological parts of any given system are, however, always mediated through the general cultural system. In humans then, any Self-system is a culturally, or as it is more commonly termed, a socially constructed reality. Language is the principal vehicle of Self and reality construction. Language, however, does not operate in isolation but is a substructure of a larger cultural system that includes a profusion of substructures and parts. In relation to language, two of the larger and more crucial substructures are values and reality assumptions. In subsequent chapters, we investigate how language, values and reality assumptions contribute to the contemporary schizoid state.

THE SCHIZOID BRAIN

Verification of the schizoid model is not limited to cognitive paradigms of mind but is likewise corroborated by brain research. Current thinking in neuropsychology indicates that the notion of linear consciousness is in error and that the brain tends to organize itself in a modular fashion. That is, instead of a group of separate organizational structures connected in series, there are independent functioning units that operate in a parallel fashion and can be totally separate from our conscious verbal self. Our conscious verbal self, what we tend to think of as our mind, is neurologically and anatomically located (at least for most right-handed people) in the brain's left hemisphere.

The first clue that there are two separate, yet interdependent, brains and hence, two potential Self-systems and even two possible consciousnesses, originated with the early split-brain studies. Prior to the neuropsychological studies, existence of other selves could also be documented, although somewhat less empirically, through

1. Altered states of consciousness such as hypnosis

2. Dreams

3. Mystical experiences

4. Drug-induced phenomena

5. Neurological studies such as the experiments of Wilder Penfield (1975)

6. Clinical observation, for example, dissociative reactions and multiple personal-ities (which are now a nosological category considered to be underdiagnosed, probably because of our theoretical ego bias)

Conclusions drawn from split-brain studies, once controversial, are now well accepted as fact. Our two brain hemispheres, although connected through the corpus callosum, can act separately. Independent functioning of the hemisphere is, of course, most evident in "split-brain patients" (those who have had the corpus callosum surgically severed) or in patients undergoing the Wada test, which allows one brain hemisphere to be put to sleep. Although these are extreme examples, best used for experimentation, to some extent the separation of hemispheric functioning occurs universally.

In general, the right hemisphere functions in an intuitive, non-linear fashion most suitable to temporal-spatial, mathematical and musical oper-ations, whereas the left hemisphere operates in an analytical, sequential manner most applicable to language, logical thinking and planning. One must beware, however, of conceiving such separations as absolute, an error that is already endemic to the media and "pop psychological theories." Carrying the fact that the brain has separate functions to its extreme would lead to a simplistic view of a holistic and quite complex organ. One can envision a new form of phrenology being the next logical step.

The true picture of the brain and its relationship to consciousness and the mind is, in fact, more complex than was originally thought. For example, Michael Gazzaniga (1985) proposes a left-hemisphere-based interpreter that accommodates, corrects and explains, in a manner consistent with our self image, any thought, emotion or behavior that might arise from another module. In studies once again employing the proverbial split-brain subject, it was discovered that the left hemisphere would provide explanations that were consistent with the subject's belief system for phenomena that the right hemisphere had witnessed.

Even if these explanations had little relevance to the observed phenomena, they were accepted as true if they were consistent and logical. Thus, in some ways part of our brain acts as an operational constructor of reality, accepting information that conforms to our image of the world, rejecting information that does not and modifying information that is marginal so that it fits our constructs. It is not quite erroneous to state then that part of our brain (for most, the left hemisphere) constructs reality. This is a key point, especially germane to the tenets of a quantum psychological ap-proach. What neuropsychology suggests is that our perception and inter-pretation of events is predetermined by a specific world view or paradigm; that is, events in the world are modified to fit our belief system. This is true not only in science but in everyday life, as well as in the three case examples provided in chapter 2. A quantum approach instructs an observer to consider perceptions and interpretations as but one out of many probabilities and thus requires an analysis of the whole situation. As the text develops, the matter of where these belief systems originate and how they affect daily interaction is explored further. Essentially, what these findings mean is that we are now working within a constructivist paradigm.

In Stanley Pribram's (1986) holographic model of the brain, the term "constructional realism" is used to describe this process. All postmodern constructivist philosophies of science likewise conceptualize the brain as being an active constructor of reality. In processing reality, our operational constructor must exclude (split, deny, repress, suppress) the parts of ourselves that are internally contradictory to our main self-construct. Put in the language of Leon Festinger's (1957) cognitive dissonance theory, one would say that two incompatible belief systems cannot exist within the same system for any extended period of time without causing a severe strain. A person, or persons for that matter, cannot live in a state of cognitive dissonance; something has to be modified—either one of the beliefs must change or be denied. In Gazzaniga's model, this denial takes place in the encoding of information within a module.

Information encoded in modules may or may not have access to the consciousness system of the socially constructed Self. The Self, or personal consciousness, is generally considered to be a left-hemisphere, language-based phenomenon. This belief exposes our cultural bias that consciousness is a language-based phenomenon, when in reality, language is not necessary for consciousness and represents but one subsystem of the entire general structure. As Gazzaniga states, information can be encoded without the language systems awareness: "The information becomes encoded in the brain in one of the many mental modules that records experiences. It is not, however, one that talks" (1985, p. 84).

Thus, it is quite possible to have within us numerous and possibly self-contradictory thoughts or feelings. The only way these alternate modules manifest themselves is through the expression of behaviors and emotions that seem strange, or "unlike ourselves." It is difficult to become aware of these alternate modules because our left hemisphere abhors cognitive dissonance and loves consistency—hence our relatively unitary and stable view of the world and ourselves.

A similar concept is espoused by Robert Ornstein (1987) who views the intrinsic organization of the mind as a group of semiautonomous "talents," "modules" and "policies," coordinated by a "mental operating system." In this model, the brain is seen as organizing the mind in a hybrid system of separate belief systems that maintain reality and the illusion of a consistent self. Ornstein speculates that our experience of reality is often illusory and our rationale for decisions, although internally logical, is often irrational. George Kelly's (1955) theory of personal constructs is a further example of a clinician who has thought about the mind in terms of a varied modular self system. Kelly is a good illustration of someone outside the sphere of clinical meta-psychology whose theories of human behavior allude to the existence of a modular self system. He is remembered as a personality theorist and the forerunner of cognitive psychology whose ideas, although popular in England, are not remembered in the United States (Jankowicz, 1987).

In terms of the Self-system, basically, these other selves represent split-off parts of the personality that the person feels are expressively unacceptable. Hence, the notion of their being hidden from others. As pointed out, it is in the expression of contradictory thoughts, feelings or behaviors that a person can first become aware of the existence of other selves. What we consider our conscious selves are to a large extent verbally tagged memories associated with the interpretations we have given our emotions, thoughts and actions. These memories, encoded in modules, can compute, remember, feel and act. In terms of mental functioning, a module is a self-sufficient entity that does not require language to encode. Modules may, then, always be reacting to the environment even if we are not consciously aware of their presence. A very simple example of this phenomenon is blushing. According to Gazzaniga,

Behavior elicited is the way to discover the multiple selves dwelling inside. Behavior is the way these separate information systems communicate with one another. It is probable that very little communication goes on internally. It is only after we behave in a way that is contrary to the usual principles of the verbal system that we may discover the multiple selves actually dwelling inside. (1985, p. 356)

Therefore, within this neuropsychological model, where our "self" is really a collection of "selves," preverbal experiences are, at least theoretically, all present. It is at this juncture that the overlap between schizoid phenomena and a quantum approach should start to become apparent. As R. D. Laing (1966) points out, the concept of Self includes not only oneself but direct, meta- and meta-meta-perceptions of ourselves and others, all of which are included in our personal construct of Self. How I perceive myself is constantly being modified by how others see me, which in turn modifies how others see me, which in turn modifies how I see myself. Therefore, the concept of Self is basically a process construct that allows for a great deal of input, output, modification and *interaction*. Within this perspective, quantum factors along with the four key principles (complementarity, consciousness, interaction and non-linearity) assume a significant level of importance. Because schizoid processes affect all aspects of the Self-system, it is the *interaction of these parts and processes that quantum psychology attempts to address*.

Of significance is that splitting mechanisms that occur within the Self are quite different from the defense mechanisms that occur with the ego. Although the ego may repress a thought or wish or instinctual urge (a singular unit of mental functioning), schizoid splitting entails the separation of entire self systems (modules, in neuropsychological language) so that the development of separate selves occurs. In an attempt to clinically explain the process of splitting, these splits have often been dichotomized along dimensions such as, true versus false self, real versus unreal self or authentic versus unauthentic self. In reality, however, the situation is even more complex because there are probably numerous selves, within both dimensions, within each person.

Ego defense mechanisms may be conceived as operating on a molecular level, whereas schizoid phenomena operate on a molar level. It must be remembered that within Gazzaniga's neurobiological model, the self is conceived as a module and each module is conceived of as potentially having its own independent hierarchical organization—id–ego–superego. The conceptualization of the mind as having separate hierarchical organizations is corroborated by general systems theory as well as Arthur Koestler's (1978) and Gregory Bateson's (1972) holarchical mode of the mind.

The self may be aware, unaware, partially aware or only symbolically aware of its other selves. The more unaware the self is of other selves (that is, the more complete the splits), the greater the degree of schizoid pathology. R. D. Laing (1966) applies the term ontological insecurity as a description of the person who is split off (out of touch with parts of the self) yet unaware of the split. Schizoid problems can exist on any level—for example, linguistic (oedipal) or prelinguistic (preoedipal)—although the tendency toward deep schizoid states seems to originate in very early stages of development. Earlier splits will inevitably result in more damage to the wholeness of the personality and the general health of the person (Balint, 1968).

The classic obsessional character who constructs for himself an obsessional existence within an obsessional profession creates an island of obsessional safety for himself. Such a person remains forever cut off from experiences that might threaten his obsessional defenses and therefore is constantly in a state of ontological insecurity, that is, an insecurity of being or of existence itself. What is being defended against are not only feelings associated with a spontaneous non-obsessional mode of existence but an entire way of being, the separate secret, or split-off, selves that perhaps feel needy, vulnerable, good or bad, dirty or clean, grandiose or unlovable. The split-off self that is beyond, in this case, the obsessional character's consciousness, corresponds to what D. W. Winnicott calls the true self.

The true self (a more accurate term would be true selves) is the repository of all real responsiveness to the world and, in this sense, is based on basic biological and psychological needs of the organism—to be warm, satiated, dry, secure and protected from excessive impingement. For most warm-blooded creatures, these factors are determined by the basic qualities of the mothering figure as related to the mothering function—holding, nursing, kissing, rocking and soothing the infant. Winnicott calls these functions good-enough mothering and suggests, in agreement with Fairbairn (1952), that it is the failure of good-enough mothering to provide a warm holding environment for the infant that leads to the schizoid process of a false and true self-system. Therefore, it is the failure of the subjective and objective internal environment that leads to schizoid development. Because there is no possibility of the infant's needs being perfectly met at all times, it follows that the schizoid condition *is a universal and a relative* concept. Fairbairn (1952) was well aware that the generality of schizoid phenomena was subject to criticism; in reference to which he states:

Actually I am quite prepared to accept this criticism, but only with a very important qualification—one in the absence of which my concept of "Schizoid" would be so comprehensive as to become almost meaningless. The qualification which confers meaning on the concept is that everything depends upon the maternal level which is being considered. The fundamental schizoid phenomena is the presence of splits in the ego; and it would take a bold man to claim that his ego was so perfectly integrated as to be incapable of revealing any evidence of splitting at the deepest levels, or that such evidence of splitting of the ego could in no circumstances declare itself at more superficial levels . . . the basic position of the psyche is invariably a schizoid position. (p. 8)

QUANTUM PSYCHOLOGY AND SCHIZOID PHENOMENA

Because quantum psychology involves a holistic, systems understanding of consciousness, it must concern itself with schizoid phenomena. This, in fact, it does. There is a striking similarity between the passage from Gazzaniga quoted at the beginning of this chapter and the following statement from physicist F. A. Wolfe:

But do these separate worlds ever interact? Indeed they do. It is their interaction, or better said, their superposition which creates new possibilities. . . . Yet, each world is essentially unknown to the other. Thus, each edition of you is aware only of his or her own world. (1988, pp. 131–132)

The correspondence between Wolf's statement concerning quantum mechanics and Gazzaniga's comment concerning the brain is startling. The four tenets (complementarity, consciousness, interaction and non-linearity) so critical to quantum psychology are in accordance with schizoid phenomena. Complementarity, which states that the universe cannot be understood in a singular, unitary fashion, but only within a multiple, overlapping reality perspective applies to the brain, consciousness and the Self as well. Each of these entities is a systems process that must be evaluated and understood within a multilayered systems perspective. As the philosopher Feldstein states,

My awareness embeds many layers, each the precipitate of a more inclusive, less penetrable antecedent subjectivity, none, even the nethermost layers absolutely unconscious or, with respect to those layers, in any clear sense conscious, and all elicited by symbolic elaboration. (1978, p. 1)

Consciousness is also crucial to understanding schizoid processes because in systems terms, if one realizes that consciousness is the supraordinate general system, then possibly it is the general system itself that is schizoid. There are splits within and between ourselves and nature that reflect a schizoid process. We always seem to be searching for either missing parts of our Selves or for parts of the world that we feel are necessary to complete ourselves. Although we are not always *aware* and cannot clearly articulate it, our consciousness is, nevertheless, a schizoid operation.

Because awareness is an interactive process, the relationship of interaction to schizoid phenomena also becomes apparent. What we are aware of depends on the contextual relationship of the systems components of consciousness. If our brains, the Self and consciousness are multilayered, then it must be through the complex and quantum interaction of these multiple layers that reality gets constructed. This is the quantum interactive Self discussed by Roger Penrose in chapter 4. Finally, a Self or consciousness that is structurally schizoid cannot be understood in linear terms alone. Non-linearity and non-locality must also play a crucial role. The modular model of the brain allows for the parallel processing of information that must, at times, result in non-linear and non-local information processing. There are clear-cut advantages for an information processing system like the brain to be arranged in parallel fashion. These benefits are

1. A dramatic increase in processing speed
2. A system that is fault tolerant and impressively persistent
3. A storage system that can accommodate large inputs of information and distribute such information so that it can be accessed in milliseconds (Churchland & Churchland, 1990)

Because it consists of separate components, parallel cerebral organization is, however, very susceptible to becoming schizoid.

CLARIFICATIONS AND SUMMARY

I assume that by now, the reader might share my feelings that some clarifications are in order. I have, after all, introduced several complex terms and concepts, most notably among these Self, awareness and consciousness. There is a key entity that I have assiduously avoided referring to, and I am afraid that, at this point, if clarification is to be possible it will be necessary to introduce it. What I have evaded is mind.

I am not exactly certain how to integrate the concept of mind into the general system of consciousness. Basically, there are two precedents that can be followed. The terms mind and consciousness can be employed identically, each referring to the same process, or the terms can be considered as separate operational systems. Although, intuitively, my sympathy is with the latter position, for now, such an approach needs to be avoided.

The main reason for this circumvention is that the difference between mind and consciousness, if not a matter of semantics, is a real distinction that requires a theoretical rationale. Again, because my support lies with the second possibility, developing such an explanation would take up too much text and I do not want to divert the reader from the basic premise of the book. Therefore, please consider that, at present, I employ the concepts of consciousness and mind interchangeably.

As for the book's basic premise, thus far, I have been constructing an argument favoring the incorporation of a quantum approach into traditional psychology. This chapter introduced the idea that consciousness, as the supraordinate system, and the Self, as a system, substructure, have the propensity to develop in a schizoid manner. Schizoid states were described as structural splits that are reflective of an unintegrated system. Schizoid splits always affect the whole person; rarely do they occur in only one psychological dimension. Sensations, images, feelings, thoughts and, ultimately, behavior are all interrelated in the matrix of consciousness. The term awareness was employed to indicate a subsystem of consciousness that operates like a special interactive "lens," illuminating, detecting or focusing on other substructures or parts of consciousness.

The following chapters, in addition to describing the relationship of schizoid phenomena to quantum psychology, will introduce observations from both personal and clinical experience. In essence, we explore the relationship of consciousness to the systems of community and culture.

From the psychological dimension, the text proceeds into the cultural dimension. Although it is usually accepted that the Self is culturally constructed, it is often forgotten that culture is reciprocally Self-constructed. As Andrew Locke states,

The concepts of Self and Culture are interdependent: one cannot exist without the other. Thus, while it has become commonplace to regard the self as a cultural product, and enquire to the "environmental" (cultural) factors that lead to the expression or inhibition of this or that aspect of the self, we must not forget the reverse perspective; that culture itself is a product of the self. (1981/1990, p. 219)

NOTES

1. For answers to this question as well as a superb review of consciousness see J. Pickering and M. Skinner (1990).

2. For an in-depth discussion of the general systems nature of consciousness, see DeBerry (1991). It should be noted that the conceptualization of consciousness in systems terms is in agreement with the position of numerous psychologists including C. T. Tart, J. Jaynes and R. Ornstein as well as the philosopher Pere Teilhard de Chardin.

Four

Sandboxes and Elevators

Steer clear of all culture.

Epicurus

At this juncture, prior to discussing culture per se, it might be helpful to first identify one of the primary themes that is developing as the text proceeds. Schizoid development represents both an historical and relative process that has, either directly in psychoanalysis or indirectly in the social sciences, been thoroughly discussed. Why then, should a preexisting entity like schizoid phenomena be made a cornerstone of what purports to be a new psychological approach? The answer can be found in what is called *postmodern culture*, a novel emergent that continuously will be referred to and leads to the following postulate:

Postmodernism can be described as a process that increases the frequency and acceleration of events that induce a concomitant escalation of interactions, combinations and associations of events that previously had minimal connection. It is proposed that the postmodern acceleration process contributes to a heightened predisposition for schizoid development. In turn, because of the principle of emergent interactionism, this mushroom effect leads to the appearance of novel emergents that cannot be explained by prior theory or analyzed by antecedent methodology. Such changes necessitate the inclusion of a quantum psychological approach in conventional, psychological procedures.

With this in mind, let us proceed with observations concerning the relationship of schizoid phenomena and the cultural system.

Because individual consciousness expresses itself through the machinations of a socially constructed Self, inevitably we must explore the social aspect of this construction. According to Pickering and Skinner (1990),

Consciousness is not just a property or function of an individual but is generated by and is dependent on interaction between individuals. . . . symbolic function and sociality are both crucial in the construction and maintenance of the cultural matrix surrounding human life. It is within this matrix that human consciousness arises, is formed and maintained. (p. 114)

In chapter 3, the association of culture to the schizoid process was introduced. Further clarification of the psychological vicissitudes of schizoid phenomena precluded an adequate discussion of this relationship. The quantum psychology of the individual could, I fear, encompass the entire text. At this point, a deliberate switch is necessary. Rather than concentrate on the intrapsychic exhibition of schizoid phenomena, let us assume an opposite tack and examine the interpersonal, or cultural, factors. I am in complete agreement with Chris Sinha who states "that we must have a new science: a science of culture rather than a science of psychology if we are to understand the determinants of human behavior" (1990, p. 182).

This is a difficult chapter to write. The challenge stems from the fact that because "culture" is a conspicuously large topic there is an excess of material to discuss. Furthermore, when discussing culture, inevitably, we move into the convoluted arena of the political/economic system. I am, therefore, going to have to limit myself. Despite restrictions, however, the chapter will undoubtedly have a generalist tone. From a broad perspective, cultural consciousness will be described and augmented by examples from specific situations.

Numerous splits exist in the way we live our lives. Because these splits are part of accepted cultural practices, they typically go unnoticed. Once again, our capacity not to notice the ordinary blinds us to the way our lives are constructed. Cultural splitting manifests itself in the individual Self and encourages the construction of distinct and separate identities. Three general areas that are familiar examples of cultural splitting are shown in figure 3. Although the right and left sides of the figure are separate, they are interconnected among themselves. In our culture, there is a strong correlation among the public, work and adult Self; likewise, a similar relationship exists among the private, social and child Self. The public, adult, work Self is serious, responsible, sanctimonious and duty bound. The private, child, social Self is playful, joyous, innocent, unpretentious and free.

This division reflects the growing disparity between work and play. Play is the property of children, whereas for adults, play is reserved for social or private times when the adult engages in behavior not evident in his public or work Self. The invention of the modern "weekend" is an example of time that is culturally set aside for play. Thus, in addition to any structural tendency of brain and mind, our *culture* also encourages a schizoid existence. The responsible and serious adult that exists from Monday to Friday is expected on Saturday to transform into the quintessential party and leisure

Figure 3
Cultural Splitting

public SELF	versus	private SELF
work SELF	versus	social SELF
adult SELF	versus	child SELF

animal. This strange split is not limited to the weekend/weekday polarity but is endemic throughout our society. Many college students expect to party through their undergraduate years and anticipate, upon graduation, an abrupt shift to serious and joyless responsibility. Children and teenagers are told that "they better have fun now" because it will be different when "they grow up." Traditional religion also has an influence on the development of schizoid sexual tendencies. One Catholic patient said that for 20 years she was taught that sex was sinful and dirty only to discover on her wedding night that she was expected to transform herself into a passionate seductress. To be chaste in public and a whore in the marriage bed was what was presumed of her. Many people have had the experience of being taught not to hurt others only to be drafted into military service and expected to kill. What our culture dictates is the development of separate systems of behavior that can be situationally evoked; in short, a *situational Self.*

The situational self is a cultural manifestation that is highly dependent on language. Across cultures, until language sets in and cultural conditioning begins, humans are very similar. In most cases, babies, toddlers and children are by nature open, joyful and loving. As culture takes over, the trusting responsivity of the infant becomes distorted. *Responding* to the world is a key element of organic life; its disfiguration represents one of the main shortcomings of the postmodern, situational self.

RESPONSIVITY

Because the concept of responsivity is central to understanding schizoid phenomena, I want to expound on it a bit. Responsivity has to do with responding. The thesaurus within my Word Perfect software provides five synonyms for the word *respond*: answer, react, rebut, rejoin, reply and return. All of these basically carry the gist of the word. The natural proclivity of any organism to respond to stimuli is exemplified in the naive reactions of children and animals. One of the pleasures of interacting with my dog, Wolfgang, or my young son, Julian, is the immediate and authentic response that I get. Duplicity or pretence, the need to hide or *edit* their response has yet to develop in Julian and will probably never occur in Wolfgang.

What happens to people after language and enculturation become established is a type of *editing* that precludes authentic responding. I especially like the word *edit* because it conveys the artificial, almost media-like process that most people in our culture go through before responding. In the service of pretence and posture, as the *situational* context demands, a role is assumed, options are reviewed and a response is *decided* on. Sometimes this editing process is conscious, but more often than not it is simply reflexive. In terms of consciousness, it is not necessary to be an animal or an infant to respond authentically. Intelligence, education and even adulthood should not necessarily prelude authentic responding. What is necessary for responsivity is first an *awareness* of what is occurring in one's personal consciousness and second an appropriate desire to express it, that is, to respond to what one is aware of. The expression may be through words or simply through action, for example, remaining in a pleasing circumstance or leaving an unpleasant situation. The *important elements are that (1) the person is aware of his response and (2) the decision to react to the awareness is a matter of conscious choice.* Response, awareness and choice represent the antithesis of schizoid behavior.

THE "TRUE" SELF

We are taught to hide what might be called our true selves, a process that is the essence of schizoid behavior. Part of the problem, as we will learn in chapter 5, is that as the *true self* disappears through the window of postmodernism; when we look inside, all too often, we find nothing. Part of the problem lies with the term *true self.* The phrase implies a romantic notion of a *core self* or *essence* that truthfully reflects that "real" person hiding within. The fact that these phrases lead to a vision of a vestigial homunculus scouring about in our skulls is a testimony to the premodern origin of the idiom. The concept of true self has probably always been a misnomer. The term represents not a thing *but a process, a way of responding without pretence and duplicity. The true self is nothing more than an organism's response minus the cultural editing process.* Let me illustrate this with the following hypothetical dialogue between two people who are attracted to one another:

Dialogue One

Person 1. Statement: "*You know, you are a really intelligent and beautiful person. I like you . . . can I be with you?*"

Person 2. (Does not respond immediately, thinks reflexively to self . . . I better not indicate how eager I am for attention, person 1 will think I am too needy, will think I cannot get anybody, if they think I am beautiful and intelligent then they do not really know me, gotta stay cool, I wonder what they really want . . .)

Response: "*No, not today, I'm busy . . . why don't you call me next week, maybe we can do lunch.*"

Dialogue Two

Person 1. Statement: "*You know, you are a really intelligent and beautiful person. I like you . . . can I be with you?*"

Person 2. Response: "*Yes . . . I feel the same way about you.*"

I hardly think it necessary to expound on the difference between the two exchanges. It is difficult to describe responsivity and the true self without resorting to words like authentic, honest, real, open, genuine, valid and sincere. Part of the problem is that these words have achieved a gold medal in cultural triteness. Nevertheless, with circumstances taken into account, responsivity does represent the initial and most honest possible reaction. In this sense, responsivity might be defined as an organism's reaction minus *inhibiting* cultural effects. Kind of a "that's how I would really like to respond" response. I am not advocating the elimination of all cultural restrictions, my argument is limited to the elements that constrain potential relatedness. The point to remember is that the *true self is a process* that represents responding in an unfeigned manner. One could say that the connection between the basic biological and psychological needs of the person and the ritualized, pseudo-expression of the needs has been partially severed. If we love or are attracted, hate or are repulsed by another, why cannot we just express it; why must feelings be concealed? The words of a schizoid but rather articulate patient ring true for an entire culture:

Why should I let people know how I feel or think? They only hurt or take advantage of you. They're just waiting for an opening so they can humiliate you. You're always asking me what do I feel . . . what do I feel? Well, why the hell should I tell you anyway? What makes you think you're different from anyone else? Why should I trust you?

Trust is a major issue in schizoid development. In terms of a person's capacity to trust, a tremendous range exists and the more schizoid a person is, the more that capacity is impaired. Furthermore, our culture directly teaches that trust is situational—"don't ever say that to the neighbors. Don't ever tell your teachers that. Wait until the holidays to tell her. Tell him while you're at work. Never be honest with someone when you first meet them (until you figure out *what they want from you*)"—are commonplace cultural admonishments. What makes the situation rather weird in an eerie sort of way is that most people *appear to be trustworthy*. Remember the last supervisor who appeared to be your friend, the last friend that seemed to be your confidant, the last doctor who acted like he was your friend?

Schizoid development is not an ontogenetic inevitability but, in subtle and indirect ways, is culturally acquired. In fact, the obsequious nature of this indirect and unacknowledged education is schizoid in itself. The situation would not be so severe if what was taught was openly acknowledged as schizoid. Because most cultures are not open and honest (the fact that no culture will acknowledge this is a prime example of the schizoid mentality), the insidious nature of schizoid development continues unabated.

The gist of schizoid edification consists of two essential elements:

1. The individual must learn that certain thoughts, feelings, images, sensations and behaviors are unacceptable.
2. These forbidden reactions must be an example of natural human responsiveness.

Several recent experiences come to mind, each one affecting different parts of the psyche.

A child, approximately two years old, is being wheeled about in a supermarket while her mother is shopping. When they reach the cereal aisle, the child starts saying, "Mommy, I'm hungry." To which the smiling mother repeatedly replies, "No you're not, be quiet now." This interchange goes on for several minutes.

A young boy of about three is playing in a neighborhood sandbox. Every few minutes a girl of about four offers the boy some of her soda. The boy, as if on cue, consistently responds to the girl's gift with hugs and kisses. The mothers both respond by separating the children and admonishing them with, "Now leave her/him alone ... don't do that." Throughout the incident the mothers never once acknowledge one another.

While on the beach, a young boy of about three wakes up crying from a nap. I hear him tell his father that he had a bad dream about the ocean. The father tells him that he has had no such dream. That he shouldn't think such things and to please stop crying and be good.

At a birthday party, a four-year-old boy is laughing and rubbing his genitals. He tells me that it feels good. Both parents hit the child and tell him not to touch himself there. They tell him he is bad and apologize profusely to me for the behavior of their son.

A young, gentle boy, of approximately three and a half, has been playing by himself. He is joined by a rather boisterous girl of four who repeatedly takes the boy's toys. When he protests, she throws sand at him. The boy cries, also throws sand and tries to get his toys back. Every few minutes, the boy's mother, who had been sitting on a bench talking, runs over and smacks the child. She tells him to "shut up and be good, to learn to share and not be so selfish." She constantly yells at him to "stop acting, talking and feeling like that." He is threatened with further punishment.

In these five incidents, the people I observed were not deranged psychotics or social misfits. Their clothes, speech and mannerisms identified them as anything but. To paraphrase the old cartoon character Pogo, we have seen the enemy and the enemy is us.

Schizoid phenomena do not represent the splitting off of bad or evil responses, but rather the splitting off of natural responses that one is *made to feel are bad and evil*. On an individual level, it is a disturbed and narcissistic parent and on a larger scale *the disturbed and narcissistic culture* that induces such development. The unaccepting scowl or rebuff in the parent or the moralistic prohibitions of the society are what cause the split. Freud and the early psychoanalysts in their work on sublimation, displacement and repression realized this but never fully comprehended the extent and depth of the breach. The conflict was simply thought to be a battle between instinct and civilization, as expressed by the id/ego duality. The contention has spread far beyond instinct and is now an entrenched part of the abstract and symbolic world we have constructed in its place. The unintegrated quality of schizoid being manifests itself within the numerous symbolic universes we inhabit.

My use of the word "natural" is not an idealistic call for a romantic return to our natural condition. I am not using the word in a "luddite"-like sense to suggest devolution to a pretechnological state. At this point in evolution, it is impossible to say what the natural condition of humans might be. The only thing natural about being alive is that life is a *response process*. It is the process of responding that the schizoid state detaches us from. *The schizoid state is static; true aliveness represents an integrative process of responding*.

STRANGERS AND SPACES

If it seems that I have been spending a lot of time in sandboxes lately, I can only say that they make good social laboratories. As proof that my world does extend beyond playground boundaries, I have included two additional cultural examples. The common thread that binds these three rather disparate territories is that they represent social arenas in which strangers come in contact with one another. Let me begin with sandboxes. My experience with the proverbial sandbox has been a cross-country affair. In various parts of the country, I have had the privilege of watching parents deposit their children in these playground sanctuaries. In terms of regional nuances, I have noticed that people tend to be friendlier anywhere outside of the Northeastern United States. It also seems that living in a major metropolitan area is less conducive to casual relationships. These observations, however, represent only my impressions and I mention them out of a general curiosity about the readers' experience. For purpose of the present text, my point in bringing these cultural illustrations to mind is that I have consistently been amazed by how alienated adults in sandboxes are.

The first thing noticeable is the almost complete loss of an ability to play or be silly. Connected to this deprivation is a similar incapacity to recognize, acknowledge or communicate, except in an inane and robotic, socially sanctioned way, with other adults. Whatever conversation does take place is almost always limited to safe, social (seen any good movies lately) interchanges. It is not that the topic itself is restrictive, only that the rules of "stranger discourse" restrict the depth to which any subject can extend. Nothing personal is allowed and the unspoken rule seems to be the maintenance of a pseudointimate superficiality combined with a blasé cosmopolitan indifference. Although there are regional differences, my general impression is that adults in sandboxes do not know how to behave. They are extremely uncomfortable with one another and, as a rule, do not make contact. The following anecdote represents notes taken from my last playground encounter:

I place Julian, my two-year-old son in the middle of the sandbox. There are three other children, a boy of about the same age and two little girls of approximately three. Almost immediately, Julian is accepted and drawn into some type of ongoing parallel play. The sandbox is rather large, approximately, 10 feet by 12 feet and is surrounded by orange-colored benches on which four adults, three females and one male, are seated. I sit on a bench directly opposite the three adults. We are separated by 10 feet of sand. I deliberately make eye contact with my contemporaries. No one immediately returns my gaze. Ten minutes pass. Finally, the other man nods at me. I return his nod and say, "how ya doing" to which he replies, "how ya doing." The women continue to ignore me. Ten more minutes pass, Julian is still engaged in play and the children are all laughing. I join them in the middle of the sandbox. Immediately, one of the young girls earnestly begins to explain to me what they are doing and I join in their play. Five minutes pass. During this time, the adults on the bench begin to constantly yell to the children: "how are you Jessica, everything O.K. Brandy, watch your shirt David," and so on. The children, who are laughing wildly at the funny animal noises that I am making, ignore the adults. I place Julian's bucket over my head and lie in the sand while the children dance about and throw sand at me. Barely 2 minutes pass; the man and two of the women are now in the sandbox. I sit up, acknowledge them and resume playing with Julian. No one makes eye contact or says anything to me. The two little girls are removed from the sandbox and transferred to the swings. I remain with Julian and his little friend. The remaining adult continues to sit on the bench her head immersed in a magazine.

The Elevator

Julian and I are in the lobby of a Holiday Inn. We get into a crowded elevator with six adults, four men and two women. Everyone is quiet, facing front and staring at the illuminated floor numbers. Between floors I turn and face people, offer salutations and make comments about the hotel. No one looks at me. They all stare at Julian and begin shuffling and clearing their throats. One woman asks me if he is my child. Later on I try the same thing without Julian. Again, everyone ignores me and becomes visibly nervous when I turn and face them. During long floor delays a man mutters and repeatedly presses the "close door" button while everyone's restlessness seems to intensify. In both cases the entire elevator encounter takes 5 minutes.

Most readers, I am sure, are familiar with the sense of uneasiness that seems almost indigenous to being in a crowded elevator. As long as an unspoken code of social behavior is followed, no one gets too nervous. By turning around and speaking I broke that code. The sandbox example is, perhaps, a little less common but is likewise an example of average social rules being violated. Both these cases are prime examples of my reference to the restrictive range of human consciousness and expression. Not only are we "cut off" from contact with one another, we are also unaware of how alienated we have become. Personal estrangement has become the cultural norm. Most people expect no more and anticipate no less. As long as experience remains within a common mean of average social interaction no one really pays any mind and we fail to notice

- How much we really ignore each other
- How uneasy we are with one another
- How restricted our range of social options is
- How nervous we get when something "unusual" occurs in our average expectable social environment.

The Beach

The beach is one of the few public places where strangers, often in rather close proximity, meet. The nature of the encounter is intensified by the state of dress or undress typical of such territory. In this situation, a beach culture, complete with its own rules of body space, a special kind of intimacy and communication evolves. Most people become anxious if any of these unspoken rules are violated. Such rules not only dictate encounters between the sexes but determine age and race relationships as well. Our culture stratifies and homogenizes the potential number of encounters people can have. I remember a man of about 70 who began playing with Julian. When I approached him in conversation and offered him some of our soda, he seemed quite surprised. It turned out that he was alone, and although he had been on the beach for several hours he could not get anyone to talk with him. The gentleman had worked most of his life as a journalist and we wound up having a very pleasant conversation while Julian played in the sand.

One of the fascinating things about beaches is that they are very susceptible to the influence of perceived time and place. Beaches that are perceived as vacation spots, locations like Club Med for example, are more conducive to making contact. These situations are advertised as "get away from it all and escape the humdrum," antidote to civilization type places. Such spots are distinguished as vacation or holiday areas and holiday time is experienced as different from "ordinary" time. Holiday time is for socializing, fun, play, abandonment of civilization's restraints and making contact with other people. I have always thought it amazing how quickly most people adapt to such circumstances and, likewise, how rapidly on return to regular living one's newfound consciousness evaporates. Feelings aroused and available during "holiday time" have come to be accepted as different and separate from "everyday life."

SCHIZOID RELATIVITY

Our schizoid condition has brought a large part of humanity to the point where free and comfortable relationships with strangers are no longer possible. Depending on one's perspective, the preceding illustrations may seem either extreme or commonplace. The important point to remember is that the reader must always consider a *relative degree of schizoidness*. The categories in Figure 1 of this chapter should not be mistaken for discreet or unequivocal Self identities. Rather, they represent a *range of possible schizoid detachment* that has permeated the strata of ordinary social intercourse. Schizoid phenomena represent *ordinary* events and should not be confused with overt psychopathology. For example, although related, schizoid splitting is not the same as multiple or split personality. The latter represent an extreme version of psychic dissociation that, as mentioned in chapter 4, is often confused with schizoid states. *A general rule to remember is that the term schizoid refers to a class of values ranging from extremely to slightly schizoid. Schizoid phenomena are a matter of degree. Everyone is schizoid; the question is not, "are you schizoid?" but "just how schizoid are you?"* As Erich Fromm states,

Inasmuch as consciousness represents only the small sector of socially patterned experience and unconsciousness represents the richness and depth of universal man the state of repressedness results in the fact that I, the accidental social person, am separated from me the whole human person. I am a stranger to myself, and to the same degree everybody else is a stranger to me. I am cut off from the vast area of experience which is human, and remain a fragment of a man, a cripple who experiences only a small part of what is real in him and what is real in others. (1960/ 1990, pp. 264–265)

Figure 4
Range of Schizoid Condition

EXTREMELY SCHIZOID   SLIGHTLY SCHIZOID

Multiple, split or ————————————▶ integrated
dissociative   personality
personality

Concerning the influence of culture and the construction of the Self, Fromm assumes a very powerful and extremely perceptive perspective. Although not concerned with schizoid phenomena per se, Fromm was nevertheless acutely aware of society's influence in the construction of what has been termed a "false, social or inauthentic" self. The important point to remember is that schizoidness is not an either/or phenomenon, but rather represents a wide range of possibilities. Figure 4 provides a rough schemata of this range.

My concern is not with the extreme end of the scale, the obviously psychopathological entities that psychologists are familiar with. It is the ordinary that the text concerns itself with—the conventional and prosaic Selves of everyday that move so easily among us. Our commonplace cultural figures are the focus, because it is the ordinary folk of our society that increasingly are encouraged to develop schizoid tendencies. Many people would, perhaps, consider encouraged too mild a term and prefer the word *conditioned* in its place. I have little objection to conceiving this process as conditioning except for one important qualification—that cultural conditioning not be totally viewed as the deliberate manipulations of a select agency or privileged class. Intentional orchestration by a select few is only partially true and accounts for but a minor proportion of what befalls the individual. Blaming the rich, the government, the CIA or European white males is a dangerous red herring that does nothing more than perpetuate an already impaired cultural system. It is our response (or lack of it) to the *general system of industrial technological culture* that needs to be modified. The general system is so vast, complex and imbedded that we hardly notice it. Contemporary culture, like the Frankenstein monster, has tak   on a life of its own well beyond the intentions of its creators. What began prehistorically as a mechanism of survival is now in control.

In evolutionary terms, culture, an organ of adaptation, has become a cancer, and the cancer has become our master. For over 50 years Erich Fromm has been one of this perspective's most eloquent spokesman. Although I find it disheartening that few of his insights have seeped into the general culture (the book I am about to quote from was last borrowed from the library in 1987), I nevertheless find Fromm's ideas valuable and worth attending to. The following statement is germane to the present position:

A specter is stalking in our midst whom only a few see with clarity . . . perhaps its most ominous aspect at present is that we seem to lose control over our own system. We execute the decisions which our computer calculations make for us. We as human beings have no aims except producing and consuming more and more. We will nothing, nor do we not-will anything. . . . How did this happen? How did man, at the very height of his victory over nature, become the prisoner of his own creation and in serious danger of destroying himself. (1968, pp. 1–2)

Schizoid development is only a neurotic defense, a means of coping with the extreme profundity of the *general system itself.* As with any neurotic defense mechanism, it is a partial and inadequate means of resolution. In order to change our schizoid position, first, we have to acknowledge its presence (make it Self-dystonic), second, we have to understand it and finally, we have to construct alternative means of contending with it.

Let us return to Figure 3 and the sample of basic Self splits that affect the individual. If one were, perchance, to meet someone from work at a social situation it is not as if he or she would be unrecognizable. To assume this perspective would be another manifestation of the human tendency to notice only aberrations and extremes. What our culture defines as normal and accepted behavior can be represented as a point on a curve. If we measure a large enough sample we arrive at the so-called "normal" or Bell curve that every psychology undergraduate is familiar with.

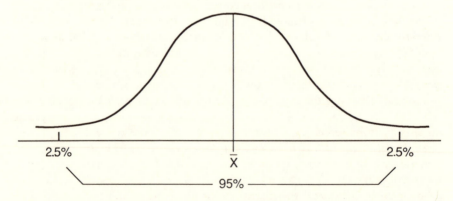

As a culture and perhaps, even as a species, humans manifest a tremendous myopia toward anything in the middle. We tend, as a rule, to lump together and perceive homogeneously, anything that occurs in this enormously wide range of values. Elementary statistics teaches that 95% of all possible values occur within this range. Ninety-five percent is, of course, an arbitrary assignment, the point being that the bulk of all measured behavior gravitates about a certain mean. The area around this mean, however, encompasses a rather wide range of possibilities and it is within this range that we tend to perceive everything as similar. This is the territory of the average citizen and the accepted neighbor. It is an area perceived as common and safe, an expanse we feel comfortable moving about in. Yet, it is a land deadly to human "aliveness"; our blindness and tendency not to notice is paving the way to destruction. Once again, Erich Fromm echoes these sentiments, stating that

We may begin by saying that the average person, while he thinks he is awake, actually is half asleep. By "half asleep" I mean that his contact with reality is a very partial one; most of what he believes to be reality (outside or inside himself) is a set of fictions which his mind constructs. *He is aware of reality only to the degree to which his social functioning makes it necessary. He is aware of his fellowmen inasmuch as he needs to cooperate with them; he is aware of material and social reality inasmuch as he needs to be aware of it in order to manipulate it.* (my emphasis) (1960/1990, p. 264)

THE DR. RUTH EFFECT

Connected to the idea that people are conditioned to notice the extraordinary at the expense of the ordinary is what I like to call the Dr. Ruth effect. The Dr. Ruth effect is related to the concepts of congruity and incongruity, terms that imply either an equivalence or sameness, kind of an "everything fits" mentality, or conversely a discrepancy, contradiction or incompatibility. What I am suggesting is that principally, we pay attention to phenomena that are culturally incongruous. Most readers are probably familiar with the psychologist, Dr. Ruth Westheimer. Dr. Ruth is a tiny, actually rather shrivelled is a better description, stylishly dressed old European woman with a heavy accent who virtually oozes grandmotherlyness. The first incongruity is that she has a strong psychoanalytic flavor to her ideas and speech. This discrepancy is slight compared to her principal contradiction which is the explicit and graphic clinical discussion of intimate sexual behavior. When I first saw Dr. Ruth on television I was dumbfounded. There on my television screen was this little old lady talking about lubricating vaginas and hard thrusting penises. At first, I thought it was a comedy act, but soon realized that millions of people either call in or listen to this woman give sexual advice. In all likelihood, her show is internationally syndicated.

One of the reasons so many people pay attention to Dr. Ruth's sexual advice without getting anxious or feeling guilty is the incongruity of the situation. In our culture, sexual activity is not associated with older people.

It is extremely safe for Dr. Ruth to discuss sex because she is not considered a sexual being. She is a grandmother and a doctor, a wise old Viennese analyst who cannot arouse sexual feelings or conflict in those that listen to her. One of the reasons her advice, although often clinically sound, is pragmatically ineffective is that her image tends to perpetuate the split between sexual feelings and consciousness. An attractive young man or woman openly discussing what Dr. Ruth talks about would make many people extremely guilty and anxious. Certainly, it would make many people uncomfortable and might even evoke strong sexual feelings. On one level, there is nothing incongruous about a young, attractive person speaking *privately* about sex. But, on another level, and this is where culturally mediated reality shifts into high-gear meta-reality, there is something very incongruous concerning a young, attractive person *publicly* discussing sex. Unless it is expressed within the medical, health or pornographic venue, such sexual openness, by anyone young, attractive and sexually active, is taboo. Incongruities that make us culturally anxious are disallowed or split off into separate parts of the culture, such as the pornographic underworld, a cultural territory visited by many but acknowledged by few.

With one exception this cultural example is totally representative of a socially constructed reality. The exception, a fact rarely acknowledged in contemporary mainstream culture is the connection between aliveness and sexuality. To be alive is to be sexual. I have never met a healthy older person who in some way or another was not sexually alive. All the other associations, the connections between age, appearance, expression and sex are cultural fabrications, metarealities of a socially constructed genesis.

The human proclivity not to notice anything that conforms to average social norms is compounded by the fact that our brains seem programmed toward short-term or immediate problem solving. As a species, humans manifest a marked inability to plan ahead. Robert Ornstein and Paul Erlich (1989) suggest that our brains are still programmed for the immediate actions necessary for prehistoric survival. The cognitive capacities conducive to adaptation 40,000 years ago are hardly appropriate to the complex and rapidly changing world we presently inhabit. Although cognitive styles are culturally modifiable, they are, nevertheless, difficult to change, especially if underlying brain structure is conditioned toward short-term changes. This recalcitrance is, for example, apparent in the energy and economic strategies of the United States. The government's and corporate structure's emphasis on fossil fuel, maximum profit attainment, deficit financing and short-term growth although effective in the present, are an anathema to future generations. Our cultural tendency to embrace the "quick fix" solution promotes a false reassurance in the status quo and an equally spurious sense that everything is alright as is. Short-term thinking combined with cultural myopia can have a deadly synergistic effect.

Let us return again to the hypothetical meeting with our schizoid acquaintance mentioned earlier. What might this social encounter with a colleague be like? Well, if the person is well integrated, little difference would exist between the person's work self and social self. In both situations, the person would appear to be the same. This similarity would be manifest across all dimensions of the Self—the person would act, feel and think alike (images and sensations are for the moment excluded). Nothing germane to the situational context about the person would be hidden.

The last sentence represents a crucial element in adequately understanding schizoid phenomena. Their importance is concerned with the fact that having a work and social self that are in correspondence does not mean that one socializes at work or, conversely, works at socializing. Being aware of one's Self does not mean that one has to always express the awareness. It is simply sufficient that it be available. In this example, what a well-integrated personality implies is that the social aspects of the Self are, depending on the contextual flavor of the situation, potentially available to the person. A popular way of phrasing this is "the person is in touch with themselves." The word *themselves*, although grammatically incorrect is, nevertheless, accurate, because, as already stated, we are a collection of several selves. The question is, just how separate are these selves? The more separate, uncommunicative and unintegrated the Selves are, the more schizoid the person is.

As Michael Gazzaniga (1985) points out, because separate selves do not communicate internally they can only be discovered through expression. What this means is that they have to be pointed out, attention has to be drawn to them and one's consciousness has to become *aware* of them. But, because our culture encourages the construction of separate lives, this is becoming an increasingly difficult thing to do. All too often, it requires either the occurrence of a life-changing, peak experience or, perhaps, the help of a talented psychotherapist. Talented therapists and peak experiences will be discussed later. For the moment, let me illustrate my point with two clinical examples.

Brian, a 35-year-old musician and high school substance abuse counselor states that

Depending on whom I'm with, I have to screw all these different heads on. The parents want me to be one way, the school another, and the agency I work for demands yet another me. Even most of the students want me to be someone else. Only "troubled students," sent to me because they "need" counseling, allow me to be myself. With everyone else it's like I'm a lamp socket. I let them screw in whatever bulb they want and turn me on.

Brian is less schizoid than most people. He is at least aware of this culturally imposed and enforced, occupational false image. The parents want him to say he never drinks, the school wants him to appear serious by dressing like a professional (collar and tie), the agency wants him to cut his hair and shave and the majority of students want reassurance that everything in life will turn out fine. Essentially, Brian rightfully assumes his position is inauthentic and that his job is to not tell the truth, that is, through image and appearance to maintain an illusion. The illusion that our culture encourages is of a black and white world where through simplistic formulas and conformistic behavior, everything will be alright. It is a culture of manipulated appearance and deliberate image, of posture and pose, pretense and deception. It is a culture where one has to have secrets. Not everyone, as the next example illustrates, is as healthy as Brian.

Michael is a 29-year-old telephone company supervisor. He is a high school graduate who worked his way into the job and is one of the youngest people to ever hold this type of managerial position. Michael came into therapy because of anxiety, recurring headaches and disturbed marital relations. Michael feels that he cannot be himself at work. What is demanded of him in supervising others forces him, he feels, to be methodical and act in a tough, authoritarian manner. By nature, Michael seems quite jovial, easy going and relaxed. Michael feels that his job is impairing his health and interfering with his marriage. At work, he is terrified of being discovered. That it will be revealed that he is not what he pretends to be.

Michael did not stay in therapy long enough for me to learn what his secrets were. I surmise that he was also terrified that I too would discover who he "really is"—the monster that lurked beneath the surface. What were his secrets and just who was this perceived monster? In the brief period that I knew Michael, I was able to learn that he was a gentle soul who had a rough beginning in life. His parents, although always present, were emotionally aloof and distant. Michael's mother was described as "bossy and domineering" and his father as quiet and passive. The children, like household pets, were always kept at a distance and viewed as "things" that needed to be raised. Michael enjoyed writing and told me that he had written a lot of poetry. Prior to ending his sessions, he began bringing some of his poems to the sessions. The poems revealed a great deal of his inner self and were, I fear, the cause of his abandoning our relationship. The following is an excerpt from Michael's poetry:

> alone in shadows, I walk where no one sees,
> my longing for embrace, is not heard
> the desire for oneness, in the heart of another,
> remains unknown.
> all must be hidden . . .
> the teacher enters, I cannot be seen.

Parts of one's Self are usually kept hidden because the person has been made to feel guilty or shameful. The feelings that one is bad, dirty, sinful or no good are common expressions of this unfortunate phenomenon. The child's sense of shame and guilt is conveyed, usually through parental figures who feel equally shameful. Both parent and child are victims of a morally defective culture that hides its own "shameful" handicaps through overly rigid and schizoid moralistic prohibitions. These cultural defects have reached a new zenith in the United States. Our stance toward pleasure, sex, abortion, marriage and family are recent examples of a confused culture that is not only unaware of itself but is unable to engage in the critical thinking necessary to correct its deficits. Michael is only a small part of this culture. Although he was 29 there was a childlike and adolescent quality to Michael that definitely emerges in his poetry. At an early age, Michael must have been made to feel bad about himself, so bad that he had to lock the bad parts away.

Michael's family would be considered an average American family that easily falls within the mainstream of accepted behavior. The same holds true for Brian's counseling position at the school. What is demanded of both Michael and Brian is considered average and expectable cultural behavior.

THE "ISM" CULTURE

Expected cultural behavior is becoming increasingly schizoid. The fragmentary nature of schizoid phenomena is reflected within the numerous accepted and, lately, encouraged schisms that exist on all levels of American society. Sexism, racism and classism represent only a fraction of the covert but very visible divisions of American culture. In contemporary culture, what is alarmingly different about *schism* phenomena is that they are being advocated. People are being increasingly persuaded to isolate themselves in segregated identity clusters. Reconciliation of differences between blacks and whites, men and women, Muslims and Jews and Latinos and caucasians (particularly European white males) are, we are told, impossible. Better, therefore, to divide into separate camps and achieve some type of mutual détente. Groups of designated people are encouraged toward ethnic, sexual and religious isolation. "Get back to one's roots," we are told and thus, insidiously but assuredly, we stop talking to one another; we isolate and disconnect even further. The rich fertilization and genesis of new ideas, people and cultures that results from cross-category combinations is explicitly being discouraged. This is evident not only in the "identity ghettos" in which people live but also in something as routine as adoption laws. Most adoption agencies have an official policy of placing babies with corresponding identical families. In the United States, on the underground adoption market "white" babies go for top dollar, and if one desires a white baby of specific religious background, for example, a Jewish or Catholic infant, the price becomes astronomical. This practice is not limited to caucasians; the National Council of Black Social Workers as an official policy advocates that black babies must only be adopted by black couples. Thus, increasingly, we are being encouraged to create more separation. The area of gender and sexual relations is likewise victim to this trend.

HOMOSEXUALITY AND SCHIZOID IDENTITY

In the mid 1970s homosexuality was officially removed from the American Psychiatric Association's list of pathological disorders. The reasons for this had little to do with the nature and structure of homosexuality itself, but rather with changes in the political and cultural acceptance of sexuality. The growing cultural acceptance of gayness, however, has had quantum effects quite beyond the good intentions of its progenitors. The identification of quantum effects that represent non-local and unforseen consequences are a key feature of a quantum psychological approach. In the case of homosexuality, the quantum effects have to do with personal identity because, in essence, it has become easier for people with identity disturbances to "be" homosexual.

Although there is no doubt that true biological homosexuality exists, it is still a relatively rare phenomenon. The majority of the homosexuals I have had experience with were not hormonally predisposed, but rather manifested extreme identity confusion and disturbed interpersonal relationships with the opposite sex. In many cases, what seems to be happening, now that it is more culturally acceptable to *be* homosexual, is that people with specific interpersonal and identity conflicts can *assume* a homosexual identity. By *assuming* a homosexual personality (Jung's notion of persona would perhaps be a better term) a person can avoid the turmoil and conflict intrinsic to relating to unresolved, or split-off, parts of the self system.

The Case of Regina

Regina is a 29-year-old Latin-American female who came into treatment for feelings of depression. Regina had a difficult, almost traumatic childhood during which she experienced the early death of her obsessive father combined with the numerous affairs of her childlike and narcissistic mother. After her husband's early death, Regina's mother wound up marrying his best friend.

During junior high and high school, Regina found herself feeling very awkward and uncomfortable with men. In college during the late seventies, Regina decided that she was gay. She reports feeling tremendously relieved by this decision, as if "a weight were lifted from my shoulder." Regina found relationships with women much easier to tolerate.

Over the next 10 years Regina continued her gay relationships but began to grow increasingly depressed. In numerous encounters with psychotherapists who followed a classical psychological perspective, Regina was always encouraged to accept herself as gay. Earlier psychotherapists had surmised her problem as one of low self-esteem combined with an inability to cope with the demands of her homosexuality. Her guilt and anxiety were diagnosed as *direct* derivatives of her inability to accept her gay identity.

Eventually her depression brought her into psychotherapy with me. At an early point in treatment, it became clear that Regina was living an *inauthentic* existence under an *assumed* identity of homosexuality. I wondered if her sexual identity was the result of a quantum ripple effect related to society's increasing openness and tolerance of gayness; a thought that soon proved to be true. In order to avoid the pain of early childhood, it was almost *as if* she were *acting* or *pretending* to be someone else. Her homosexuality was an *illusion*, a manufactured cultural pretense that enabled her to continue living at the price of being only half alive.

Many radical homosexuals advocate zero contact with the opposite sex. Even for more moderate gays, intimacy with the opposite sex is either painful, avoided or only tolerated in controlled situations. The solution of assuming an identity that precludes intimate contact with people of the opposite sex is a tragic and incomplete attempt at healing the Self. Furthermore, the identity and relationship confusion of contemporary culture affects not only homosexuals but all people, regardless of sexual preference. The fact that cross-sexual relationships are in a deteriorated state is, perhaps, one of the reasons some people retreat into same-sex affairs. Such behavior is reflective of another cultural schism and does nothing to really alter the schizoid condition.

THE PUBLIC AND PRIVATE SELF

The average and accepted behavior that our culture encourages fosters the development of one of the paramount splits of modern existence, the construction of a public and private Self. Although historically, the Self is thought of as a relatively consistent and omnipresent phenomenon, our present conception of the Self is really a recent cultural construction. At the earliest, the birth of the modern Self can be traced back to the late renaissance period but, in all likelihood, the Self we are now accustomed to is a product of the enlightenment period and seventeenth-century rationalism. In advanced technological areas, the modern Self is already shifting into an enhanced version called the postmodern Self. When discussing the postmodern Self, Kenneth J. Gergen (1991), much in accordance with my position speaks of multiphrenia or the saturated Self. The postmodern Self represents the ultimate schizoid paradox and will subsequently be discussed in greater detail. Because the postmodern Self is a magnified edition of the modern Self it also reflects the public private dichotomy.

We inhabit a socially constructed world in which some thoughts and feelings are readily revealed to others, whereas others are best kept secret. Paradoxically, it has been stressed, most notably by Ernest Becker (1973), that postmodern life entails a substantial loss of privacy. The Self is assaulted with a barrage of agencies, data banks and assorted others who are privy to vast amounts of information. The government, the bank that holds my mortgage, my health insurance company all know things about me that years ago would have been considered private. What do these agencies really know about me? In essence, except for a handful of statistics, very little; in fact we all know very little about each other. Becker was not completely aware of the extent to which the paradoxical nature of modern privacy affects people. This is partially because of his failure to comprehend the extent of the public/private Self schism. What is known or readily revealed to others is the public Self—a.k.a. the persona, social, outer, or false Self— whereas the private Self—a.k.a. the inner, core, true, or authentic Self— remains hidden. It is the public Self that our electronic, computer spawned, information saturated world has exposed. The private Self has turned inward, its retreat nothing more than a misplaced, well-intentioned defense against civilization's onslaught. The problem is that this so-called true or inner Self is lost and as the song goes, "cannot find its way home."

What is missing, what we have misplaced, is of course, a process; the operation of authentic responding. The public Self is a totally inauthentic sham, a constructed contrivance of perception and image. Its responsiveness is not dictated by need but rather by image and appearance. The question becomes not What do I feel? but rather What do I want to look like? What image would I like to convey? As fluid as the artificial construction of an image can be (as in changing fashion or hairstyles, for instance), it is virtually static when compared to the dynamic aliveness of nature and what consciousness could be.

RESONANCE

The loss of authentic responding has likewise led to decrease of an experience that in quantum psychological language could be termed resonance. The *interpersonal process* of resonation occurs when several system levels of one person(s) correspond to the identical system levels of another person or group. Psychological resonation is very similar to the definition of its physical cousin—the reinforced vibration of a body exposed to the same frequency vibrations of another body. The experience of resonation intensifies and expands whatever sensory process is occurring so that when it occurs, the person reports knowing, feeling and essentially experiencing it on all levels of being. Resonance is a systems phenomenon applicable to all general systems in which a parallel meshing of related systems occurs. The ensuing system becomes a suprasystem in which all systems processes are augmented and, if only temporarily, transformed; thus, *resonance represents the ultimate experience of responsivity*.

Resonance may sound like quasimystical, New Age dribble but, in reality, it represents what was once an ordinary experience. Popular language contains numerous phrases that characterize the process as in "we are on the same frequency, vibrating, or in sync together." Intense and enlightening conversation, creative or eureka experiences, peak experiences, spiritual, mystical or transcendent phenomena, passionate encounters (see chapter 8) and, perhaps most common, the initial phase of "falling in love" are some examples of resonance. In order for resonance to last or occur with greater frequency an integrated Self-structure is required. As the postmodern self grows more schizoid, structural fragmentation of system levels severely limits the probability of resonant encounters. A critical dilemma, however, is that a schizoid self-structure precludes awareness of this loss, so for most, shifting to a new, less resonant way of relating becomes the accepted norm.

POSTMODERN RELATIONSHIPS

Postmodern relationships are characterized by a relatively unique style of interaction. Kenneth J. Gergen describes what he terms the postmodern Self as going through three distinct stages: strategic manipulation, the pastiche personality and the relational Self. Gergson's relational Self is not a responsive self but a self of utilitarian interaction, a pseudo responsive derivative of its manipulative and role-playing predecessor. This relational Self is mainly the public Self simply out for its own image aggrandizement. If the postmodern Self is increasingly only an image, what then, do we really know about each other?

What we do know takes the form of information—statistics and data. We know *things* about each other and yet we are extremely unaware of how, for example an *Other* might feel. In fact, some people view emotions as nothing more than cultural performances. One of the tragedies of the postmodern Self is that feelings, sensations and images, the inner experiences of the person, are becoming superfluous to relating. The relatively recent trend toward meeting people through personal ads is a prime example of the incongruities in the expression of the public and private Self. Following are two examples from a popular magazine.

SWJM 32 y.o. man, 6'11", 185 lbs, intelligent and successful, handsome, athletic, likes animals and the outdoors desires romantic involvement with attractive and thin but well built woman between 24 and 30 who likes to laugh.

SWCF 28 y.o. woman, 5'5" athletic and very attractive, intelligent, likes romantic evenings, animals and the great outdoors is tired of the same old stuff and wants loving adventure with similar, nonsmoking man between 26 and 34 who has a sense of humor.

It would certainly seem as if these two people would be inordinately compatible. Yet, as readers familiar with personal ads know, such harmonious meetings are rather rare. What these people have revealed about themselves is nothing more than information, a series of data that represent only an abstract skeleton of the real person. There are ways of knowing an Other that can not be expressed through an information network or computer terminal. Feel and touch, taste, smell and the tone of vocalizations represent modes of relating common throughout the animal kingdom. Among humans, such ways are vanishing and increasingly, as a way of associating with others, we rely on vision and language.

How people appear and sound are becoming the essential factors by which we measure people. The recent trend toward *politically correct* behavior is a movement that places heavy emphasis on appearance and language. Out of all our sensory apparatus, vision and language represent the two most abstract methods of processing information. Vision is the most detached of all sensory operations and our addiction to it amplifies the schizoid problem, allowing the image of a person (as in photography) to evoke a visceral reaction *as if* the person were real. For many people, the reality of the image, as in *Playgirl/boy* models, has superceded the blood and guts actuality of a living person. Popular polls repeatedly indicate that men desire women who are constructed like video image models. Contemporary trends in fashion, make-up and especially cosmetic surgery reflect this tendency. Like vision, the symbolic constructions of language can substitute a world of indications for corporeality. We respond to a symbolically mediated universe and act as if it were the real thing.

The schizoid structure of consciousness, in combination with an over-reliance on appearance and image, has definitely affected the way people relate. This effect is significantly apparent in both love and marriage. In contemporary society, the notable increase in the divorce rate is partially attributable to the fact that people are marrying only "parts of each other." A relationship based on one part of the Self that is presented may change drastically when other self systems emerge. The statement, "I never knew that side of him/her existed until we were married" is becoming a common postmodern lament.

Very often, couples remain together as "part" or transitional objects for each other, partially content with what is being satisfied but, always longing for something more, additional gratification for the self being neglected.[1] Although such couples might appear to be happy, in reality they are acting out a culturally sanctioned public role on the level of social appearance and obligation. The connection that exists masquerades a terrible loneliness and isolation. The writer John Cheever eloquently describes this condition:

The terrifying insularity of a married man and woman, standing figuratively toe to toe, throwing verbal blows at each other's eyes and genitals. Their environment is decorous, a part of their culture. The clothes they wear are suitable for this part of the world, this time of year, this income bracket. There are flowers (hothouse) on the table (inherited). Children sleep or lie awake in upstairs bedrooms. The man and woman seem well rooted and native to their environment as the trees on the lawn, but at the height of their quarrel they seem to stand in some crater on the moon, some arid wilderness, some Sahara. Their insularity is incomprehensible. This is an abandoned place. (1991, p. 27)

Concerning bad relationships, few people are as honest as John Cheever. The image and the posture, the public self of marriage, becomes painfully obvious while what is left of an inner or private self begins to wane. If the principal structure of our relatedness has become word and image, what then does our loss of privacy entail? For one, it means that information about ourselves, in the form of appearance and language has become public domain. The loss of privacy and the ascendence of the public person produces, however, a far more insidious repercussion. The consequence is that what remains of a responsive inner Self begins to atrophy; feelings, sensations, and images become more cut off and less available to consciousness. Because the schizoid state is matter of degree, some people walk around in agonizing awareness of their isolation, whereas others hardly notice it at all.

"HAVE A GOOD DAY"

This saying, a phrase that began as a sincere sentiment, has now attained the pinnacle of banality. In that we no longer notice or care, this well-intentioned expression has become a trite cliché, a testimony to the forgetfulness of consciousness. Because politically correct behavior seems to demand that business transactions conclude with this phrase, in many sections of the country it is now almost impossible to complete a transaction without the clerk muttering this epithet. It does not really matter if the clerk really cares, notices you or even makes eye contact; personal acknowledgment is not an essential ingredient here, all that is necessary is that the incantation be stated. Recently, a young oriental girl concluded our grocery transaction by evoking the sacred phrase. I smiled and inquired if she knew what she was saying meant. Haltingly, she smiled back and stammered that she did not speak English. I left wondering how such a well-intentioned act could achieve such a degree of schizoid sterility. In the stupor of modern life, this phrase, along with many other aspects of ordinary existence hardly get noticed. People no longer really notice themselves or each other but rather monitor one another. As long as nothing unusual occurs, as long as behavior occurs close to the mean, to the average expectable behavior we are conditioned to, everything appears fine. "Have a nice day" no longer has anything to do with whether or not I am having or will have one; in fact, it no longer has anything to do with me at all. Myself, the reader and the young oriental clerk are replaceable and interchangeable; as Pink Floyd sings, our presence is totally secondary to the meta-message being conveyed.

The meta-message is quite similar to other mindless and common exchanges between people. "Good morning . . . How are you? . . . How ya
doing? . . . How's the wife and kids? . . . Hot enough for you? . . . What
about those METS? . . . What's new? . . . Seen any good movies lately?" are
all classic contemporary examples of this genre. The meta-messages contained here are those of reassurance and denial. They are an expression of
underlying suspicion and anxiety concerning the intentions of the other.[2]
Our schizoid world precludes expression of suspicion or anxiousness, so
instead we say, "How ya doing, hot enough for ya?" If the other responds
in kind with "Fine, how are you doing, yeah it's pretty hot," then a covert
social contract has been reached. Implicitly, the contract states that there is
no need for suspicion, we are of the same ilk and are safe together. The
sense of safety brought about by this ordinary social transaction also implies
that certain topics will not be discussed. The meta-communication is that
we will not get too close or intimate, our private selves will not be touched.
In brief, such meta-communication states that the world goes on as is. In
the words of another schizoid patient:

My world continues, everything is safe . . . there is no need for worry. There are
things that make me anxious. . . . I do not wish to talk or think about them. . . . I
do not wish to know myself or reveal myself to others. . . . I will remain inside,
secret . . . known neither to myself or others. . . . I will talk about the latest movie
I have seen.

One is reassured and comforted by ordinary, prosaic things proceeding
in a rational and predictable order. The meta-implications of language are
discussed more in chapter 5, the point for now is that language can be used
to conceal and obfuscate. For many students of the human condition, language is considered the ultimate schizoid vehicle, a device that allows for
the construction of an "as if" existence.

THE "AS IF" PERSONALITY

Michael's poetry (see page 86), like so much of contemporary writing,
music and adolescent lamentation is not only a cry for love but also a plea
for wholeness and honesty. I employ the term adolescent lamentation not
in a negative or condescending sense but as an accurate depiction of what
many people are aware of. In the words of another young patient, "growing
up is no fun," or as a contemporary aphorism says, "life sucks, then you
die."

Adolescence is an extremely difficult period, a transition phase that many
teenagers see as a step toward deadness. The enculturation process that
begins in infancy with the ascendence of language reaches its critical mass
in adolescence. Within this phase, reactions range from the complete in-
ternalization of dominant cultural values to violent rebellion. Adolescence

is a time of decision, a period in which one's cultural *role* must be decided on. Typically, it is an interval of hero worship and role rehearsal. It is developmentally appropriate for adolescents to *assume*, or *try on*, many different roles without actually internalizing or believing in the role itself.

Adolescents pretend, they strut, posture and pose and, in essence, act as if they were in a play. There is a certain quality about modern and especially postmodern cultures that allows for a pathological extension of this developmental phase. This distorting "quality" is related to disturbances in cultural values especially as reflected in the cultural ethos. An ethos does not exist in isolation but is connected to numerous cultural system levels that are discussed in chapter 5. For now, the critical point is that contemporary culture fosters the development of an extended adolescence. There are some very positive qualities about healthy adolescence, two of them being a sense of unlimited time and a sense of endless possibility. These are not, however, the qualities sustained by a narcissistic culture that overly values the image of youth. In contradiction again, the young do not value themselves for a sense of time (or lack of it), or spontaneity, but for the tendency to be virile and attractive and detached and aloof.

In a culture that values image and pretence, the values of love, honesty and openness become secondary to being *cool*. Learning to be cool is an accepted cultural ritual. Coolness entails many traits; being tough, clever, emotionally strong, attractive, and detached are just a few examples of "cool" cultural values. Being emotionally strong does not imply strength of emotional expression but, conversely, the ability to hold one's feelings in. The tendency toward emotional coolness has been especially valued for its survival potential among poor and minority citizens. As one young black teenager told me, "You let people know how you feel in my neighborhood and you're dead."

Adolescence does not necessarily end in blatant conformity or antisocial rebellion. Another more insidious process is afforded by contemporary culture, a schizoid mechanism termed the "as if" personality. The "as if" being represents the postmodern culmination of schizoid development. The "as if" person *acts* like he is part of the cultural system and appears to embrace the values of the system. This is, however, a cleverly produced illusion that is destructive to both the person and the general system. In fact, the preeminence of "as if" phenomena in contemporary culture and especially within the political system is one of the primary reasons both the system and the individual remain ill. "As if" behavior fosters the split between inner and outer, or public and private. In public, the individual can appear one way and yet act and feel in contradictory ways in private. Separate and distict lines of inner and outer Self-development become manifest. Kenneth J. Gergen calls this self the ersatz being, stating that

Daily relations in the postmodern world seem highly problematic. Deep relations become an endangered species, the individual is fragmented over an array of partial and circumscribed relationships, and life is lived out as a series of incoherent posturings. As the constructed character of ersatz identities becomes increasingly evident, the self loses its credibility to both actor and audience. Daily life seems transformed into a game of superficial shamming, a scherzo of triviality. (1991, p. 186)

Because we live in an age where appearance and image are openly worshiped, celebrities and politicians are most vulnerable to "as if" actions. Ronald Reagan and George Bush can act as if they care about human life, drug addiction or inferior education; Jim Baker, Pat Robertson and assorted evangelical gurus can act as if they really care about spiritual matters but, on closer inspection, nothing about what they *seem* to be talking about gets affected or translated into action. In "as if" phenomena, what is attended to are words, gestures, mannerisms; indications rather than actualities become important. Very few people take a closer look and most are relieved that the illusion of safety continues.

Pretending to embrace certain values allows the general cultural system to become more entrenched and enables the "as if" personality to contribute to the social construction of the quintessential, situational Self. Postmodern, "as if" people assume a chameleon-like demeanor, which they take great pride in. As one corporate executive recently told me, "when the deal comes down to money and profit, I can be whomever you want me to be." "As if" behavior weakens not only our connection to our Selves and Others but attenuates our role as parts in the larger cultural system. We dissociate to the point where nothing seems real and all that remains is illusion. Inside we remain empty, while outside we persist and pretend to be full; making believe that things and accumulations make us happy, we act happy. Nietzsche, perhaps for other reasons, said that all is vanity and illusion, but the words of the German poet Rainer Maria Rilke, perhaps, say it best:

We discover that we do not know our roles; we look for a mirror; we want to remove our make-up and take off what is false and be real. But somewhere a piece of disguise that we forget still sticks to us. A trace of exaggeration remains in our eyebrows; we do not notice that the corners of our mouth are bent. And so we walk around, a mockery and a mere half; neither having achieved being nor actors. (1975, p. 141)

SUMMARY

This chapter introduced ordinary cultural factors that contribute to the construction of a schizoid Self. The schizoid Self was described has having numerous possible splits, the most prominent being the polarity between the public and private Self. This division has contributed to the formation of the "as if" personality, a postmodern temperament characterized by pretence, performance and image.

Three key ideas were introduced: the concepts of responsivity and resonance and the description of the true Self as a process. Responsivity represents the antithesis of schizoid behavior, whereas a process description of the true or core Self reflects a necessary quantum modification of an outdated Cartesian concept. Resonance epitomizes one of the ultimate expressions of responsivity in which several system levels between people connect and behave identically. These ideas are discussed in greater depth in the chapter on the ecology of being. At this stage in the text, numerous questions arise, three of the most pertinent being

1. What does a quantum psychological approach have to do with schizoid development?
2. If schizoid behavior is so culturally entrenched, what are its adaptive values? Is there anything positive to be gained from being schizoid?
3. If culture is the milieu in which schizoid development is acquired, then what are the principal vehicles by which such maturation is transmitted?

The last question inevitably brings us to the issue of language and *value* transmission, important matters that are covered in chapter 5. The reader should not feel that further discussion of a quantum approach has been abandoned to the description the schizoid condition. Schizoid phenomena are so central to quantum psychology that such lengthy exposition was necessary. Chapter 6 will begin with a brief summary of the association between the schizoid condition and the principles of quantum psychology.

NOTES

1. See case of Tony in DeBerry (1991, p. 98).
2. For interesting discussions of the deceptive nature of language see M. Engels (1984) and W. Lutz (1989).

Five

The Deconstruction of the Self

The pathos of distance.

Nietzsche

This is a good point in the text to pause and clarify the general themes being developed. A central point of this volume is that we are becoming increasingly unaware of ordinary consciousness. The everyday process of life has simply been accepted as "the way things are" and no one very much bothers to consider the systems implications of ordinary existence. As long as everything seems O.K., society embraces a type of don't rock the boat philosophy. As Frances Moore Lappe states, "What we have today, flawed as it may seem, is the best we can realistically hope for, we are told. Better not touch bedrock rules governing our social world or we will end up with something much worse" (1989, p. 15).

I have proposed that certain cognitive tendencies tend to augment our species' proclivity for cultural myopia. Consistently thinking in a linear, logical fashion is one of our first handicaps. Linear processes lead especially to developing analytic and reductionistic tendencies that not only amplify linearity but increase the fragmentation of consciousness. Under these circumstances, the general system of consciousness evolves in a circumscribed and splintered manner that may be termed schizoid. Within schizoid consciousness, awareness becomes a subsystem limited by the restrictive demands of a linear culture that restricts the natural responsivity of the organism. We become aware of only the components of consciousness that cultural survival requires us to be aware of.

Within any given cultural or subcultural system, what is demanded for survival becomes the accepted and dominant fashion, and any deviation from this mode is appraised as abnormal. Within this system, psychiatry and most of psychology emerge as *the official gatekeepers of normality*, and the criterion of abnormality can become the deviation from a very arbitrary statistical norm. Under these circumstances, the tendency to notice only the extraordinary or abnormal becomes magnified. Fromm comments succinctly on this phenomenon, stating that "people will be afraid to feel the wrong thing; they will become more accessible to psychological manipulation which, through psychological testing, tries to establish norms for desirable, normal, healthy, attitudes" (1968, p. 45).

Thus, a synergistic process of system amplification develops in which these properties (linearity, reductionism, abnormality) become more entrenched, and consciousness becomes more fragmented. The entire procedure may be compared to the algae-choking effect that occurs when a lake is overly nitrogenated. Both are examples of dynamic ecological systems transformed into limited and static structures. A derivative of this operation of diminishment and a substructure of consciousness is the Self-system. The last two chapters focused on the manner in which the Self-system develops in a schizoid mode. At this point, the issue that must be addressed concerns the adaptive value of schizoid processes.

THE ADAPTIVE VALUE OF SCHIZOIDNESS

When it comes to schizoid behavior, culture and individual cognitive processes operate in tandem. Because humans are a social and, hence, a cultural species, their behavior becomes extremely malleable, as throughout history we have been able to adapt to and accept as "normal" a rather wide range of cultural conditions. The mental prerequisites necessary for adapting to the information-saturated, technological/industrial late twentieth century include at least the following:

- The ability to understand and process a tremendous amount of information
- The ability to encounter and negotiate with an enormously large number of people, nations, cultures and ethnic groups
- The ability to tolerate and adapt to an exponentially accelerated and crowded pace of life
- The ability to quickly adapt to new technologies and events

As Kenneth J. Gergen discerningly points out,

The essence of postmodern existence is the *saturation of the SELF*. . . . As we become increasingly conjoined with our social surroundings, we come to reflect those surroundings. There is a *populating of the self*, reflecting the infusion of partial identities through social saturation. And there is the onset of a *multiphrenic* condition, in which one begins to experience the vertigo of unlimited multiplicity. Both the populating of the self and the multiphrenic condition are significant preludes to postmodern consciousness. . . . So we find a profound sea of change taking place in the character of social life during the twentieth century. Through an array of newly emerging technologies the world of relationships becomes increasingly saturated. (1991, pp. 49, 79)

One meaning of postmodernism concerns itself with the fact that events occur in greater numbers and at faster speeds. Postmodern culture is modernism magnified and amplified from a predominantly linear level of interaction to a quantum amalgam. New things begin to happen and emergents, never before experienced, become characteristics of everyday life. New levels of reality interaction are constantly created. Novel subsystems, substructures and parts emerge, and their interaction increases the possibility potential. The principle of emergent interactionism introduced in chapter 2 begins to assume an almost prosaic identity. Events no longer affect a person, community or nation—they affect an entire planet. One reason for this exponential distortion is the incredible technological changes that quantum physics has ushered in.

On the night of September 17, 1991, air traffic to three of New York City's major international airports came to a complete standstill. Incoming flights had to be rerouted, outgoing flights were unable to leave and a tremendous backlog of people, packages and information occurred. The effects of the delay were felt not only locally but on a worldwide level. The problem began when telephone communication between the respective air traffic control stations became blocked. At the time of the mishap, it was speculated that a possible cause of the problem could have been a malfunction in a single optic fiber switch. Optic fibers utilize laser beam transmission and, although no larger than a human hair, are capable of transmitting approximately 10,000 separate bits of data. Obviously, loss of one optic fiber cable can have tremendous repercussions. The original method of transmitting telephone information was through copper wire; one wire, one phone conversation. Although fiber-optic transmission represents an incredible technological breakthrough, when it does malfunction, difficulties are no longer local but global. An individual air traveler, whether he likes it or not, is now part of an interconnected and global network. Such are the ramifications of postmodern existence.

The rapid increase in both information and interconnection produces a complex interdependence of previously detached systems and parts. For example, interdependence is now such a salient feature of the global marketplace that a factory closing in Sandusky, Ohio, can affect what a family in Botswana is having for dinner. Almost overnight, the world seems to have mushroomed in complexity, a fact directly related to the adaptive value of schizoid structures.

The connection is both obvious and simple; schizoid consciousness is the easiest and most efficient means of coping with the postmodern plethora of changes. *Schizoid consciousness is postmodern consciousness*; an extremely neurotic form of consciousness, but consciousness nevertheless. I employ the term neurotic not in an etiological sense but rather as a descriptive term designating a maladaptive way of resolving a conflict or problem. Schizoid behavior may be compared to a person facing a painfully difficult encounter who suddenly develops a phobia or anxiety attack that allows the situation to be avoided. Although a neurotic solution partially succeeds, the price is always high. Another facet of the problem is that far from being an incapacitated self, the schizoid self is highly adaptive to postmodern culture. A. W. Lerner has characterized the emerging postmodern culture as being manipulative and makes a similar comment concerning the manipulative personality:

Such a society is not incapacitated—far from it, just as the high-achieving narcissist for example is not incapacitated; just as the Machiavellian, the gamesman, and the hardball player are not incapacitated. Rather, it is frequently tense, frequently deceptive and self-deceptive, grandiose in its plans, and in a deep sense infused with tragic elements amidst outward engagement. It has its "moments" both of functional success and severe internal depletion. (1990, pp. 136–137)

Lerner's point is well taken. In our society, the schizoid person can be a *functionally* successful person; in fact, for professions like law and politics the ability to be withholding and secretive is a veritable prerequisite. As we will see later in the chapter, a schizoid structure maintains the personality profile thought necessary for postmodern survival. But, what of the inner depletion Lerner is referring to? The depletion is connected to the profound alteration in relationships that first modernism, and now postmodernism have ushered in. The schizoid person does not have difficulty with achievement or cultural survival but with intimacy. It is only within the arena of closeness and intimacy that any kind of Self-pathology becomes evident. The tactic assumed by the schizoid system is simply to avoid closeness or, more likely, to *appear* to be intimate without really being intimate at all.

In place of recognizing, understanding and integrating technologically induced postmodern changes, one can simply compartmentalize them and ignore them. The splitting of consciousness and the subsystem of Self into parallel modules enables the organism to efficiently negotiate a rather complex reality. The schizoid organization of the brain and mind is not solely a modern phenomenon and, in all likelihood, has been in operation since the dawn of language and civilization. In earlier times, life was not as compressed and complicated as today, and being schizoid did not extract such a high price. The industrial revolution produced a major shift in consciousness and now the ascendence of the information-saturated technological revolution has spawned another (Gergen, 1991; Toffler, 1980). Our original schizoid strategy of adaptation has become not only passé but dangerous to the survival of our present definition of being human. Humanity may survive, not as we are accustomed to but in a radically different manner. When a system moves from one level to another a "causal decoupling" occurs in which the new level, although connected, bears little resemblance to its predecessor.

THE POSTMODERN SELF

The Self, for example, is dependent on the operations of the brain. The brain in turn is dependent on the mechanisms of biological processes, which are dependent on the laws of chemistry, which are contingent on the laws of physics and so on. Yet, the system level that the laws of physics operate on bears scant resemblance to the final product; in this instance, the reader. At numerous junctures in the system, a causal decoupling occurs that transports an operation to a new level of identity.[1] This is, I believe, exactly what is happening to the very definition of being human. A definition of humanity is emerging that is creating a new system level, defining "aliveness" and Self in terms drastically different from those we have been accustomed to. A similar position is espoused by O. B. Hardison (1989) who suggests that "the idea of what it is to be human (is) disappearing, along with so many other ideas, through the modern skylight." W. T. Anderson likewise sees human identity in the postmodern world as undergoing significant changes. Anderson calls these changes meta-trends and describes them as changes in the way things change. Anderson identifies them as

1. Changes in thinking about thinking (shifts in the public psychology)
2. Changes in identity and boundaries
3. Changes in learning
4. Changes in morals, ethics and values
5. Changes in relationship to traditions, customs, and institutions (1990, p. 254)

The image-conscious, situational Self of the ever expanding postmodern era, although a relational Self, experiences relationships in a manner drastically different from its predecessors. Like the Self, relationships are also becoming situational and transient, dependent on image and the temporary needs of relativistic encounters. The relativity of images and their dependence on a shifting collage of media signals distorts human relations to a new height of abstraction. At the cost of emotionality and visceral feelings, we are beginning to relate almost exclusively through an abstract, language-dominated, image-saturated consciousness. Such consciousness includes a limited awareness that falls far short of our premodern biopsychosocial potential. From the bubbling cauldron of full aliveness we have been transported to the arid desolation of abstraction. We are, indeed, less alive. As Joseph Campbell stated,

People say that what we're all seeking is a meaning for life. I don't think that's what we're really seeking. *I think that what we're seeking is an experience of being alive* [my emphasis] so that our life experiences on the purely physical plane will have resonance with our innermost being and reality, so that we actually feel the rapture of being alive. (1988, p. 3)

We must confront the issue of our deadness or, as Ernest Becker (1973) so aptly said it, our denial of death.

THE RELATIONSHIP OF SCHIZOID PHENOMENA TO QUANTUM PSYCHOLOGY

Before we explore this area further, let me again clarify the relationship of quantum psychology to schizoid phenomena. Readers interested in the first summary should refer to the section in chapter 3.

Quantum Psychology is a Postmodern Psychology

Because the schizoid constitution reflects the quintessence of the postmodern character, quantum psychology is also a psychology of the postmodern schizoid condition. The inclusion of non-linear as well as linear factors makes quantum psychology an ideal paradigm for understanding the multitude of intrapsychic and interpersonal interactions the postmodern Self must negotiate. In part, the postmodern Self consists of a multilayered, fluid assemblage, a collection of situational image constructions and modifiable postures. This is the Self that most people interact with. The protagonist, Jean-Baptiste Clamence of Albert Camus' *The Fall* makes the following apropos statement:

I navigate skillfully, multiplying distinctions and digressions, too—in short I adapt my words to my listener and lead him to go me one better. I mingle what concerns me and what concerns others. I choose the features we have in common, the experiences we have endured together, the failings we share—good form, in other words the man of the hour as he is rife in me and others. With all that I construct a portrait which is the image of all and of no one. A mask, in short, rather like those carnival masks which are both lifelike and stylized so that they make people say: "Why, surely I've met him!" (1956, p. 139)

The interaction is, of course, situationally dependent so that at times the adult Self will be present soon to be followed by the child Self, the play Self or the moral Self. There are also other Self-systems that, within the postmodern framework, go unacknowledged, for example, the subsystems of affect, sensation and imagery. The postmodern person stands before you, a vast and colorful collage, unaware and cut off from itself. Within such a complex system the probability of non-linear and non-local interactions increases and necessitates the incorporation of a quantum psychology into the traditional and accepted linear format of contemporary psychology. In addition, the sheer number of potential interactions that postmodern humans must confront accelerates the intrinsic *emergent* tendencies inherent to complex systems. As more molecules are packed into a limited space, the potential for novel interaction increases. The same is true for consciousness and the Self-system. As more interactions between selves are made possible, more new properties and processes emerge. As emergents manifest, their interactions produce as yet unfamiliar existential scenarios. Quantum psychology is an attempt to incorporate the emergent interactions of the postmodern self—a self that is explored in greater detail in this chapter.

Because the Self-posturing operates in the rarefied atmosphere of images, abstractions and language it is an easily manipulated Self. Because the postmodern individual experiences no core being or "true Self" to retreat to, there is no internal anchor, and manipulation becomes easier. In fact, being manipulated can become desirable. Manipulation by powerful external forces can ameliorate existential dread and provide the illusion of safety and meaning. Thus, the postmodern individual, very much like his premodern ancestors, is buffeted by forces that he is usually unaware of. A quantum psychological analysis is a step toward addressing these forces. The complementarity principle of quantum psychology emphasizes an ecological understanding of human activity that includes within the individual clinical situation the cultural forces that affect the person. By broadening individual or intrapsychic inquiry and incorporating cultural elements—history, politics, economics, art, religion—everything that has led to the construction of a particular Self or situation is examined. All of these different subsystems interact, and none can be studied in isolation. Often the interaction is discernible and linear but, as the postmodern schizoid Self becomes more complex and fragmented, more often than not the interactions are of a quantum nature, that is, non-local. A clinical illustration might augment this point.

Robert is a 43-year-old graphic artist and musician who came into therapy for feelings of depression. Robert is of Latin descent and comes from a family of nine siblings. He began his life in abject poverty and he is now wealthy and successful. Robert is involved in his third marriage and has five children. Three children, all in their twenties, are from his first marriage, another 12-year-old daughter is from his second and a two-year-old son is from his third. Robert claims to still have "intense" and meaningful relationships with all of these people. His oldest son recently returned from Africa with a wife and child and has moved in with him. Robert himself has lived in several countries and is fluent in at least three languages. His mother, who he is very close to, has just been diagnosed has having terminal cancer. His stepfather, whom he loves dearly, has been on a three-month trek in South America. Recently, his biological father has returned to the scene. Robert was just offered a lucrative music contract that would include a great deal of touring.

Robert's presenting complaint was depression. There are several very good clinical theories that could partially explain why Robert is depressed. The paradigms of learned helplessness, internalized anger, biological predisposition or negative cognitions might all be applied here. Even so, regardless of which theory one chooses an essential ingredient remains missing—why is Robert helpless, angry or negative? In other words, what is the *story* of Robert's life and how can one make sense of it? The principles of emergent interactionism that underlie a quantum psychological approach state that because new levels of events cannot be explained by what was known previously, an original perspective must be assumed. The little I have told you about what already has occurred in Robert's life far eclipses the potential possibilities faced by his historical predecessors. Although common today, the nature of the relationships, interrelationships and meta-relationships inherent to Robert's life is something that rarely existed 50 years ago. A half century ago, Robert's life would be the substance of fiction, but today, yesterday's fiction is today's postmodern fact. Such "facts" need to be placed within an explanatory framework. Because people need to make sense of their lives, placing one's problems within an explanatory framework is an essential ingredient for positive change. Before anything can be accomplished one must first have understanding.

Quantum Buttons and Effects

The multitude of interactive possibilities and interrelationships of an accelerated and often novel postmodern existence requires a whole new way of looking at things. Situations, interactions and relationships, improbable yesterday, are more than possible today. Robert's clinical situation requires an openness to understanding the numerous ways in which the above factors (which represent but a sample of Robert's life) interact. Quantum psychology calls for a new understanding of the separate parts of the person to themselves as well as the Self to the culture. Behavior needs to be explained by understanding connections between very disparate parts of the Self-system. Connections that in a traditional, linear psychology of Newtonian cause and effect would be either impossible to identify or dismissed as random, "nuisance" variables, extraneous to the situation at hand, within quantum psychology assume a new importance.

In the chapter on the quantum model I introduced the concepts of quantum buttons and quantum effects. Quantum buttons represent emotional triggers that may produce wave- or ripple-like effects in the Self-system. Because the Self-system has a predominantly schizoid organization, different elements of consciousness—thoughts, memories, feelings or sensations— are stored in separate and non-communicating modules. This structure renders a person vulnerable to having self-modules activated that one might not be aware of. Unpredictable activation of modules may occur when the person encounters unexpected situations that may activate a quantum button. For example, a person who is very schizoid in relation to sexual feelings may have a quantum button pressed by an unexpected seduction or exposure to sexually explicit material. Involvement in certain situations related to highly "emotionally charged" issues such as abortion, race, religion and even sports sometimes elicits intense and extremely unpredictable emotional and behavioral responses. The recent Louisiana gubernatorial election in which the covert racist and ex-Ku Klux Klan member, David Duke, ran for office was, according to news reports, one of the most emotionally charged and unpredictable events in the state's history. When intense and highly polarized emotions are aroused, split-off emotions and self-systems can become activated. Often this results in people acting in ways that they themselves do not understand.

Once a quantum button is activated, the split-off part of the self becomes available to consciousness—one becomes *aware* of thoughts, feelings, sensations or images that formerly were unavailable to consciousness. Such circumstances are quite confusing and are often intensified by the ripple-like quantum effects of a previously unavailable self-system being activated. The process of adding formerly unavailable factors to the system of awareness increases the probability of new interactions, which manifest themselves in behavior, for example, the person finds himself *responding* in novel ways and new behaviors, thoughts and feelings begin to emerge. The appearance of these *emergents* can be distressing and necessitate a new way of understanding one's situation. For example, to continue with the above example, the newly activated sexual subsystem may cause the person to be

1. Depressed at home
2. Seductive with the boss
3. Aloof and removed from the children
4. Impulsively purchasing a new wardrobe
5. Questioned curiously by other family members and friends
6. Short tempered with colleagues

Obviously, the possibilities become endless, a fact that a quantum approach is quite cognizant of. As I have stressed and will emphasize throughout the remainder of the text, the unpredictable newness and sheer magnitude of postmodern possibilities increases the probability of quantum effects. Robert's depression was related to feelings activated by the sudden presence of his first son's (whom he had not seen for 10 years) beautiful wife. The insertion of this young and beautiful woman into Robert's daily life activated a quantum sexual button that had long been split off. The presence of new and unfamiliar sexual feelings affected Robert's relationship with his wife, his mother, his career, his self, his children and, in short, his entire world. Such situations can be quite disruptive and need to be placed within a fresh perspective that both relieves and illuminates.

What, for instance, does a person's economic position have to do with a clinical depression? In traditional psychology the relationship is considered absent or minimal and the focus is nearly exclusively intrapsychic, or at best interpersonal. A quantum approach necessitates the inclusion of the economic system into the analysis of an individual's condition. Again, an economic system cannot be explored in isolation but requires the inclusion of a host of personally relevant cultural factors, such as, ethnic and historical information, geographic and educational data, religious and idiosyncratic details. *In formulating a true understanding of a person's situation, once we step out of the artificial constraints of the "intrapsychic," the entire constructed system of consciousness must be dealt with.* Such investment requires the recognition and acceptance of *emergents*, the novel patterns, events and relationships that develop between the self and an increasingly postmodern world culture. Emergents always increase the probability of a quantum effect occurring.

A quantum approach incorporates a holistic perspective that attempts to analyze as many relevant system levels, and interactions and emergents as is possible. Quantum psychology is in accord with the thinking of A. W. Lerner who in discussing the work of Harold Lasswell states:

The notion of emergence has aided in overcoming many old dualisms. . . . What appears to be antithetical is reconciled on a new plane. I represents a position which Lasswell has repeated time and again in his various writings when he enjoins us to *occupy as many observational standpoints as possible in the analysis of individual, social and cultural phenomena.* (my emphasis) (1990, p. 21)

This is exactly the perspective that contemporary psychiatry and clinical psychology so assiduously avoids. When teaching differential diagnosis to psychiatric residents or psychology interns, I usually include a section on cultural factors that contribute to individual psychopathology. Repeatedly, my experience has been that both students and faculty, although finding such associations "interesting," place little emphasis on their importance and prefer to remain within the boundaries of biological symptoms and intrapsychic conflict. Such avoidance exists for a variety of reasons that will be described in greater detail in the chapter on quantum diagnosis.

Thus, quantum psychology is an ecological psychology of consciousness that explores the interaction of individual consciousness with culturally constructed, situational contexts. Within this model, consciousness is understood as *the larger, more inclusive system* and as described in chapter 3, individual *awareness is conceptualized as the "interaction" of consciousness with the social context.* As the culture becomes increasingly schizoid, the interaction of split-off parts becomes more complex, bewildering and often anxiety provoking.

THE DECONSTRUCTION OF THE SELF

What is, perhaps, most anxiety inducing about the present human condition is the deconstruction of the Self. If modern science ushered in the death of God as we knew "him," then its accelerated version, postmodernism, has wrought the death of the Self as we once knew it. The elements of Self that contemporary humans so prided themselves on are changing. Metaphorically, we are being taken apart and put together again; reconstructed, if you will. This deconstruction/reconstruction process is a matter of no small importance because metaphors, despite their abstract nature, have tremendous practical implications. As K. J. Gergen states, "As we live long and comfortable within these metaphors, they turn literal; they take on the appearance of solidity, and seem sincere reflections of the truth within themselves. Indeed, the literal is simply the metaphor grown complacent" (1991, p. 223).

The prize package of most humans, their object of highest veneration is the true, real or core Self. Belief in this premodern vestige of a more romantic period is tenaciously clung to. A patient who works as an institutional insurance broker for a major corporation told me: "You know, underneath all the bullshit that I have to engage in at work there's still a me and I gotta figure out what that me is. That's why I'm seeing you. I know that whatever it is . . . that it's more real than the mask I put on for them."

No one wants to discard the feeling that there is "something" inside, that apart from the fashionable fabric of society lies a true and often much "nobler," individual Self. As the song goes, "I gotta be me, I gotta be me," and, yet, most people are now in the bewildering situation of searching for the real "me" only to encounter either empty space or a swirling mosaic of collective identities, none more "real" than the other. Throughout history, the romantic and idealist position has often been a healthy reaction to the demands of restrictive cultures. The problem is that the traditional metaphor of an inner true Self is becoming increasingly irrelevant to postmodern life. In fact, the true Self is becoming a mythical and symbolic image of that "better time" that many people long for. Like the "ghost in the machine" metaphor, to look inside is truly to see but a suggestion of what was once thought to be there. Again, to quote K. J. Gergen:

Under postmodern conditions, people exist in a state of continuous construction and reconstruction; it is a world where anything goes that can be negotiated. Each reality of self gives way to reflexive questioning, irony, and ultimately the playful probing of yet another reality. The center fails to hold. (1991, p. 16)

Thus, as a socially constructed entity, the composition of the Self is undergoing drastic modification. Most people hardly notice the dramatic changes taking place, whereas the majority of those who do seem to notice are rather incapable of arresting the process. This is understandable because as consciousness becomes more schizoid, the Self gets parceled into separate "parts" that are unaware of each other and fail to notice what is happening. Furthermore, the postmodern process of accelerated technological change cannot really be stopped, perhaps delayed a bit, but not completely suppressed. In fact, because luddite reactionism is not the most helpful of responses, such progress should not be discontinued. Pushing the clock back to the mythical "good old days" is not the point, rather we must learn how to modify our response to technology. *Technology is not the enemy*; if anything, it is our deranged attempt at adaptation that will destroy us. We have created a cultural climate of competitive struggle and survival; as Lester C. Thurow (1980) and Frances Moore Lappe (1989) call it, a *zero-sum society* that promotes one individual's advancement at the expense of other individuals and the larger community. Under these conditions, living is reduced to personal survival and the situational Self that is most adept at surviving becomes the dominant Self.

The Dominant Expression of the Postmodern Self

This is going to be an important but difficult subsection, a fact that partially explains my taking so laboriously long to arrive here. The section is important because it refers to critical postulates concerning the nature of the evolving postmodern self. As such, it is essential for developing a postmodern psychology of the Self. The section's difficulty has to do with the general and abstract quality of these postulates. There will be some readers, I assume, that share my perspective, and for these readers there should be little problem in understanding my position. On the other hand, there are undoubtedly readers who do not share this perspective and it is for this group, especially, that I have taken the time to develop my argument. One of my contentions thus far has been that the expression of the contemporary Self has evolved in a schizoid fashion that is reflective of a general disturbance of consciousness. In terms of consciousness, we are now at a point where the text can go into greater detail as to where we are, why we are here and where it is that I think we are going.

The ultimate expression of the postmodern Self is a relational and situational Self. I am in complete agreement with K. J. Gergen's position that "in this era the self is redefined as no longer an essence in itself, but relational. In the postmodern world, selves may become the manifestation of relationships" (1991, p. 146). Within this relational system, one can not really speak of a true or dominant Self but rather a process of Self—integration, awareness and expression, always in relation to other processes. The Self, necessitated by postmodernism, is a relational and process Self that is *always* correlated with the *entire* general system of culture and consciousness that provide the fundamental constituents of its social construction. As clearly stated in the preceding pages, it is a central contention of this book that the *process* itself is distorted. It is our estrangement from *process*, therefore, that exacerbates our schizoid traits. What becomes dominant is not so much a consistent "core" Self but rather a solitary and situational Self, whose principal goal is survival. Commenting on recent historical trends, the writer Stephen Schiff states,

But if the sixties divided America in half, the economic cataclysms of the seventies subdivided it again and again, almost beyond recognition. Survival became the new byword. Americans retreated into themselves, aerobicizing, gulping down multivitamins, flocking to gurus, and generally straining to turn themselves into little gods, impervious to the upheavals wracking their lives. (1990, p. 46)

As Schiff alludes, because very few people want to acknowledge what is occurring, the process is ignored and split off from everyday awareness. The schizoid contortion of consciousness and the Self, in combination with the general cultural ethos, has resulted in a self cut off from its Self. By this I mean that people have been misled into thinking that

1. Individual survival is primary
2. Survival means having a successful image
3. Maintenance of the image is contingent on compartmentalizing the irrational components of consciousness
4. Such irrational components of consciousness are emotions, images, sensations, thoughts and behaviors that do not mesh with the successful image.

The Interactional Self

The preceding factors precipitate at least two major changes in the Self-system. The first, the collapse of the Self into a unidimensional and schizoid non-process, has been adequately discussed. The second is that if the post-modern Self is a relational Self, then it is a relational Self that is almost totally "out for itself." Relationships, for this *distortion* of what the post-modern Self *might* be, are relationships of self-benefit and self-improvement. The Self makes associations based on what the Self can acquire from such associations. Manipulation of other Selves for purposes of self-profit and gain, whether the gain be emotional (I needed to be loved that night), monetary (I can make a lot of money from this friendship) or personal advancement (my career will benefit from this affair) becomes the raison d'être of the survival-oriented situational Self. The Self, therefore, becomes a posture, a mere sham and pretense, its demeanor determined by where it is and what it can negotiate. Once again, Jean-Baptiste Clamence, the protagonist of Albert Camus' *The Fall*, provides a relevant illustration, stating:

> To be sure, I occasionally pretend to take life seriously. But very soon the frivolity of seriousness struck me and I merely went on playing my role as well as I could. I played at being efficient, intelligent, virtuous, civic-minded, shocked, indulgent, fellow-spirited, edifying. . . . In short, there's no need of going on, you have already grasped that I was like my Dutchmen who are here without being here; I was absent at the moment when I took up the most space. (1956, p. 87)

Camus, in discussing the role playing of the existentially alienated person anticipated, perhaps, the emergence of the postmodern interactional self. The interactional self plays for its own benefit; it plays at being loving, being sincere or smart, or even at being President, but this type of self no more believes in what it is doing than a studio commercial actor believes in the cigarette he is endorsing.

This is a Self cut off from the totality of others, its environment and itself. In fact, it is not a Self at all. From this point on I will use the upper case *Self* to refer to the total ecological system process of an integrated consciousness, whereas the lowercase *self* shall refer to its postmodern cousin, the incomplete situational self.

Another qualification is warranted at this point. The evolving postmodern self, although relationship oriented, is not a "loving" self, not at least in the more traditional ways in which loving relationships are conceived. Although it is realized that relationships exist for a multitude of reasons and purposes, most people will still recognize romantic love as the golden nugget. The human expression of love and all that is connected with it, in a very premodern and lingeringly romantic way, is still perceived by many as the ultimate connection—a relationship by which all other alliances are measured.

For now, suffice it to say that for the situational self, relationships do not exist for *reasons of mutual benefit* but rather for purposes of self-gain. The situational self is not really a relational self but an interactional self, an entity that has learned to successfully negotiate a multitude of rapidly changing interpersonal situations. The postmodern self gets involved not for purposes of relating, but for reasons of efficient interaction that insure survival, preservation and profit. This analysis of the postmodern self is very similar to the *manipulative self* described by A. W. Lerner (1990) and the *narcissistic self* depicted by C. Lasch (1978). The manipulative/narcissistic self is an egocentric self of gamesmanship and sensationalism. As Lerner states,

> We have a picture of a highly manipulative personality. The profile incorporates access to an empirical record of favored manipulative ploys and interpersonal style for effecting them, the Machiavellianism literature. The profile also incorporates

access to a dynamic theory of inner mental processes, the self-psychology literature on narcissism. (1990, p. 89)

The interactional self is neither universal nor inevitable; it does not operate in isolation but is a constructed product of culture. In the United States, it is the cultural ethos and primary value system of competition, acquisition and individualism under which varied systems of the situational self get activated. This ethos is expressed in an overemphasis on individual competition and achievement and singular gain and accumulation. This ethos and value system is conveyed through the vehicle of an increasingly abstract language system.

First, we will focus on the avenue of expression, and second on the content of what is being expressed. Concerning language, it is a fundamental hypothesis of this text that *contemporary consciousness is a language-dominated consciousness that represents a complete deconstruction of the Self so that in true deconstructionist fashion, nothing exists but the text itself.* The text is language, and it is this text that we will now explore.

LANGUAGE AND THE DECONSTRUCTED SELF

Whoever controls the language, the images, controls the race.

Allen Ginsberg

We are a linguistic species. The degree to which language dominates our consciousness and shapes our lives has been known for years. As the species matured, awareness of the effects of language evolved so that by the late nineteenth and twentieth centuries, human communication became a major philosophical and scientific subject. Philosophers such as Ludwig Wittgenstein (1958/1990) and Alfred North Whitehead (1925/1990) along with the linguistic theoreticians Benjamin Whorf (1957) and Noam Chomsky (1988) have extensively explored the genesis and power of language. [2]

The literature on the topic of language is vast, and I am certain that countless contemporary investigators could be included with these names. It is not the purpose of this section to expand on a thesis so substantially covered by a host of brilliant others. Rather, I wish to take the topic in a somewhat tangential direction. The basic posture of my reasoning is summarized by Aldous Huxley as follows:

To formulate and express the contents of this reduced awareness man has invented and endlessly elaborated those system-systems and implicit philosophies we call languages. Every individual is at once the beneficiary and the victim of the linguistic tradition into which he has been born—the beneficiary inasmuch as language gives access to the accumulated records of other people's experience, the victim insofar as it confirms him in the belief that reduced awareness is the only awareness, and it bedevils his sense of reality, so that he is all too apt to take his concepts for data, his words for the actual things. That which, in the language of religion is called "this world" is the universe of reduced awareness expressed and as it were, petrified by language. (1954, pp. 23–24)

Huxley's statement, especially his use of the term petrification sums up the position I have been developing—that awareness of the full potential of consciousness has been reduced and along with it, its subsystem, the Self, has been diminished to a fragmented and superficial self. The postmodern variety of the self lives primarily in an abstract, overly saturated world of symbols and images. But, because our symbols have been removed from their animate, existential base—*the organic responsive process*—they have become inert and lifeless.

Words, which in the beginning were constructed as *symbols of process* (compact and condensed representations of experience), have now assumed a reality of their own. Divorced from their intuitive and sensual base, words have become powerful but barren symbols. Their power lies in the fact that what we consider consciousness is almost exclusively a language-dominated consciousness. In essence, language is all we have, and as such, it becomes extremely powerful. Because it is very simple to change reality by modifying language, words become a powerful postmodern tool for manipulating behavior. We have, so to speak, put all of our eggs in one basket. Yet, cut off from the sensual and intuitive systems of consciousness, it becomes a rather stagnant basket. The postmodern self is a system, deconstructed from its organic wholeness and reconstructed as a unidimensional, language-driven entity.

What has occurred, as K. J. Gergen suggests, is that we now inhabit a metaphorical world that has become literal. To compound matters, we seem to have forgotten as much, so that we are now in the rather ironic and paradoxical position of actors who have forgotten they are in a play. We have pretended and acted for so long that we have forgotten that we are pretending and acting. An ever expanding, spiraling whirlwind of linguistic meta-realities pulls us forward, meta-realities that are encouraged and enhanced by the incredible technologies of our age. Communities and relationships form through computer networks while phone machines answer calls and respond for us. A depressing new development in contemporary culture is to have the machine answer with just numbers; "hello, you have reached 212-515-2040 . . . at the beep please leave a brief message . . . have a nice day. . . ." As we "relate" through computers and have sex by telephone, computer spawned "salons" and "networks" become the electronic communities of the postmodern world. The past few years have witnessed the growth of the "phone sex" industry into a sophisticated multibillion dollar affair. The technology of the computer has also led to the development of what is known as "virtual reality," a method of viscerally being connected to the computer so that what one creates is experienced as being real. It is interesting to note that for males, the most desired form of virtual reality is the construction of a sexual partner.[3]

In terms of technology, we are at a point where our reliance on language can construct worlds of ideas that people live their lives by. Susan Sontag's work on illness as metaphor as well as the recent "linguistic construction" of the government orchestrated "reality" of the Persian Gulf war are two examples of how artificially created, linguistic realities become dictums for living.[4]

THE META-LEVELS OF LANGUAGE

> Our perception of "reality" is the perfectly achieved accomplishment of our civilization. To perceive *reality*! When did people stop feeling that what they *perceived was unreal*? Perhaps the feeling and the idea that what we perceive is real is very recent in human history.
>
> R. D. Laing

The tangent of this section is that language is not as sterile and unidimensional as we believe it to be. What this means is that not only has organic *responsivity* been reduced to a linguistic dimension but the linguistic dimension itself has been diminished. Ordinarily, language is conceived as a fairly homogeneous phenomenon that follows a common and consistent logic. To explain this we must explore some of the ideas of Ronald David Laing.

Laing is probably best known for his work on psychosis and the Self which were published in *Self and Other* (1965b) and the *Divided Self* (1965a). His theories became highly politicized and were embraced by the growing counter-culture movements of the sixties and seventies. His wide acceptance by this movement, in combination with his literary penchant for poetic allusion, are part of the reason Laing is virtually ignored by traditional psychology. Political activism and effusive metaphor are not, as a rule, widely embraced by conventional science. My experience in presenting Laing's ideas at "mainstream" scientific meetings has been most disconcerting. He is usually dismissed as a "pop" philosopher with outlandish and untestable theories. The problem is not so much with Laing's ideas as with the i erpretation others have given them. R. D. Laing, who is now unfortunately deceased, was a genius whose ideas, which are very similar to a quantum approach, were definitely ahead of the times.

Many of Laing's postulates concerned the complex and convoluted nature of language, a fact that is essentially ignored by many people. In 1966, Laing, along with two English psychologists, H. Phillipson and A. R. Lee, published an obscure book called *The Interpersonal Perception Method*. The psychologists were able to transform Laing's theories of interpersonal communication into a rather long and time-consuming test (The Interpersonal Perception Method) that was able to measure what Laing was talking about. The cumbersome and very mathematical form of this test was, I believe, one of the reasons that the test itself never caught on. When completing my master's degree in general/experimental psychology, I intended to utilize the test for my thesis but was denied permission to do so by the graduate faculty. The master's committee informed me that the Interpesonal Perception Method lacked reliability and validity, and thus my thesis was rejected on methodological grounds. In the social sciences, conventional wisdom dictates that if something cannot be measured, then that something either does not exist or is irrelevant. Because they could not be adequately *measured*, Laing's ideas were dismissed. Perhaps Laing's mistake was to get involved with psychologists.

What R. D. Laing et al. were trying to say could be summed up by the following, poetic passages from the book:

The human race is a myriad of refractive surfaces staining the white radiance of eternity. Each surface refracts the refraction of refractions of refractions. Each self refracts the refractions of other's refractions of self refractions of others refractions. (1966, p. 3)

Farther on, the text becomes a bit more scientific, although equally abstract, stating:

If we obstinately continue to regard human beings as persons, then it is clear that there can no more be "simple location," in Whitehead's sense, in the human scene than anywhere else. But many languages (English included) express a further complexity, arising from the refractions a person undergoes as he is seen from different personal perspectives. Language expresses this by forcing the one person through various pronominal transformations according to his relation to the signifier. . . . My field of experience is, however, filled not only by my direct view of myself (ego) and of the other (alter), but of what we shall call *meta-perspectives*—my view of the *other's* (your, his, her, their) *view* of me. I may not actually be able to see myself as others see me, but I am constantly supposing them to be seeing me in particular ways, and I am constantly acting in the light of the actual or supposed attitudes, opinions, needs, and so on the other has in respect of me. (1966, p. 4)

What Laing and his colleagues are referring to is the incredibly "spiralling" capacity contained within most relationships. Such relationships refer not only to people but to the relationships among all objects in the universe. Laing's theory is essentially a quantum approach that recognizes the complex interconnectedness of all things. As such, it recognizes the principles of complementarity as well as the possibilities of non-local and non-linear relationships. It is not that these relationships do not exist, but simply that we are incapable of noticing them. This is precisely the point Laing is making about language—that a plethora of interpersonal refractions of self, self-self, and self-other perspectives enter into everything we do or say. The final product, the sentence, "I love you," for example, is an end product, a unidimensional distillation of this amazingly complex process. Language reduces an incredibly wonderful and rich history of process into a set of symbols that are *assumed* to be universal. That is, we all seem to think we are saying the same thing, when in fact, we are not and unfortunately, more often than not, are light years apart.

Laing termed our personal view of ourselves the *direct perspective*, our perception of an other's view of our self as the *meta-perspective* and our perception of what we think the other might think we perceive about our self as the *meta-meta-perspective*. Fortunately, he stops here, because as Laing points out and is often evident in creativity and psychosis, the meta-perspective is perfectly capable of extending indefinitely into the meta-meta-meta-meta, or the I think you think I think you think I think you think I think spiral. Interestingly enough, this is exactly what often happens in the convoluted arena of world affairs when different interests, cultures or national powers negotiate.

The sense or feeling of personal validity, expressed in terms of feeling understood or misunderstood, is a central theme of the interpersonal method and is most relevant to the present discussion on language and the deconstruction of the Self. Thus, as the authors state:

There is a peculiar satisfaction in feeling that one understands another person, and in feeling that one is being understood. Patently, however, two people may neither understand each other completely nor wish to. They may understand each other while supposing that they do not understand. Understanding may be greater over some issues than in others. The relationship may be relatively symmetrical, in that each understands the other to about the same extent over the same issues, or it may be lopsided, one person, in Jung's sense, being the container and the other the contained. The feeling of being understood entails feeling that the other person's meta-perspective is correct, in other words, that one's own meta-meta-feeling corresponds to one's own direct perspective. *One is now operating between all three levels* [my italics]. The feeling of being understood or misunderstood may be desired or feared. Its presence may be comforting or disconcerting. Its presence may mean of sense of being together, its absence a sense of solitude. (1966, p. 30)

Laing and his colleagues place interpersonal relations into the quantum arena where they truly belong. The possible permutations, combinations and interactions, linear and non-linear, in this model are virtually infinite. Obviously, one's system of consciousness becomes critical to this scheme because it is the contents of consciousness, whether one is aware of them or not, that determine the direction and nature of the potential interactions. Furthermore, what makes Laing and his colleagues' ideas central to my contention that the postmodern usage of language has contributed to the

deconstruction of the Self is this ability to translate interpersonal observations into a linguistic format that can be measured and operationally defined.
Language reflects the interpersonal meta-refractions that the authors are
discussing. Words are our vehicle for expressing our sense of understanding,
being understood and feeling understood. What this implies, as Laing, Phillipson and Lee point out is that words can be utilized in defense of the
schizoid posture.

People will vary as to whether or not they would rather be understood or understand.
An important aspect of each person's *self*-concept is the extent to which he feels
capable of being understood. An important aspect of one's image of the other is
the extent to which one feels the other can or does understand oneself. (1966, p. 34)

What Laing is describing is the interpersonal structure of the quintessential, *interactional self*, where language is the modulator of self-revelation.
The postmodern schizoid self employs language as a tool that measures just
how much of one's Self will be revealed. Not everyone wants to be, or is
capable of being, understood; however, certain people can tolerate the
thought of being understood but not the feeling. Feelings are dangerous
and disruptive to schizoid organizations that must conceal affect in order
to survive. The basic thrust of the schizoid person is to be secretive—not
honest about all the selves in the entire Self system. Now the schizoid
condition itself usually precludes awareness of other selves by the situational
self currently in operation. Thus, the situational self may be estranged from
its own sense of being misunderstood and may continue to operate as if
disharmony between itself and the world (or another person) did not exist.
Once again, the proverbial question arises that if all of these linguistic levels
operate intrapsychically and interpersonally, then why aren't we at least
somewhat aware of them. Why is humanity unable or unwilling to halt an
interpersonal estrangement that is spiralling out of control? The answer to
these questions is contained within the general theme of the book and has
been alluded to since the text began.
    If, as a species, humans accept the notion that they are evolving in a
schizoid manner, then the last two questions can begin to be answered.
When it comes to language, for example, we assume a very unidimensional
perspective and recognize very little beyond our direct, narcissistic perspective. Humans are becoming an "I," interpersonally estranged from the
"Thou," that the other can be related to as. The experience of resonance
described in the preceding chapter is an affair that, under these conditions,
is hardly possible. We ignore the vast complexity, the innuendo richness
of our words and phrases. Hardly anyone pauses to think of language as
having complex meta levels; most settle for a flat, bland version of what
true communication can be. The postmodern utilization of language represents the ultimate deconstructor of the Self. As an efficient manipulator

and negotiator of situations, language is employed as the universal defender of the situational self. Through its obfuscative constructions, it can perpetuate schizoid fragmentation, all the while maintaining the illusion that such fragmentation does not exist.

The deconstruction of the Self is not an inevitable quality of language but rather a product of the way *we use language*. Language is employed in defense of the schizoid position; it is utilized to conceal from consciousness the entire range of human responsivity. Language is wielded as the transformer of *process* into non-process; language symbolically reduces the vast complexity "between things" into abstractions. As symbols of the responsive quantum process of *aliveness*, the postmodern usage of words has left much to be desired. In their work on mythological symbols, both Joseph Campbell and Carl Jung stated that for our ancestors, one of the most crucial things symbols provided was a rich and mysterious feeling of being alive—alive in the sense of being connected to a greater reality than the personal self. This concept of aliveness bears a striking similarity to the quantum idea of resonance and suggests that postmodern consciousness is vastly different from premodern consciousness.

One of the truly amazing aspects of this postmodern linguistic transformation is that by "ancestors" we are talking about people who lived only a few hundred years ago. What is so frightening is that these changes have occurred in a time period that represents but a small fraction of recorded human history. If we extend recorded history back to the time when Cro-Magnon people first appeared, approximately 40,000 years ago, then it becomes apparent that enormous changes in the consciousness of the species are occurring at light-year speeds. What postmodern unidimensional language does is reduce language to an abstract and impersonal dimension where other systems of consciousness (feelings, images, sensations) do not count. Postmodern identity represents *being* estranged from the body—people alienated from the blood and guts corporeality of existence. As Wittgenstein pointed out at the turn of the century, most of our modern conflicts are *conflicts of ideas and concepts*, not conflicts of reality. We inhabit a world of ideas and employ language as its navigator. Our inventiveness has enabled us to modify reality to fit our idea of what reality should be. Through technology we rearrange the world, whereas through cosmetic surgery we alter our bodies to appear as we would like them to be. As I have stated throughout the book, we severely constrict the full system of consciousness, and in doing so, we constrict our usage of language as well. There is, however, a way out, an antidote, partial, perhaps, but an antidote nonetheless. Communication between people must be enlarged to include the other selves; especially, it must be augmented to include emotions. If language is the postmodern deconstructor of the Self, then emotions are the deconstructor of postmodern (unidimensional) language. Before we cover proposals for improving our alienated condition, there is one more area that begs to be explored; the relationship of language to law, culture and the ethos of contemporary civilization.

SUMMARY

In a deconstructionist mode, this chapter examined our employment of language as the ultimate dissembler of the Self. The text shifted from discussing a whole, but fragmented, Self to a newly constructed interactional self. The interactional self is a postmodern development and an outgrowth of the situational/relational self of modern times. Schizoid consciousness was described as the postmodern consciousness *erroneously* thought necessary for survival. It was postulated that the sheer number of interactional possibilities inherent in an accelerated, information-saturated, postmodern world necessitates a quantum methodology for understanding the human narrative.

The principle of emergent interactionism, first introduced in chapter 2, was used to explain novel emergents that the postmodern self must encounter. It was further suggested that postmodern existence leads to a causal decoupling of human identity to a new level of definition. The interpersonal theories of R. D. Laing were introduced as an illustration of how contemporary people ignore the full meta-implications of relationships and language. Before leaving the topic of culture and discussing a postmodern ecology of being human, a final but important illustration of contemporary social life is examined.

NOTES

1. For a thorough discussion of causal decoupling, see H. Pagels (1989).
2. See chapter on language, DeBerry (1991).
3. For an informative as well as interesting introduction to virtual reality and "cyberpunk" see the magazine *Mondo*, published in Berkeley, California (of course).
4. The Center for Public Integrity, a Washington, DC, based group has recently issued a report describing the type of linguistic and visual manipulation used to distort the full impact of the war.

Six

Ethos and the Domination of Law and Market

Civilized life requires a state of illusion.

Camille Paglia

Recognizing a cultural system is a step toward identifying the manner in which a civilization maintains its identity and perpetuates its continued existence. In that their evolutionary purpose is survival, adaptation and advancement, cultures are teleological in nature. The end product of any culture is identical, it is the means that differ. By means, I refer to the parts or substructures of the cultural system that carry out the basic cultural system operations. Both between and within species, cultural operations manifest an incredible range of possibility. In the case of linguistically dominated humans, cultural variability has reached its zenith; a pinnacle, however, that is always changing. Part of the problem inherent to the interactional self concerns the evolution of culture. As the world moves toward a global or planetary society, the question of culture and consciousness becomes critical. As a species, are we culturally evolving in a homogeneous manner, or are distinct paths of culture and hence consciousness developing? To an extent, I believe both these possibilities are occurring and, therefore it is incumbent on us to understand the divergent processes affecting our future.

Cultural fluctuations are indicative of the paradoxical nature the global cultural system finds itself in. One of the precipitants of this paradox is related to two opposing macro forces operating antagonistically. By macro, I refer to large-scale pressures that affect entire cultural systems; externalized consciousness and the greenhouse effect are two examples of large-scale forces that have a global effect. In the present case, one force represents the historical constraints of contemporary cultural systems to homogenize consciousness—to make everyone alike. To borrow Herbert Marcuse's (1955) phrase, "unidimensionality" of thought enables a civilization to manipulate parts so that the system operates efficiently with minimal friction. In this case the parts are, of course, people. The opposing force has been termed cultural devolution, a movement that emphasizes national and ethnic diversity. A prime example of devolution is now occurring in Eastern Europe and the Soviet Union, where different nations and cultures are attempting to separate and establish autonomy. Devolutionists are concerned with establishing a unique and separate identity based on distinctive values expressed in culturally indigenous customs. In the United States, the now fashionable trend to emphasize one's ethnic origins, especially as manifested by the preservation of native languages and customs is another example of devolution. Four decades ago, I remember my mother's grandparents going through great efforts to lose their southern Italian accents and peasant ways. Today, such dialects and customs are in vogue and people are taking great pains to "return to their roots." Devolution is a global tendency that manifests anywhere a distinct individual group attempts to establish ethnic, religious and cultural autonomy.

The paradox with devolution pertains to the way the tendency toward devolution fuses with the global drift toward unidimensional thought. Although these macro forces are antagonistic, they are by no means equal, the tendency toward homogenization of thought being the more dominant of the two. Unidimensionality of thought refers to the postmodern proclivity to process reality in a common and singular manner. The general structure of this processing style has already been extensively discussed as schizoid. As schizoid consciousness becomes a global phenomenon, devolution offers little chance of escape, because the devolved culture will tend to be a devolved schizoid culture. However, devolution, because it implies a breakdown of monolithic cultural substructures, such as racism, communism, totalitarianism, or rampant capitalism, can be a positive process. Not only can it be exhilarating but it can lead to examination of previous cultural norms that results in a beneficial reorganization of the manner in which things are accomplished. By things, I am referring to the vicissitudes of work and love (play), the principal concern of any culture. Although devolutionists want the chance to express an individual cultural identity, underlying this intent is the more fundamental desire to improve the manner in which people work and play. If these fundamental modes of human relatedness do not change, any devolution process will lead to nothing more than alterations in window dressing. Things would appear, in a media image manner to have changed—people might dress distinctively, speak another language or celebrate different holidays—but, substantially, nothing will really change unless the manner in which people interact with one another changes.

ETHOS AND CONSCIOUSNESS

Unless an important system modification occurs, attempts at devolution and ethnic and national freedom are doomed to only limited success. In chapter 5, I cultivated the notion that it is our response to the industrial/technological, postmodern system that must undergo modification. One way to begin to alter this less than positive response is to change the systems ethos. Ethos refers to the enduring and distinguishing characteristics of a nation or race—the daily habits or "ways of doing business" on a personal, social, business, professional and governmental level. The ethos refers to the general and unspoken rules by which a culture operates and conducts its daily affairs. A derivative of ethos is the word ethical, a term commonly employed in reference to the standards by which professions or businesses operate. Because ethos represents a more inclusive term that encompasses all aspects of human interaction, I am giving it precedence over its more familiar cousin.

More often than not, people are unaware of the prevailing ethos. This tendency is related to our inability to notice ordinary consciousness, an inclination that is compounded by our cultural inability to engage in dialogue, to seriously and meaningfully discuss important issues. This nearsightedness is so ingrained that if, as it usually does, the prevailing ethos *gradually* changes, whether positively or negatively, we fail to notice it. What we are cognizant of, however, are alterations in awareness. An example of a positive shift is the experience of holiday or vacation. On holiday, we behave differently and notice that emotions and thoughts have assumed a distinctive and novel quality. Sensations and images, dormant and long forgotten, suddenly become paramount and eclipse the more mundane elements of our psyche. We begin to feel more alive, we are on holiday from ordinary life.

The experience of holiday or vacation offers vivid illustration of the incredible covert power of a systems ethos. I have numerous friends and patients who survive because they are able to take time off and travel. The ethos under which a tropical resort or a foreign vacation operates provides the opportunity for consciousness to change. Many people, on coming back from such a holiday, typically wonder why they are returning from such a wonderful state of being to a highly stressed and personally inadequate way of life. This is an important question and certainly one that deserves a better answer than many of us have been able to come up with. Most people behave differently on holiday, for example, the only time sex is pleasurable for some people is when they are on holiday and away from their usual routine.

Another critical point concerning ethos is the *top-down effect*. Inevitably within a system, the ethos is determined from the top of the hierarchy. The leader, or principal system, sets the ethical tone and eventually the ethos filters down to subordinates or subsystems. The following example provides a good illustration of the top–down effect of systems ethos.

A director of a mental health clinic cared little for the lower-middle class community the clinic was located in. The director, a wealthy physician, lived in an affluent suburb miles from the clinic. The director assumed a very laissez-faire attitude toward clinical treatment and was basically indifferent to the psychological needs of the community. This ethos filtered down to the psychiatrists, who, at the expense of the clinic and community, devoted most of their time to personal affairs and private practice. Despite the fact that their actions represented a gross injustice and were basically criminal in nature, because the behavior was unofficially condoned from above, little could be done to improve the situation. Eventually, this ethos became so ingrained that the entire clinic staff worked only what was minimally necessary to get by.

Now, because *ethos is hardly ever apparent in language,* the Director never directly condoned this behavior or expressed these ethical beliefs. *In postmodern language words are employed to obfuscate, conceal and distort the ethos.* Language is used to make people believe one thing is happening while, in reality, an entirely different set of circumstances exists. A similar situation exists in terms of governmental policy, concerning health care, racial bias, sexism, drugs or education, where one thing is stated while another actually occurs. What literally happens is determined by the silent ethos, allocating from the top echelons of government and trickling down through all strata of society. Ethos is only manifest in the behavior, actions and life-style of a person. It is evident not in the words but in the manner in which a person lives. The cultural ethos suggests what is covertly required of people to function within a society. For example, the cultural ethos of the United States emphasizes functioning, productivity, individualism and competition.

Ethos, like consciousness, is subtle and insidious. Like clean air, a cultural ethos is usually taken for granted. People tend to be aware of an ethos only when sudden cultural changes, as in war or natural disasters, force "normal" cultural operations to change. Under ordinary cultural conditions, most people do not pay much attention to the ethos they are operating under. In this case, an ethos can slowly and imperceptibly change and reach a new system level that is simply taken for granted—it will appear that this is "the way things are and always were." Although I can think of a lot of cultural illustrations, three examples that come to mind are rock music, driving and lingerie.

AUTOMOBILES, ROCK AND ROLL AND UNDERWEAR

What would Walt have thought of this? One new realm of the ever-expanding Disney empire is its recently launched Hollywood Records label, which is pushing a leather-clad heavy metal band called the Scream. The label is clearly aimed at a more adult audience than other Disney enterprises. But the Scream screams lyrics that Mickey would never whisper to Minnie. (Let's just say the words "push" and "honey" are used in creative ways.) *Disney calls the music "very normal rock and roll."* (my emphasis) (*Newsweek*, November 11, 1991, p. 8)

A few weeks ago, I visited a friend in the store where he works. Rock music was playing and my companion really liked a song and inquired if I felt the same way. I replied that I really liked the group's sound but felt that something was wrong. "The lyrics," I said. "Doesn't anyone hear what these guys are saying?" No one really knew or cared what I was referring to and told me "just to listen to the music and stop being so analytical."

The music was good, but the lyrics vividly described a man sexually abusing a young girl who had mistakenly entered a less than desirable section of town. Everyone in the store (I conducted an informal survey) thought the lyrics were quite ordinary and actually quite reflective of "the way things are." I have had similar discussions with teenagers who claim to think that the lyrics they are listening to represent banal statements.

I remember a time not too long ago, perhaps approximately 25 years, when popular rock lyrics were quite different. Many groups were singing about love, peace, enchanted people, mystical states and, in general, conveyed a distinct sense of harmony and human respect. In no way am I implying that all songs were of such a genre but, nevertheless, the prevalent musical ethos of the late 1960s and early 1970s was dramatically different from the musical ethos of today.

Driving provides an example of another gradual but dramatic shift in ethos. What I am specifically referring to is the relationship between people and cars. The area I live in is approximately 50 miles north of New York City, and here, it is quite clear that in terms of "right of way," cars take precedence over people. Cars do not stop for people, in fact, drivers seem to rarely notice people; if and when they do pedestrians are usually viewed as a nuisance or impediment to the vehicles' continuous onslaught. I am not just talking about street crossings but public parking lots, malls and parks as well.

If I stop my car to allow someone to continue walking, a bombardment of horn honking quickly ensues. Furthermore, people whom I stop for appear shocked and are usually too terrified to accept my offer, or if they do continue walking, they do so quickly, with a perplexing look of suspicion and gratitude, almost as if I were doing them a favor or they were breaking the law or committing a social faux pas. As far as I know, there is no law stating that cars in a supermarket parking lot have the right of way over people. The law has not changed but the ethos under which people drive

has. This ethos has changed so insidiously that no one seems to remember
there was a time when an individual's promenade took precedence over an
automobile's trajectory.

The contemporary dress ethos is another good example because in relation to clothes, most people will simply say that fashion is always
changing. Although this is true, what also changes over time is the
ethos that a particular style may represent. Lately, I have noticed that
people are very comfortable wearing pajamas, underwear and frilly lingerie in public. A young girl recently came to her therapy session
dressed in what used to be thought of as a woman's bedroom clothes.
Of course, no one thinks they are wearing underwear, just as almost
everyone forgets that only 20 years ago no one would be wearing what
people often wear today. The cultural fashion ethos did not allow for
clothes that looked like private garments to be worn in public. There
was a separation of public and private dress that today no longer exists.
Lacy, frilly, seductive or relaxed clothes are no longer restricted to private showings, they have become public and in doing so convey a certain cultural message, reflective of a shift in ethos. The contemporary
ethos has altered the symbolic message of clothes—for example, the
sexual connotation of lingerie à la the Madonna image is not supposed
to be acknowledged. This is, of course, incredibly schizoid, because it
separates what for many is a covert sexual message from public consciousness—that is, sexual arousal cannot be openly acknowledged. This
is an extremely confusing and convoluted process that leads to unacknowledged meta-messages. The direct communication might be "this is
my style and the way I like to express myself." The meta-message
might be "do you find it sexually arousing?" Whereas, the meta-meta
message could be "if so, do not feel or act on it." Adolescents do not
remember a time when dressing in a risqué manner conveyed a sexual
message; for them, the fashion ethos has not changed, but for many it
has and this change can be both puzzling and frustrating.

The point of these examples is that we are usually unaware of the prevailing cultural ethos, the unspoken "rules" by which we socially construct
our daily lives. So ingrained is the dominant ethos that as a result of what
is often an extraordinary experience, remarkably few people attempt to alter
or reexamine their life. Even when an earnest attempt is embarked on, the
prevailing ethos is usually so powerful that most ventures are tragically
short lived. One patient, a highly stressed, self-made business entrepreneur
was so impressed by the Latin custom of taking siestas that he attempted,
unsuccessfully, to incorporate the habit into his style of life. The daily and
usually unnoticed habits imposed by the dominant ethos of the U.S. culture
doomed his endeavor to failure. Not only is the ethos difficult to notice, it
is likewise absurdly difficult to change.

THE CAPITALISTIC ETHOS

> A democratic capitalistic society is, in principle, uncommitted to any one vision of a social order.
>
> Michael Novak

With an important qualification, the cultural ethos that I am discussing refers to the system in the United States. The qualification is that the U.S. ethical system is fast becoming a global system. This system, which affects all aspects of daily life and human relatedness, is politically intertwined with the economic system of capitalism. The term capitalism, which usually is thought to refer to a fairly consistent and homogenous method of conducting economic business, actually represents a rather diverse range of economic practices. The point is that there exists a wide range of capitalistic styles, each with their peculiar benefits and liabilities.

Capitalism, U.S. style, represents one of the worst manifestations of this economic system. U.S. capitalism is capitalism run amuck, what Michael Harrington (1989) and Fredric Jameson (1991) call advanced, late phase and casino capitalism—a way of doing business fueled by the synergetic effects of a cultural ethos that emphasizes

- Excessive and wasteful competition
- Wide speculation, short-term growth and immediate profit
- Individual and community dispensability
- Singular achievement and individual hoarding

These statements represent only the tip of the iceberg. My position on capitalism is similar to my opinion concerning technology—that is, that it is not capitalism per se that is unsuitable but rather the nature of our interactive cultural response to capitalism. It is not my intention in this chapter to elaborate on the detrimental interactive effects of late stage capitalism, such explications have been more than adequately covered by others, among them Albert Einstein, whom I feel compelled to quote before leaving this discussion:

The profit motive in conjunction with competition among capitalists, is responsible for the instability in the accumulation and utilization of capital which leads to increasingly severe depressions. Unlimited competition leads to a huge waste of labor and to a crippling of the social consciousness of individuals. The crippling of individuals I consider the worst evil of capitalism. Our whole educational system suffers from this evil. An exaggerated competitive attitude is inculcated into the student who is trained to worship success as a preparation for his future career. (Schwartz & McGuiness, 1979, p. 169)

The direction I wish to take involves an exploration of the subsystems that are correlated with and support the capitalistic ethos, U.S. style. These are the contemporary subsystems of law and values.

POSTMODERN LEGALISM

The United States is a litigious culture in which the ratio of lawyers to people is greater than in any other nation in the world. Because postmodern law is very different from its premodern predecessor, to understand it is to understand the culture we live in. For one thing, the concept of justice, except in a very metaphorical and, perhaps, mythological way, no longer exists. Let me provide a personal incident as an illustration.

In 1989 I was scheduled to give a presentation on consciousness at the American Psychological Association's annual convention, which that year was located in New Orleans. Because my wife was 7-months pregnant, we decided to drive from New York in a small camper. The first night of the journey, while parked and resting in the back of the truck, we were hit by a teenage drunken driver who had lost control of her vehicle. Both of us sustained serious bodily injury, but Linda, because of her pregnancy, was forced into premature labor and Julian, who I have been referring to throughout the book, was precipitously ejected from his embryonic sanctuary to make a hasty, 31-week entry into the world. It is totally due to the incredible advances in neonatal technology that Julian is alive at all (actually, as I write this chapter he is slightly over 2 years old and doing quite well—his existence is one of the paramount reasons I am not against technological advancement).

The reason behind this personal revelation concerns the rather odd legal world the accident catapulted us into. I will spare the reader the litany of convoluted legal tactics employed by the driver to avoid prosecution and punishment. Anyone familiar with contemporary legal affairs will know what I am referring to. My point is this: at no time in the last 2 years, except in a rhetorical sense, did the concept of justice and retribution arise. There has never been any direct contact between the woman that hit us and ourselves, all contact has been through lawyers and insurance companies, disinterested third parties who are invested in this case for the following reasons:

- Money
- The efficient administration of the law
- The management of a plurality of interests

Our notion of law has been removed from all vestiges of personal and direct involvement. Law, in becoming an abstract and impersonal vehicle of efficient managerial deployment, has become increasing schizoid. This is true not only in the above illustration but on other occasions as well. I have had the twilight zone experience of watching opposing lawyers viciously attack each other in the courtroom, pause at recess to share lunch at "the Club" together, inquire about each other's families and plans for the weekend only to return to the courtroom and resume fighting. What lawyers do has nothing to do with whatever human tragedy may have occurred; what lawyers do has to do with the law. Postmodern law is the ultimate example of deconstructionist principles, nothing exits but the text itself. There is no concept of individual or community truth, only the truth of the text—the law.

The deconstruction of legal processes removes the full human system element from consideration. All the elements of consciousness that we have been considering—thoughts, feelings, images, sensations, behaviors—are irrelevant, what matters is the law. This creates the surreal circumstance where intuitively, some things that "feel" right are illegal while actions that decidedly "feel" wrong are sanctioned. The problem is that the law has become increasingly schizoid. In calling the law schizoid, I am suggesting that although the *concept* of justice has remained the same, the *process* of justice—the actual day to day operations of the legal system—has become increasingly inauthentic. This inauthenticity is further compounded by the unacknowledged accumulation of decades of racial, ethnic, religious, sexual and economic bias. These prejudices, although thoroughly discussed outside of the system, have never been directly and openly acknowledged or rectified within the legal system itself.

Part of the reason for this neglect is that our legal system fails to directly acknowledge anything. What the system initially recognizes is the *implication* of an act within the law and, second, through an almost metaphysical transformation, the law itself. Id est, the act becomes divorced from its human element and enters a new system level of abstract legalese connections. Within this level, dialogue concerns itself with technical legalities, precedents and methodologies and is not directly concerned with human suffering. Legal proceedings are more concerned that procedures be legal. What this odd tautology implies is that for postmodern law, maintaining a consistent internal validity—concentrating on the law rather than the deed—is what is important. This was evident to me not only in my own case of trying to prosecute a drunken driver but in the U.S. response to killing Iraqi children or Panamanian civilians. Once these situations were examined in the legal arena, the actual impact of what happened to people became irrelevant.

Human experience plays a minor role in legal proceedings or is given only cursory or sensationalistic acknowledgement. The recent proposal that African-Americans be economically compensated for their period of enforced slavery is an example of a new attempt to heal an old wound. But these suggestions have been made before, and, like attempts to reconcile the horrible tragedies of the holocaust and ethnic genocides of World War II, have fallen on deaf legal ears. In an attempt to balance a plurality of interests, postmodern law has become an agency of efficient administration. In a culture of optimal administration, the *image* of the law becomes more important than even the letter of the law. Thus, law is removed not only from the human element but from itself as well. In the United States, postmodern law represents a legal system frantically trying to balance the plurality of interests inherent to an interactional age. As we retreat into the abstract world of litigation and law, we accomplish nothing more than exacerbating the schizoid condition.

In reference to contemporary American culture, the writer Stephen Schiff states that "the central fact of American life as we enter the nineties is the intensity of our pluralism. We're a nation of 250 million nations, a commonwealth with almost nothing in common. We are, each of us, particles; never in this century have we felt so atomized" (1990, p. 44).

The administration of efficient law represents government's attempt to balance this plurality. Within this legal system, the purpose of government becomes the maximization of individual rights as a means of maximizing individual profit. Because there is a plethora of special interest groups, each clamoring to have their needs met, the goal of government becomes the ensurance of fairness. In order to accomplish this, law and government pretend to be value free. According to Edward Sampson (1989), "the state was to remain indifferent and neutral, neither taking sides nor espousing any one purpose over any other beyond ensuring that no single purpose would dominate" (p. 915).

Within a governmental system that is required to balance an extraordinarily skewed plurality of interests, certain skills are required. As Max Weber noted, it becomes necessary to have a vast and complex bureaucracy of efficient management and administration. Management and administration, as dictated by the law, are the postmodern hallmarks of government. The question then becomes, can such a system be value free? The answer, of course, is no. What the system can do, however, is pretend or appear to be value free. Acting one way while pretending to think another exacerbates the schizoid condition and fosters the split between what appears and what is. The fact that government policy is inauthentic only serves to increase individual confusion—confusion that becomes even more blatant as the inauthenticity is denied.

To compound the confusion, the emphasis on efficiency and administration applies to lobbyists who now orchestrate highly technological and insidiously complex influence campaigns. Contemporary lobbying efforts demonstrate the postmodern confusion between appearance and actuality. The key to a successful lobbying campaign is to make it appear to represent a consensus of that increasingly ethereal body, *the American people*. For example,

Firms now employ sophisticated techniques to hone in on constituents who back their position and will take action. A group of major retailers last year hired Reese Communications Companies to block a protectionist textile bill that would in effect raise the price of imported clothes. Reese started with 3 million names from its own database and rented mailing lists and then began weeding out the unreliable. . . . *The key to any carefully planned effort is to make it look like a natural explosion of raw democracy.* (my emphasis) (Waldman, *Newsweek* May 6, 1991, p. 35)

One reason for this dilemma is that our legal system still conceives of itself in premodern, romantic terms, whereas it acts in a very postmodern fashion. This romantic image of the legal system is apparent not only in movies and television shows about lawyers, cops and judges but in the mythological images and dictums the profession itself pretends to follow. Law, like postmodern democracy, bears only a vague linguistic similarity to its ancient origins. At one point in history, law represented the principles of a just and fair negotiation between the actions of individuals and community. In making this claim, I am not saying that premodern law was always fair and just. There is an inherent danger in idealizing "the way things used to be," and I definitely wish to avoid this conceptual pitfall. What I am implying is that there was more of a direct connection between the act, the person and the community (or state). This directness was possible, in part, because of the small size and homogeneity of most communities and nation states. It is difficult, perhaps, to remember that just 192 years ago the population of the planet was approximately 4–1/2 billion less than it is today. The Greek, Judeo/Christian concepts of law and democracy originated roughly 2,700 years ago in a time when populations were modest and most people, in comparison to contemporary standards, lived in relatively small nation sates. If we accept the evolutionary evidence that homo sapiens began evolving several million years ago, it becomes almost startling to realize that it took millions of years for the human planetary population to reach the 1 billion mark. This occurred approximately around 1800, and by 1930, only 130 years later, another billion humans were added, and so, we come to 1992 where in perhaps 5 years the global population will reach the 6 billion mark. The legal rules that guide the fate of 6 billion are a universe apart from the rules for thousands of Athenians, Judaens, or Carpathians, and yet, to a large extent, we pretend this is not so. Our pretence is based on an entrenched romantic image of the law that contaminates the reality of the law in our vastly different postmodern age.

This schizoid polarity between the *image* and the *actual* contributes to a panoply of confusion and conflicting interests. As a nation, we are confused over all facets of birth, living and death. We quibble over when and how life begins and the manner in which it should end. Nineteen nations have infancy mortality rates superior to the United States, a nation in which the majority of infant deaths occur principally to Black and minority status babies. The infant mortality rate among Black Americans in the nation's capital averages near the so-called third world rate and is higher than in Costa Rica and Jamaica. In discussing the infant mortality rate, *Newsweek* columnist George F. Will, hardly a flaming liberal, states that

The rate among black American babies is worse than among Hungarian and Polish babies. Nothing that happens in Bangladesh should be as interesting to Americans as the fact that a boy born in Harlem today has a lower life expectancy than a boy born in Bangladesh. Between 1978 and 1988 the number of babies born with syphilis increased seven fold, the number born with AIDS is increasing, and 100,000 babies born each year may be chronically handicapped because of their mothers' use of cocaine. (1991, p. 78)

Many people are blind to the implications of such facts, and because the ethos is both invisible and unacknowledged, people become passionately involved in heated debates over abortion, affirmative action and sexual harassment in an incredibly limited and short-sighted manner. Everyone thinks they are right, each asserting a privileged access to truth. Ideas and principles are zealously defended but no one stops to discuss long-term ecological effects such as what happens to unwanted babies after they are born or how the continuance of racial inequity affects a community and nation. If people had to actually live with the outcome of their beliefs, the situation would be quite different. To paraphrase Ludwig Wittgenstein (1958/1990) our conflicts are conflicts of ideas, when it comes to the actual necessities of reality we are more in agreement than we would care to realize. The postmodern world is a world where people are increasingly fighting and dying over the relationship between ideas. This would not be so troublesome if people were equipped to fight over such abstractions, but, unfortunately, when it comes to conceptual battles we are an ill-equipped army. Furthermore, those more enlightened are usually passive and withdraw from direct involvement allowing most of the action to be handled by zealots and fundamentalists.

In the United States where less than 50% of the population votes in national elections, with the exception of well-orchestrated interest groups with money and a specific agenda, the abandonment of true political activism has reached a zenith. To compound the problem, as Robert Bellah and his colleagues have pointed out in *Habits of the Heart* (1987) and *The Good Society* (1991) our cultural ethos still emphasizes a variation of Lockean individualism. People in the United States feel that they can live a life of their own choosing, independent of whatever powers that may be. Brian, the high school musician and student counselor mentioned in chapter 4, is an excellent example of this phenomenon. Brian pretends to be whatever the system demands of him yet feels he is "in it but not part of it." It is an axiom of quantum physics and a quantum psychological approach that once systems interact they become correlated with each other. In reality, it is no more possible to be part of an inauthentic system and to claim one is not part of it, than it is to simultaneously sit and stand. As Bellah and his colleagues (1991) point out, social institutions have an enormous and usually unrecognized influence on us—that influence being the ethos I have been addressing.

Again, I want to stress that I am referring to the U.S. legal structure and, by fiat, the entire system of government. Here, we act one way while thinking another. Because the world is not uniformly postmodern, there are still regions where deeds and principles are more in accordance. The Soviet Union is a nation undergoing incredible changes on almost every system level. For a period in the Fall of 1991, over a matter of legal principle, the city council of Moscow participated in a 4-week hunger strike. There is no way I can even remotely imagine U.S. lawmakers fasting for even a day—and for a matter of legal principle, never. The point is that even in contemporary Russia there is a concordance between a premodern, romantic vision of the law and individual action. In the United States, where lawmakers exist in the rarefied atmosphere of rhetoric, euphemism and political jargon, this connection does not exist. By our ethical standards, the actions of the Moscow city council are probably viewed as irrational, although, from another perspective, it can be stated that only someone who truly "feels" an injustice can act in such fashion. In the linguistic, metaphoric world of legal terminology, feelings have no place. Only the linear and logical elements of language and rationality are accepted. Law is a profession dominated by linear rules of language in service of efficient administration of interests. As such, it bears little connection to the ecological fullness of the community or individual. In reference to this, legal professor Mary Ann Glendon states that

We've put a lot of weight on the law. There is a question of whether law can bear all the weight we've put on it, and whether it's really desirable for the law to be such an important value carrier in society. Montesquieu and Tocqueville, among others, thought that what was really important was what undergirded the law— *manners, customs and mores. If a law wasn't grounded in the mores, the philosophers didn't think there was much hope for it.* (my emphasis) (Moyers, 1989, p. 471)

Governments do not pay much attention to philosophers any longer and as for manners, customs and mores, the ethos I have been talking about, such standards could be summed up by consumption, profit and competition—the values of the market.

THE MARKET ETHOS

Our overemphasis of the market ethos has affected consciousness in a troubling variety of ways. For one, it has virtually eliminated critical dialogue on the issues I have been raising. Cornel West, in reference to the market ethos states that "it makes it very difficult to hold on to non-market values, such as commitment in relationships, solidarity, community care, sacrifice, risk, and struggle. Market values encourage a preoccupation with the now, with the immediate" (Moyers, 1990, pp. 102–103).

The prevalence of the market ethos has also contributed to the continuing deterioration of community. The word community has lost its original meaning and is now used in a very abstract sense to refer to *any common group of people independent of geographic location*—professional communities such as the scientific community, racial communities such as the Black community, business communities such as the financial community or electronic communities such as computer networks. Because community no longer demands communal involvement, the postmodern enlargement of the term has made daily personal contact irrelevant. In the United States, we inhabit ersatz or pseudocommunities in which most people live in a state of perpetual alienation. We are removed from the daily involvement of mutuality, interconnectedness and community—what binds us is law and what law serves is the vested interest of the market. The market ethos replaces community and relatedness with impersonal social contracts that appear to be personal but, in reality, are extremely dispassionate.

Commenting on these recent changes in the American way of life, Alan Wolfe states that

Although they like to think of themselves as neighborly, Americans increasingly resort to ways of resolving their disputes that are more formal than friendly. The increasing litigiousness of American society, the new role of insurance companies as makers of public policy, the formalization of trust, the increasing use of binding arbitration, the increasing privatization of government services all represent steps away from a community based on kinship within a common tradition (Gemeinschaft) toward one based on impersonal social contracts (Gesellschaft). . . . The net result is a change in the texture of everyday life, one felt in places as diverse as the physician's waiting room, the courtroom, the local prison, and the suburban shopping mall. (1991, p. 38)

The principle connection a family living in Westchester county has with a Seattle, Washington, family is increasingly being reduced to economics and law, and increasingly economics and law are becoming one. The average local political campaign now costs hundreds of thousands of dollars. When we reach the level of national politics, multimillion dollar campaigns confront the contender. The U.S. Senate, a legislative body composed primarily of millionaires, recently raised its annual salary to approximately $125,000. The sheer cost of running against incumbents has transformed the House of Representatives into a quasipermanent political employer. It is simply too expensive to run against an entrenched, elected official. For example, according to former California governor Jerry Brown:

In fact, if you judged from how our elected representatives spend their time, you would conclude that government had become a cover story for political fund-raising. Like a perverse form of natural selection, the system sorts out candidates by how much money they raise and spend on "public" airwaves. In California, for example, it costs $18 million to run for the United States senate, which translates to about $10,000 for each working day during a six year term. In mid-size states, $5 million to $7 million is common. Such sums are not gathered by the faint hearted but only by those candidates who can exploit without shame their time, notoriety and their public office.

But the situation is even worse than it looks at first glance. The important campaign money comes in the most undemocratic way imaginable—from a fraction of the citizenry, mostly those in the top 1 percent of income earners. And it is principally these few for whom politics still works, as they watched their after-tax incomes grow in real terms from $190,500 in 1977 to $400,000 in 1990. (1991, p. 84)

The marketing of the democratic process has alienated a large portion of U.S. voters. For an industrialized Western nation, the United States has the lowest percentage of election voter turnout (50.1% in the 1988 presidential election and 36% in the 1990 election). Voting is, likewise, skewed by income; in the 1980 general election 70% of those with incomes above $25,000 voted, whereas only 25% of those with incomes below $10,000 a year did (Ahlberg 1991, p. 81).

Such financial prerequisites to government service also distort the cultural ethos, which in turn debilitates community. As E. J. Dionne states,

Because of the flight from public life, our society no longer fosters a sense of community or common purpose. Social gaps, notably the divide between blacks and whites grow wider. We have less and less to do with each other, meaning that we feel few obligations to each other and are less and less inclined to vindicate each other's rights. (1991, p. 78)

The loss of community is not a novel trend but, in Western civilization, has been occurring since the end of the nineteenth century. In discussing the breaking up of twentieth century culture Robert Phelps states that

Since 1900—give or take a decade—individuals have been conscious of the passing of community, of losing the sense of unconditional belonging which every culture before us has taken for granted. It was something which happened slowly but persistently, on every social and economic level, and in every form of community from the family and the church congregation to the city and nation. The forms themselves did not vanish. Many appear to go on functioning as solidly as ever. But now they are under siege. They have to be force-fed and defended, they are no longer simply given, as cards dealt out in a game of poker. And more and more people, in their hearts, no longer feel with assurance that they belong to anyone, or anything, anywhere. (1965, pp. 17–18)

There is a deep and profound sense of alienation involved in the loss of community, an estrangement that directly leads to the overdevelopment of schizoid structure and the propagation of the postmodern interactional self. A key phrase in the Phelps passage is "many appear to go on functioning," because appearance and function are two critical composites of the interactional self. In the schizoid, interactional world of postmodern existence, *appearance is valued over essence and functioning over vitality*. This subtle but crucial transformation of what could be called "basic reality assumptions" is a cornerstone in the development of a postmodern quantum psychology and is discussed in detail in the chapter on quantum diagnosis. In terms of the current exposition, the basic point is that the universal worship of the late capitalistic market ethos distorts both consciousness and community.

In discussing the relationship of capitalism to community Michael Harrington (1989) quotes from Irving Howe's book *Socialism in America* (1985):

Who does not feel the continued poignancy in the yearning for community which seems so widespread in our time? Who does not respond in our society, to the cry that life is poor in shared experiences, vital communities, free brother and sisterhoods?. . . We live in a time when the yearning for community has been misshaped into a gross denial of personal integrity, when the desire for the warmth of social bonds—marching together, living together, huddling together, complaining in concert—has helped betray a portion of the world into the shame of the total state. (pp. 162–163)

Howe's point is well taken. The totalitarianism that occurred under communist rule distorted socialism and terrified the average American citizen that socialist tendencies would seep into democracy. In the United States, the fact that socialism and democracy are not antithetical is lost on a nation in which 49% of the population thinks that wheat is the main ingredient of oatmeal (*Harper's Index*, November 1991). Not only can socialism blend with democracy but with capitalism as well. The ethos of contemporary U.S. capitalism needs to be tempered by the cooperative and community orientation of modern socialism.

I have followed a bit of a political digression here, but it is one that I shall return to repeatedly in the remainder of the text. The reason I raise these issues now is to illustrate how awareness of important issues (consciousness, culture and economics) can become narrow and restricted. Although numerous reasons contribute to our limitations, a principal one must be identified as the market ethos. In the culture of the United States, everything is entwined with money and becomes a marketable commodity. This economization of areas formerly independent of financial concerns is becoming a major obstacle to progress. Education, health care, decent housing, the arts and even social and scientific research are increasingly yoked by the constraints of grants, loans and financial restrictions. In this sense, almost everything, including the democratic political process, becomes a marketable commodity. Thus, under postmodern conditions, the law also becomes a marketable commodity. But, if law and money are becoming synonymous, so are government and the legal profession.

In contemporary Western politics, where few people outside the legal profession are allowed entry, government and law are virtually synonymous. The only exception seems to be actors and celebrities whose media image and overvaluation by a media-riveted society provides access to the political arena. But even in these cases, such people function as figureheads and props of vested interest groups. What we seem to be witnessing in the United States is the marketing of political leaders. In fact, the U.S. society represents a culture in which anything, from the death of a child to a war, can be transformed into a marketable commodity. The fact that accounting nomenclature has seeped into everyday language is a pernicious yet subtle example of this cultural transformation. The expression, "the bottom line" is now an accepted part of normal conversation, and deciding the "pluses minuses and profits" of a decision represents a customary way of thinking. During the Persian Gulf war, infant and civilian casualties were referred to as "collateral damage," but the epitome of this trend is best exemplified by WQXR, the New York City radio station of the New York Times, which began all war coverage with a statement about how "The Market" responded to battle "fluctuations."

In his work on postmodernism and the cultural logic of late capitalism, Fredric Jameson (1991) refers to the work of Gary Becker (1976), quoting the latter as saying,

Let me emphasize again that commodity output is not the same as national product is usually measured, but includes children, companionship, health and a variety of other commodities . . . this most scandalous of all market models is in reality a production model! In it consumption is explicitly described as the production of a commodity or a specific utility: in other words, a use value which can be anything from sexual gratification to a convenient place to take it out on your children if the outside world proves inclement. (p. 267)

How have human experiences and values become so distorted?

VALUES, REALITY ASSUMPTIONS AND VALUE EXPRESSIONS

> To hear is to forget, to see is to remember, to do is to understand.
> Confucius

In attempting to answer the above question we are confronted with a serious but often ignored enigma. Values represent a subsystem of the general system of consciousness that has also been designated attitudes, beliefs, opinions, preconceptions, axioms of certainty or a priori assumptions. In general systems theory, values may be considered suprabiological structures that regulate consciousness. By influencing perspective and modulating the focus of attention, values partially determine our construction of reality.[1] The enigma, which pertains to the origin of values, is illustrated by the following example:

In one of my graduate psychology classes with a very diverse ethnic student body, a discussion on values was started. On a scale from 1 to 100 students were asked to identify the values they most related to with numerical ratings. As with most surveys on values, priority items on the list were: love, respect, friendship, truth, justice, dignity and fairness. The confusion began when I assigned people with similar professed values to separate groups and asked them to discuss *how* they would express these values. In the abstract, there was almost unanimous agreement over what the foremost of human values should be; in the actual, there was little agreement over how best to express these values. If this experiment was enlarged to include living together, creating a community, having intimate relationships, building families and raising children, I am certain there would be even less agreement.

A great deal of confusion exits concerning values. Part of this confusion concerns the failure to differentiate between stated values and the expression of values. As a society, we seem to be searching for common values, a quest, which as Stephen Schiff (1990) points out, "makes societies simple minded and intolerant." This intolerance is partially caused by our persistence in (1) disavowing our schizoid condition, a denial that contributes to (2) unacknowledgement of critical changes in the Self, a situation that leads to (3) refusal to recognize the vast changes that a postmodern culture has wrought, all of which are correlated to (4) overreliance on simple, linear and reductionistic formulas for improvement, which contributes to (5) the cultural inability to engage in meaningful and productive dialogue, which is associated with (6) a ridiculous nostalgia for the "good old days," which in turn leads to a growing intolerance of what we are actually experiencing.

Values represent an arena where romantic, premodern notions of reality persistently clash with a postmodern, interactional world. Like my psychology class, although most people will claim to know what values are, they will be at a loss over how to act on them. This confusion is endemic within all strata of American culture. Meg Greenfield, a chief editor for *Newsweek*, in attempting to write about American values reflects this confusion. First she states that

Americans should be encouraged to reclaim their cultural roots. But there is also an important, binding, shared American identity now—political, philosophical and cultural. It is big enough to hold everyone, tough enough to take (and profit from)

our continuous complaints and efforts at improvement, and indispensable to the well being of every individual and group in this country. (1991 p. 68)

Sounds terrific, doesn't it? But what are these cultural roots we need to reclaim, and what is our all important and binding shared American identity? Here, Mrs. Greenfield, like most politicians, is a bit vague and evasive. Her next few lines contain reference to the numerous nostalgic mythologies that the culture still clings to: "marching bands, Desert Storm, cub scouts, the American Legion and patriotism." At this point, in that it seemed our binding identity was not going to be explained, I was feeling a bit disappointed. My disillusionment, however, was premature, for a few lines later the common values I share with my fellow Americans are identified: "Yes, patriotism. The culture is shared and familiar: *hot dogs, watermelons, ice cream, beer, flags and fireworks*" (my emphasis).

This passage exemplifies the simpleminded, reassuring images that are spoon-fed to an increasingly alienated population. As a common bond, a collective group requires more than nostalgic and marketable images; it requires collective and mutual behaviors and purposes. Our collective ethos has contributed to the disintegration of common values, enabling symbols and images to be confused with feelings and mutual ways of doing things. According to Lewis L. Lapham,

What we share is a unified field of emotion, but if we mistake the sources of our energy and courage (i.e., if we think our uniqueness as Americans rests with the adjectives instead of the noun) then we can be rounded up in categories and sold the slogan of the week for the fear of the month. Political campaigns deal in the commodity of votes, and from now until November I expect that all of them will divide the American promise into its lesser but more marketable properties. (1992, p. 45)

When it comes to values, an essential question should be how we can learn to live together and express our values in actions. The actual demonstration of values needs to be distinguished from the verbalization of values. This is a significant task, the exploration of which is well beyond the focus of the present text. Briefly, I can offer the following suggestions. In order to understand how values are constructed, the developmental origins of values must be explored. The precursors of values may be termed macrovalues or reality assumptions. Because they determine the customary nature of a response, reality assumptions can be conceived as general response regulators. Karen Horney (1973), although not designating them as such, identified what she called three basic personality types: those who move *toward*, those who move *away* and those who move *against* other people. In that these three personality types influence and determine the way one perceives reality, they can also be considered reality assumptions. The fact that the three are clearly embedded within a relational framework associates each with a certain response style. This variance of responsivity affects the manner in which values are expressed. Two people may claim to have similar values, but if their reality assumptions are different, the values will be expressed differently. This renders values as culturally constructed beliefs and hence artifacts of language and implies a relative futility concerning the study of values, at least as we currently understand and attempt to measure them. Self-disclosure is probably the least useful way to study and measure values. By asking people what they value, all one is going to secure are *verbalizations that reflect designated and accepted cultural values—the predominant socially constructed reality*. What needs to be explored is not what people say, but how people interact. This rule can be extended to larger groups like communities, organizations and nations. Ask almost anyone in the United States if they value life and the answer will probably be yes. How each individual *acts* on these values is partially determined by reality assumptions.

There are numerous ways in which reality assumptions may be classified. Three reality assumptions that I have described before are: fatalistic-tragic, idealistic-romantic and existential-ironic. The following clinical examples provide useful illustrations.

John is a 29-year-old male who was referred to therapy by an employee assistance counselor because of symptoms of depression. John is married, has five children and works two jobs to support his family. He is in financial debt and because of his inability to provide a down payment, currently rents a house. Needless to say, John has very little time to spend with his wife and children. He considers enjoyment or relaxation to be a waste of time. Beneath John's symptoms lie certain fatalistic-tragic reality assumptions. In a session John stated that "you know, my dad had to do the same thing, he worked his life away . . . hey what are you going to do . . . that's what a guy's gotta do . . . that's just the way things are."

Scott is a 26-year-old male patient whose underlying suppositions about life reflect an idealistic-romantic reality assumption. Scott is a postmodern renaissance man. He is a part-time musician, carpenter, graduate student, actor and investment counselor. Scott is a charming, intelligent individual who has been married twice and is currently having an affair with another woman, a circumstance that reluctantly, at his wife's request, brought him to therapy. The patient is not depressed, has very high self-esteem and does not feel he has a problem. Scott loves to be in love, in fact, "since love is what we came here for," he views his attitude as an asset. In a session Scott stated that "I know I am kind of an idealist, but, why shouldn't I be . . . after all, I'm talented and life is for having fun."

Finally, Melanie presents a good example of the existential-ironic dimension.

Melanie is a 32-year-old graduate student who has a very perceptive but extremely cynical view of life. She basically came for psychological treatment because: "I've tried everything else and now I want to give therapy a try." Melanie has experimented with drugs, sex, travel and money and still feels that life "is empty and useless." Although she is quite attractive she has never had a long-term intimate relationship. When we talked about relationships and being close the patient replied "what for . . . people always leave you in the end and if they stay, they either trick you or turn out to be jerks."

Reality assumptions are extremely difficult to modify and are rarely addressed in contemporary psychotherapy. This tripartite classification represents only one categorization of reality assumptions. More can be included, and because reality assumptions are neither independent nor mutually exclusive, a wide range of potential permutations exists. For example, the musician/counselor Brian, mentioned in chapter 4, maintains an especially difficult combination—the fatalistic-romantic perspective. My point in providing these clinical vignettes is to illustrate how interaction and *responsivity* to the world can be globally predetermined. Reality assumptions act like directional filters that can predispose a person to take a certain direction in life, for example, tragic or idealistic. In that they tend to frame a distinctive, existential ambiance, reality assumptions tend to "flavor" a person's life.

Before we leave this topic I would like to briefly discuss the origins of reality assumptions. Reality assumptions develop from early childhood interaction with the world. They originate from the child's early assumptions concerning his or her relational position in the environment. Thus, reality assumptions are based on the child's early experience of the world. This is essentially what humanistic philosophers and psychoanalysts have been saying for years. Another format for analyzing reality assumptions can be found within developmental psychology, such as the psychosocial stages of Erik Erikson (1963) or Margaret Mahler (1975).

Politically Correct Values

In that it attempts to modify the way people behave, political correctness can be construed as an attempt to establish a specific value system. The recent controversy over "politically correct" language has spread from its academic origins and now affects all levels of culture. Because of its overvaluation of *words and phrases*, the contemporary emphasis on politically correct language (and behavior) represents a unidimensional pseudosolution to a plethora of complex cultural and existential problems. It almost seems that emergent interactionism has taken the experience of language to a new level. The shallow, insipid and dogmatic nature of political correctness contributes not only to the recalcitrance of the market ethos but also to the decline and confusion over values and reality assumptions. Political correctness achieves this through its zealotry and insistence on language as the sole indicator of human expression. Confucius' remark that began the section on values illustrates my position: "to hear is to forget, to see is to remember, to do is to understand." Only in *doing* can the complete spectrum of human consciousness be activated and, hence, a true change of consciousness occur. Speaking and hearing the proper words is, at best, an incomplete and shortsighted approach.

My introduction to politically correct thought came during a graduate seminar where I used the words (in separate sentences) Black, handicapped, and Indian and when, in describing a patient, said (which I thought was very pertinent to the case) "she had a really nice body." After class I was informed by several students that my words implied that I was racist, a sexist and that I discriminated against people who are different. I was informed that the "correct words" were African-American, Differently Abled and Native American. As for women, I was assured that remarks in relation to their physical appearance were offensive, and that women had no need to listen to references concerning their bodies. I must point out that this was a small graduate seminar in which the students and I had a good relationship. The above, was, therefore, expressed in a kind of collegial, friendly, and almost helpful manner, as if they were saying "Dr. DeBerry, for your own good we think you should know this." Because I was aware of the quarrels over politically correct speech, I thanked the students and told them I would take their advice seriously. I was well aware of the serious ramifications that other university faculty members had experienced over saying the wrong thing.

The movement to advocate politically correct language originated within colleges in *just* response to culturally skewed curricula, biased historical interpretation and various discriminatory practices. However, the movement's solid overemphasis on the linguistic dimension of reality makes it typical of a postmodern, unidimensional attempt to influence. In the autumn of 1991, a Smith college student handout stated: "As groups of people begin the process of realizing that they are oppressed, and why, new words tend to be created to express the concepts that the existing language cannot" (Taylor, 1991, p. 37). As the author of the article pointed out, "making people watch what they say is the central preoccupation of politically correct students." The movement spread from language to include other external "indicators" of consciousness like appearance so that now we have environmental and ethnic correctness. Although I applaud the intent to make people accept and understand each other, I deplore the notion that language and appearance are the sole indicators of consciousness. Even more problematic is the aversion that advocates of political correctness have to dialogue. The following passage bears directly on my last sentence:

Of course, to make such a statement is invariably to provoke a charge of racism. But part of the problem with this reaction is that it trivializes the debate. In fact, it makes the debate impossible. But that is just as well, according to the new fundamentalists. Debate and the analytic thinking it requires is oppressive. It's logocentric. It favors the articulate at the expense of the inarticulate. It forces people to make distinctions, and since racism is the result of distinctions, they should be discouraged. (Taylor, 1991, p. 40)

The fact that the politically correct movement has emerged in the late eighties and nineties, a period in recent U.S. history when racism and discrimination are at a peak, illustrates the futility of the approach. Political correctness likewise exacerbates the decline in authentic dialogue concerning experience. Like a savvy acquaintance of mine recently told me "I may hate you but, these days I would never admit to it." In that it does not change the entire system but only what people say, political correctness is of only limited value.

The significance of "correct" language to political correctness has a strong parallel to legal proceedings. Political correctness and the law both make people wary of their language. So that clarity could be achieved and ambiguity avoided, the "language of the law" originally represented a succinct and precise method of phrasing. This legal explicitness has now expanded to the realm of common discourse and behavior. The culture's zealous scrutiny of language and behavior contributes to a general distortion of what was once considered accepted behavior. For example,

- A grade school teacher is disciplined for sexually inappropriate behavior because he lets a 6-year-old girl sit on his lap.
- A parent loses custody of her child because in a therapy session she mentions that she sometimes feels like killing him.
- A distressed young woman is involuntarily hospitalized because she tells her therapist that she sometimes feels like killing people.

As purpose, intent, meaning and innuendo are collapsed into a single stretch of literal meaning, we lose the ability to evaluate the full dimension of language. For fear of litigation, words are interpreted at their face value. The three people described in the above list eventually became my patients. The teacher was a caring and empathic individual who never even considered the possibility that he was doing something wrong. As for the women, both of them stated they had no intention of hurting anyone and were simply blowing off steam. As one woman said, "Haven't you ever been so angry Doc, that you feel like killing somebody . . . not that you would ever do it, but, you know, you just gotta say it?" The truth is, of course, that myself and many others have felt that way. In a politically correct world, however, this is a dangerous thing to admit to. Unfortunately, like many facets of postmodern existence, it is something best kept secret.

Sexual Politics

A dogmatism similar to political correctness has emerged concerning relationships between the sexes. Further impediment to relationships in a nation that is already sexually repressed, confused and deficient in understanding *sensuality, erotica and joy* is, indeed, a tragic disappointment. Once again, this new obstacle to open relationships stems from a metamorphosis in linguistic meaning. For example, if we examine the new concept of date rape, it is approximated that one out of four female students have experienced it. According to journalist Stephanie Gutmann (1991), this figure is grossly misleading because it reflects a change in the definition of cross-gender relationships: "the real story about campus date rape is not that there's been any significant increase of rape on college campuses, at least of the acquaintance type, *but that the word rape is being stretched to encompass any type of sexual interaction*" (my emphasis) (Taylor, 1991, p. 39). As a Swarthmore college manual states, rape is no longer restricted to actual intercourse but includes "acquaintance rape and spans a spectrum of incidents and behaviors ranging from crimes legally defined as rape to verbal harassment and inappropriate innuendo" (Taylor, 1991, p. 39).

The tendency to employ language both as an indicator of consciousness and a means of controlling behavior is increasing. My objection to this in no way detracts from the actual tragedy of real rape and sexual abuse, phenomena that occur at alarming rates in this country. Focusing exclusively on what a certain group defines as "the correct language and behavior" totally belies the duration and complexity of the problem. The United States, like most other nations, has a long history of cultural, racial and sexual prejudices. The schizoid condition and the interactional self of the postmodern age further complicate and divide not only relationships between the sexes but the relationship of everyone to everything else.

The essential point regarding the reduction of relationships and behavior to language is that such an approach ignores the effects of a multitude of interacting subsystems and structures. Consciousness does not need to be reduced to a unidimensional perspective but, to borrow an old phrase, needs to be *expanded* to include an understanding of how these different systems interact. Social problems are incredibly complicated and will not simply go away because a person says the right things, wears the right clothes and appears to act the right way. We can all act; in fact, acting is a postmodern calling card. One of the problems with postmodern actors is that they all want to be directors. We are generating a nation of 250 million actors, directors and writers, each insulated and immersed in their own scripts. Another script, even a politically correct script, is just another example of the single-minded reductionism and linear thinking I have been deriding throughout the text.

In 1867, Emerson said that "things are in the saddle and ride mankind."

Relying exclusively on language simply makes it another thing—another thing that controls us. There are, I believe, several ways out of this control dilemma. Some of them might seem pretty obvious but, as the Taoist aphorism states, "the way out is by the door . . . why is it that no one uses it." In Chapter 7, we explore the difficulty in finding the door.

SUMMARY

The present chapter explored how the increasing American proclivity toward developing a legalistic culture can combine with a market-dominated ethos to produce a monolithic society. In this milieu, appearance is valued over essence and *functioning* becomes the principal criteria by which life is measured. Within this system, a formalized linguistic structure becomes the dominant mode of interpersonal discourse. Explicit social contracts replace friendlier, less formal arrangements, while community shifts from an informal network of mutual obligations to prescribed and precise patterns of interaction. The schizoid condition intensifies and the full potential richness of consciousness is further restricted. A vicious cycle ensues and reality assumptions, the early precursors of interpersonal development, evolve in an increasingly malignant fashion.

Although my observations are derived from my direct relationship with the culture of the United States, the increasing trend toward globalization of the economy makes them applicable to other localities as well. The collapse of the majority of communist societies creates the opportunity for vast economic and political changes and makes people especially vulnerable to the propagation of the unwholesome ethos that can insidiously envelope an entire people. Global economic changes are inevitably transformed into simple, daily decisions of living. The quality of life, in essence the very definition of being human, is affected by an incredible acceleration of events. In a potentially global society, it is necessary that these events be understood in their totality.

NOTE

1. See the chapter on values in DeBerry (1991).

Seven

The Ecology of Being

Only connect.

E. M. Forster

Recent years have witnessed a burgeoning interest concerning the physical environment. People are becoming increasingly aware of the interdependence and interconnectedness of the material world. Yet, interestingly and paradoxically, except in a cursory manner, the enthusiasm of this preoccupation has not generalized to the world of human relationships. Environmental ecology clearly supercedes what might be called *humanistic ecology*. This is, perhaps, partially because of an almost universal preference to discuss and explore the external world. The inner dimensions of consciousness seem trite and esoteric, worthy of little more than a stint of psychotherapy, a flirtation with religion and philosophy or a few weekend "relationship" workshops.

Nothing could be further from the truth. Inevitably, the internal world transposes to the relationship nexus, which translates into simple everyday affairs and common exchanges—in short, the gist of existence. As a social species it behooves us to learn all we can concerning the nature of our interactions. There are, therefore, important reasons to consider the ecology of being human. An ecological approach to human identity extends significantly beyond the internal world to include the external factors that contribute to the construction of inner consciousness. Because it assumes a "package" approach to human experience, humanistic ecology is in accord with a quantum psychological model that attempts to

• Make statements of probability and potential
• Understand the interaction and correlation between different system levels

- Synthesize intrapersonal and interpersonal elements that seem complementary—i.e., mutually exclusive
- Account for the influence of consciousness
- Accept the possibility of distant (non-local) and synergistic (non-linear) influences

Because we are a social species, humanistic ecology describes the interconnectiveness of the self, in relation to itself, other selves and *community*. Like its environmental sister, humanistic ecology seeks to describe the conditions optimal for the development of the Self as part of mutually interactive suprasystem. The concept is a systems approach that has strong ties with field and gestalt theories of interaction. Humanistic ecology perceives existence as a product of relationships; the milieu or environment in which these relationships form represents the interpersonal matrix from which identity and consciousness develop. As has been repeatedly stressed, this matrix is determined by culturally induced reality assumptions. Quantum psychology incorporates humanistic ecology as a way of studying the expression and interaction of the intrapersonal and interpersonal system levels and, hence, disparate reality assumptions or "world views." The idea of an ecological approach to "being" is certainly not new and emanates again as a healthy reaction to the isolating tendencies of schizoid development.[1] As such, human ecology is a precursor of the more formal quantum diagnostic approach that is explored in chapter 8.

THE CONDITIONS OF ALIVENESS

Aliveness is a necessary condition of human ecology. Although all organic life is alive, aliveness manifests itself on many different system levels and, for humans, an extensive range from the biological to the transpersonal exists. Each point on this range represents a different system level (cellular, organelle, or Self). Because a quantum psychological approach is concerned with the ecological conditions that best allow the Self-system to develop, we are involved with an *interpersonal ecology*. The Self-system level is extremely paradoxical as it can produce intense self-absorption (narcissism) or passionate communal concern. Both are possible, and if the Self is to continue to evolve, each is necessary. Part of the postmodern dilemma, a predicament that is an historical culmination of a problem that in all likelihood has existed since language gained dominance, is that as a species, we are increasingly evolving in a distorted manner—one of intense self-absorption. In evolutionary terms, psychological imbalances, like environmental deformities, culminate in extinction. Unless a balance ensues, humanity, as we currently know it, may cease to exist. This chapter endeavors to introduce concepts that could help achieve a more balanced ecology of the Self.

E. M. Forster's admonishment to connect enumerates the essence of aliveness. Aliveness is a process, a responsiveness—a dynamic and evolving association, not of things, but of responses and reactions. In this sense, the universe may be conceived as a vast multilayered, interactive field system. Everything in some way affects everything else and the proverbial question shifts from the absolute inquiry of *who am I?* to the relativistic notion of *who am I now or, what is my response?* Who we are is discovered in our response. Because of the inherent danger of assuming a position of *moral relativism*, the idea of relativistic responsivity is a difficult concept to develop. As the text proceeds, however, the reader will see that response relativism does not necessarily imply moral relativism. From the perspective of quantum psychology, *Responsivity* represents the ultimate condition of aliveness.

If an organism is truly responding to its environment, the probability of full development greatly increases. The course and outcome of development cannot be predicted, but an approximation of potential direction can be deduced. This is to say that from the general conditions of an organism's life, the quality of the present and future can be partially determined. This applies to any level of system organization from simple organisms to complex societies. Conditions that allow responsivity to flourish can be the yardstick by which a system's total health and aliveness can be measured. Thus, there is a direct relationship between the aliveness of a system and the system's degree of responsivity. An ecological approach should identify the system conditions (interpersonal, intrapersonal and impersonal) that best promote responsivity. I have identified two of these conditions as experience and dialogue.

Experience

Responsivity is directly related to experience. The term experience is not employed in its contemporary fashion where it has come to be equated with training, knowledge, or the acquisition and accumulation of specific skills. Rather, my usage of "experience" concerns the feelings, observations and general sense of living and being that our sensory apparatus has given us. To experience life is to feel life in all ways possible.

Dialogue

Because words dominate consciousness, language represents a significant factor in terms of responsivity. In addition to widening access to the other domains of Self and consciousness, ordinary communication itself can be improved. Dialogue represents a way of thinking and talking that promotes responsivity and, thus, intimacy, understanding and constructive evolution. The concept of dialogue implies a complete connection of selves in expansive linguistic discourse.

The argument I have been developing over the preceding six chapters is that human responsivity is impaired. The interactional self of the evolving postmodern era represents a situational fact; that is, the interactive, modular self is the evolutionary reaction to rapidly changing technological and cultural conditions. Adaptation is not a negative phenomenon. What is negative is the character or essence, perchance, what one might call the temperament or personality of the postmodern self. This personality has exhaustively been described as schizoid, false, fragmented, manipulative, narcissistic, inauthentic and alienated. The present chapter suggests that it is possible to develop an alternative model of self-interaction.

EMOTIONS AND THE INTEGRATION OF EXPERIENCE

> Modern man may be ashamed of emotion, but he is all affect and temperament.
>
> Isaac Bashevis Singer

An alternative model of interaction must involve all levels of consciousness. The model of the Self that has been discussed throughout the text describes a Self-system that represents itself through thought (cognition), affect (emotion), sensation, imagery and behavior. These subsystems (as described in chapter 3) are split off from one another, causing the Self to exist in a schizoid or unintegrated state (described as the self). The predominant cultural self-systems (what people tend to think of as the Self) are characterized by reflexive posturings that depend primarily on media images and language; the unidimensional utilization of language being the fundamental vehicle for self-preservation. The preceding chapters have provided numerous concrete examples to clarify the conceptual obscurity of the preceding lines. One of the reasons this murky abstractness exists concerns a central dilemma of the topic itself—the fact that I am using words to describe a problematic situation that is, in part, caused by words. It is necessary to move beyond words to a more holistic mode of embracing experience. But, as must be apparent, not only is it impossible to totally escape language, it is also not desirable to do so. Rather, we must abandon our preoccupation with narcissistic monologue and move on to authentic and cooperative dialogue. Because thought is expressed via language, the nature of cognitions must likewise shift to a dialogical position. As for the remaining subsystems of consciousness, responsivity can be improved by integration into consciousness via experiential sensory encounters. The processes of dialogue and sensory experience are explored more as the chapter proceeds.

Animation

What I am basically referring to is the construction of a new way of being that can restrain and alter the course of schizoid development. The construction of an alternative model involves, therefore, the reintegration of a new way of being that, in reality, is a modification of an old way of being. The "old ways" have to do with the quality of animation, a feature that, in terms of relating, presumes a certain vibrancy and fullness. These traits represent the embodiment of responsivity and demonstrate that all subsystems of consciousness are integrated and available. Animation is a necessary prerequisite for aliveness, and experience a necessary condition for animation. The lack of animation in daily life drastically alters our perception and interaction with the world. The German poet Rainer Marie Rilke was well aware of this, in 1925, stating in a letter to a friend that "animated things, things experienced by us, and that know us, are on the decline and cannot be replaced anymore. We are perhaps the last still to have known such things" (1975, p. 141).

The human species has several key subsystems for grasping reality; all except the linguistically dominated cognitive system are in a state of atrophy. We do not experience reality with the full sensory potential available to us. Schizoid development precludes such possibility. Even the ascendance of language has not been a uniformly positive evolution; in effect, it has been a one-sided affair. Although part of the difficulty is what has been referred to as "the big head problem"—we tend to think and talk too much—this does not necessarily represent the entire problem. Another part of the "big head" issue is the manner in which humans think and, especially, converse. Thought and language tend to be excessively linear, reductionistic and logical; employed increasingly to obfuscate and conceal and, thus, to augment the schizoid condition. The perversion of thought and language tends to reinforce the suppression of alternate modes of processing reality and, in terms of ordinary discourse, tends to restrain dialogue, authentic interaction and emotion. These three qualities are essential elements of responsivity and are discussed in detail throughout this chapter.

Dialogue and authentic interaction have been discussed extensively by spiritual philosophers such as Thomas Merton and Martin Buber. For example, in reference to dialogue, Thomas Merton states that

To live in communion, in genuine dialogue with others is absolutely necessary if man is to remain human. But to live in the midst of others, sharing nothing but the common noise and general distraction, isolates a man in the worst way, separates him from reality in a way that is almost painless. It divides him off and separates him from other men and his true self. (1972, p. 63)

Martin Buber (1970) echoes Thomas Merton's sentiments concerning the necessity of authentic dialogue, calling it I-Thou communication. Although Martin Buber's ideas are couched in predominantly religious overtones, they, nevertheless, are extremely applicable to ordinary intercourse. Dialogue and the I-Thou encounter are important cornerstones of a quantum psychological approach and will be discussed in greater depth. For the present, I wish to focus on the subsystem of emotion. The principal catalyst for the renewal of responsivity comes from the emotional system. It is through the reintegration of emotion into ordinary consciousness that conversation can become discourse and monologue develop into dialogue.

Are people, as Isaac Bashevis Singer says, afraid of emotion? The author has not been the only writer to express such sentiment. Innumerable others have voiced similar views, the essential message being that (1) emotions are split off from ordinary consciousness and (2) as a schizoid subsystem, emotions are becoming increasingly powerful in a destructive way, which leads to the contention that (3) emotions need to be controlled. This line of thinking totally misses the point that emotions need to be experienced and not controlled, that is, *one must learn how to experience them*. What people appear to be afraid of is the sheer animal potency of emotions. We have relied far too heavily on the abstract world of language and logic and emotions seem like unfamiliar territory. As Rollo May states,

We remain spiritually isolated and at sea, and so we cover up our loneliness by chattering with other people about the things we do have language for—the world series, business affairs, and the latest news reports. Our deeper emotional experiences are pushed further away, and we tend, thus, to become emptier and lonelier.... The capacity for consciousness of ourselves gives us the ability to see ourselves as others see us and to have empathy with others.... In the achieving of consciousness of one's self, most people must start back at the beginning and rediscover their feelings.... Their connection with their feelings is as remote as if over a long distance telephone. (1953, pp. 68, 86, 105)

Emotions and thoughts are complementary, that is, they are at times mutually exclusive modes of being. They are, however, valid modes of sensory processing and, even more crucial, is that their complementariness means that *each requires the other*. Emotions and cognitions, like particles and waves, are the yin and yang of human existence; one without the other is only half the circle. Emotions, more than cognitions, are rooted in the immediacy of experience. *Emotions are now*. This, I believe, in a period of growing alienation and detachment, is what frightens people—the pure visceral, animal-like immediacy of emotional experience. Often, especially if they have been repressed or split off for long periods, emotions can be extremely disruptive to the socially constructed interactional self. Emotions demand a response, they literally force one to face the naked reality of their existence. They demand clarification. Emotions, like ideas, cannot be danced around or sequestered in abstract ivory towers of isolation but, must be confronted. As a patient once wrote, "Why do I do this? Why do I keep returning to Dr. DeBerry. All he does is make me feel. I hate feeling. It scares me. I want to disappear, to be invisible, to evaporate. I hate this.... I know I need it but it's so hard."

Discussing the work of the philosopher Pascal, Gregory Bateson makes a similar point, stating that "to Pascal, a Frenchman, the matter was rather different, and he no doubt thought of the reasons of the heart as a body of logic or computation as precise or complex as the reasons of consciousness" (1972, pp. 138–139).

For a person who has existed in a schizoid state, there is no doubt that emotions are difficult to deal with. Early experiences, the building blocks of reality assumptions, predispose development in certain directions. For the sake of example, let us consider a simple dichotomy— schizoid versus non-schizoid.

The schizoid state is one in which emotions are not directly and holistically experienced. By holistic, I refer to the fact that emotions must be experienced not in isolation but as part of the total system of consciousness. In order to be processed and understood as anything but the flow of adrenaline, rage or lust, affective phenomena require other subsystems of consciousness, that is, they need a healthy internal and external context. Without such positive context emotional arousal can be experienced as destructive. The following clinical vignette provides an apt example.

Lynne is a 25-year-old actress who came into therapy because of depression and marital difficulties. She complained that her husband of 2 years was too needy and sexually demanding. When we discussed the topics of sex and intimacy, Lynne would become visibly depressed and often cry. In the course of therapy, it became evident that whenever the patient was involved with sexual contact that was not initiated of her own volition, she would become tearful, depressed and angry.

As an actor, Lynne was able to successfully act out sexual scenes. On those occasions, or when she was acting as the seductress, Lynne was able to go through the motions of having sexual intimacy. At those times she reported feeling in control of her feelings and not being depressed. Lynne's self-system was extremely fragmented. Negative affect, like depression and anger, were split off from ordinary consciousness—she was not *aware* of these subsystems. Because her emotional system was unintegrated, when sexual contact was unrehearsed or Lynne was spontaneously aroused, the experience became disruptive and terrifying. Emotional arousal was equated with increased fragmentation of an already fragmented self. Sex was like a quantum buttom eliciting all sorts of quantum effects, such as the return of childhood rage and depression. For Lynne, the experience of sexually induced emotional arousal was an unintegrated experience.

Both the internal and external context of Lynne's affective experience was negative. A healthy or positive context is part of an integrated Self system, the existence of which depends on (1) affirmative early experiences (what the British pediatrician/psychoanalyst D. W. Winnicott referred to as "good enough mothering") and (2) subsequent culturally *validating* Self experiences. Because literature concerning the contemporary lack of healthy parenting is enormous, I wish to concentrate instead on the culturally constructed conditions that promote not only inadequate parenting but also the ensuing schizoid development of the person. Prior to directly discussing interpersonal ecology and culture there is an appropriate "parenting" anecdote I would like to tell. The story reflects a central point of the text, that we are unaware of the ordinary conditions or ethos of our daily lives.

One Saturday afternoon I was in the local supermarket with Julian. Like other toddlers, he was in the child seat of a shopping cart that I was wheeling about and, like other toddlers, when we reached the cookie aisle he demanded a cookie. As Julian munched his cookie another child, a girl, slightly older and very verbal, was wheeled up next to us. The girl, seeing Julian eating his cookie, turned to her parents and said that she was hungry and wanted a cookie. As we migrated down the cookie aisle I overheard the following conversation:

Child: Mommy, I'm hungry.

Mommy: No you're not.

Child: Mommy, I'm hungry.

Mommy: No you're not.

Child: Mommy I feel hungry in my tummy and want a cookie.

Mommy: (silent and ignores child . . . Daddy approaches).

Child: Daddy, I feel hungry in my tummy and want a cookie.

Daddy: (to Mommy) She say's she's hungry.

Mommy: (to Daddy) She's not hungry.

Daddy: (to child) You're not hungry.

Child: I feel hungry, Daddy.

Daddy : You're not hungry . . . you always want everything. Now let's go. (The family disappears into the frozen food section with a somewhat sad child in tow. Julian and I look at one another. He smiles and eats his cookies.) The End.

I was extremely curious concerning what the little girl might have been feeling or, perhaps   feeling about her feelings. What would happen the next time she felt hungry? Would she again be told that she was not feeling that way? If I am feeling, for example, emotion A and I am told that I am not feeling A, then what am I supposed to think? I might, conceivably, feel or think that I am going crazy, a distressing process sometimes called *invalidation*. At best, I would certainly doubt the authenticity of my feelings. If I were a child and depended on the external adult world for guidance, this process would probably increase my dependence on external as opposed to internal validation. That is, I would question myself and look to others for confirmation of what I am feeling. I would become highly tuned with the other, not in a positively empathic manner but rather in an indecisive and overly dependent manner. I would, in essence, lose an essential part of myself.

I also wonder how often this rather mundane scene is repeated in supermarkets and living rooms across America. Fairly often, I suspect (this is the second parent/child supermarket example I have used). What the young girl experienced could not be considered a personally affirmative experience. Self-doubt and skepticism concerning the validity of one's emotional experiences are the long-term result of repeated exposure to such interactions. A well-entrenched myth exists that disturbed adult behavior is often the result of single traumatic episodes. My sentiment is more in accord with people like Alice Miller (1984) who believes that the unnoticed, chronic, everyday experiences of childhood are what leave an indelible mark on us.

Cultural Invalidation and the Postmodern Feudal Lord

The everyday experiences of childhood are constructed by culture and community as much as they are by particular styles of parenting. By accepting the idea of a socially constructed reality, one also acknowledges that our culture inhibits and distorts the emotional processing of reality. Essentially, it allows conditions that foster the emotionally invalidating exchange described above to thrive. The cultural conditions that contribute to our construction of reality are the same conditions that reinforce our sense of alienation and estrangement.

In chapter 6, it was pointed out that contemporary U.S. culture transforms everything into a marketable commodity. As Erik Fromm has emphasized, this process transforms the ethos of the culture, community and individual from a mode of *being to one of having*. The entire concept of *Being* is a difficult one for most people to understand. This is because Being, in an existential sense, is an experience that demands no specific form of action—one does not have to do to be. In a culture consistently emphasizing *doing* that usually takes the form of *having*, the experience of *being* has little value. In fact, when they can no longer continue to *do and have*, most people report feeling lost and empty. As an experience, being includes all the dimensions of human consciousness that have been referred to throughout the text. What our cultural ethos does is restrict the types of experiences that cultivate the belief that it is not necessary to have in order to be. What the market system breeds is a collection of separate and isolated, optimally consuming individuals. In a sense, therefore, schizoid conditions are beneficial to the postmodern market.

In *The Externalization of Consciousness* (DeBerry, 1991), I introduced the concept of the postmodern feudal lord. I have since come to realize that this analogy is more valid and more common than I originally thought. What the cultural system encourages is that each individual maximize his own property, capital and acquisitions. This ethos, in combination with

the increasing crime rate, inflationary and recessionary cycles and an expanding "underclass," results in a "social paranoia" that encourages people
to isolate and protect themselves, and the contemporary home becomes a
postmodern fortress. This individualization of community is a pr   uct of
the dominant capitalistic ethos and represents one of its negative side effects.
In reference to this process Gary Becker states that

The household production function framework emphasizes the parallel services
performed by firms and households as organizational units. Similar to the typical
firm analyzed in standard production theory, the household invests in capital assets
(savings), capital equipment (durable goods), and capital embodied in its "labor
force" (human capital of family members). As an organizational entity, the household, like the firm, engages in production using this labor and capital. Each is
viewed as maximizing its objective function subject to resource and technological
constraints. (1976, p. 267)

My purpose in quoting Gary Becker is to emphasize how the capitalistic
market ethos contributes to the loss of communal involvement and the
ascendance of the isolated, individual or fragmented postmodern family.
Within almost every community in the United States, there are hundreds
of individual households each doing the same thing and repeating identical
functions that formerly were done communally. In the area in which I live,
like any other "ordinary" community in America, each household is self-
sufficient. Each has, to name but a few, its own cooking, laundry, refrig-
eration, cleaning, carpentry and recreational areas. We accept this as ordinary not realizing that life was not always this way.

The mass production and commoditization of almost everything, has
made available to the middle class acquisitions that previously were available
only to the aristocracy. Art, one of the classical symbols of wealth is now
a mass-produced commercial product easily available to the middle class.
Homes, automobiles and in essence, entire "life-styles" based on classical
concepts of wealth are now packaged and available. Because these life-style
packages encourage individual isolation and acquisition, they invite each
household to be an independent and self-sufficient unit with a feudal value
base, similar to the medieval feudal town. This self-sufficiency is reflected
by wealthy home owners, who, armed to the teeth and stockpiled with
food, cheap foreign labor and capital, can retreat into the sanctuary of
backyard pools and tennis courts and bother with no one. This insidious
trend is so prevalent that the United States is now at a juncture where the
wealthy can, in fact, withdraw from public involvement. In reference to
this tendency, the conservative Charles Murray (1986) as well as the liberal
Harvard economist Robert Reich (1987, 1991) claim that "over the next
decade, the rich will grow in number and wealth . . . producing something
very like a cast society with the implications of utter social separation"
(Henwood, 1992, p. 15).

These conditions do not encourage community or communal involvement in any way. The loss of the communal ethos is reflected in the type of interactions that a culture encourages. When one considers the experiences that our culture inhibits, this becomes even more obvious. For North American culture I have selected five neglected realms of experience: sensual, irrational, peak, communal and joyful.

The Sensual

The inhabitants of the United States are not a sensual people. Most North Americans confuse sensuality with sexuality, not realizing that the latter is but a single dimension of a much larger sphere of experience. The term *sensuality* is derived from the latin word *sensus* and concerns itself with *pleasure* related to the total sensorium—the full range of somatic perception. A sensual orientation is one that embraces the complete aesthetic appreciation and visceral enjoyment of living through all the senses (olfactory, auditory, gustatory, tactile, visual, emotional and cognitive). The last time that the first six of these sensorial qualities are used in unison is infancy; as one "matures" the culture tends to encourage the abstract realm of cognitive processing and to an extent, the most abstract of all visceral senses, vision, over all others.[2]

In the United States sensuality is associated with lavishness and lewdness and is deemed a quality to be avoided, repressed or diligently overcome. To an extent, psychology, psychiatry and, in particular, psychoanalysis have contributed to distortions concerning sensuality. This may seem puzzling as one of the goals of the above disciplines is considered to be the expression of healthy sensual and sexual behavior. Although to an extent this remains true, the basic thrust of the clinical sciences has predominantly been to set limits, and to contain sensual behavior. It is as if the clinical sciences are so worried about excess sensuality that they attempt to restrict whatever potential for sensuality might be present. Describing the debauched "cults" of the late 1960s Ernest Becker says,

In our time we would have no trouble recognizing these forms of defiant self-creation. We can see the efforts so clearly on both personal and social levels. We are witness to the new cult of sensuality that seems to be repeating the sexual naturalism of the ancient Roman world. (1973, p. 84)

Becker is a brilliant and prolific thinker who does go on to say, "I am not saying that this is bad, this rediscovery and reassertion of one's basic vitality as an animal" (p. 84). Unfortunately, because our culture manifests an entrenched centripetal antagonism toward sexual expression, statements like Ernest Becker's are often erroneously employed as a justification of the continued repression of sensuality. In *Eros and Civilization*, Herbert Marcuse

(1955) repeatedly stressed the repressive effect that modern culture has on sensuality, stating that "the salvation of culture would involve abolition of the repressive controls that civilization has imposed on sensuousness" (p. 174).

The fact that Becker was discussing the excessive worship of sensuality and not sensuality per se, does little to affect this distortion. In fact, the mental health profession remains terribly confused about sensuality, still misconstruing it for its lesser cousin, sex. A recent review of the psychological literature reveals a plethora of articles on sexual behavior but none on sensual behavior. A more recent example comes from an advertisement for a conference entitled *Erotic Mysteries: Intimacy, Sexuality and Gender in the 1990s*, presented by the Department of Psychiatry of the University of California at San Diego. The add reads, "Featured topics include: survivors of sexual molestation, obsessive love, power relations between women and men, male intimacy, male couples facing AIDS, and erotic transference in individual and couples therapy."

By no means am I inferring that these topics are unimportant, rather, I am suggesting that our approach to the erotic is becoming a bit one-sided. This distortion applies not only to sex but to all bodily functions. Through an extensive army of deodorants, American culture has become an antiseptic domain where basic somatic functions are vigorously disguised and body odors homogenized into artificial, perfume-like essences. Most homes and work places are sanitized into deodorized and disinfected landscapes, whereas the satisfying and stimulating smell of much of our cuisine is reduced to uniform and tasteless blandness. The cultural aversion to noticeable odors likewise, to a lesser extent, extends to unfamiliar tastes. Habituation of the familiar is characteristic of all cultures and is certainly not limited to American society. Because taste preferences are a highly personalized, culturally and ethnically rooted phenomenon, little beyond my personal predilections can be expressed. In terms of taste, I therefore leave the reader to his own thoughts and observations. I can, however, comment more generally concerning my observations related to the tactile modality.

People in the United States assiduously avoid excessive, non-sanctioned or informal touching. The typical cultural greeting is a firm handshake characterized by ample body space between the participants. Uninvited touching in public, when it does occur, is almost always frowned on and is guaranteed to induce a litany of apologies and excuse mes. Hugging, kissing and embracing on meeting is discouraged and, lately, often perceived as sexual harassment or inappropriate and immature behavior. Visitors to other cultures, particularly the Latin, French, Italian, Southern European, Middle Eastern and African countries often marvel at the intense physical closeness commonly expressed between people. In many cultures, hand holding between males is the standard, a social behavior that in the United

States, with the exception of predominantly gay enclaves, represents a behavior that is aggressively ridiculed and discouraged.

When it comes to the pleasures of the ear we are an equally undiscriminating people. In terms of sound, the problem is not that we discourage it but rather that most people tolerate an incredible cacophony of noises. The increasing frequency, intensity and invasiveness of modern noise is becoming a significant problem and in high density urban areas is becoming a major environmental issue. Noise pollution is a global problem especially endemic to highly industrial or developing industrial countries. In wealthy industrial nations, people are more able to either retreat into the sanctuary of their own homes or move to the quiet of suburban areas. Like the countless urban commuters hooked up to their headphones, the ability to avoid the problem in no way contributes to its amelioration.

Sounds, especially rhythmic or musical sound are commonly used by several subcultures in ritualistic or ceremonial ways. Within certain sects of Buddhism and Hinduism the ritualistic remains very connected to the fabric of everyday life. Sound is often employed as an aid to help people connect to a more tranquil level of relating or is used for meditational purposes. My experience in the United States is that music and sound is more often used to narcotize then to expand awareness.

The types of sounds that are tolerated in public areas contributes to another problem. Places of public contemplation or communal discourse are virtually nonexistent. On a city street, dialogue or even friendly chatter between strangers is becoming extinct. Commenting on the loss of even banal public conversation, Lorne Foster claims that

Sadly, the art of small talk now seems to be in a precarious state—not easy to achieve and strenuous to maintain. We now often interpret small talk as a personal invasion rather than as a soothing connection. And as our skill in the art of small talk diminishes, we can expect the quality of community life to do the same. (1991, p. 123)

Even in private space, people have become immune to discourse, mesmerized by the incessant drone of television, radio or music. Both contemplative silence and the exchange of meaningful sounds (as opposed to words) is becoming a vanishing experience.

Vision is another sensorial mode where deficiencies are remarkable. The utilization of public space along with the production of mass-produced and uniform commodities reflects a culture with little concern for the aesthetic qualities of the environment. Much has been written concerning the commercial desecration of areas of natural beauty or pristine wilderness. Our obliviousness to the finer subtleties of our visual world extends beyond the natural environment and encroaches on most urban areas. With few exceptions, notably, major civic projects or the homes and enterprises of the wealthy, little thought is given to what public areas will look like. The sordid ambience of public housing along with the commercial development of many urban coastlines is a prime example of this tendency.

Yet, when it comes to personal appearance, the culture places inordinate emphasis on what one looks like. Personal image has become a major multibillion dollar industry that extends from textiles and mannerisms to plastic surgery and style. The tendency toward overreliance on visual modalities is a key feature of postmodern life and a process that separates the visual sense from all others. Although we repress odors, ignore sounds, avoid touch and are blasé toward taste, contemporary civilization is positively entranced with the way things look. The utilization of cosmetic surgery has expanded exponentially and for certain professions, such as modeling and acting, is now considered a necessity. The ascendance of visual electronic technology in combination with a cultural celebrity obsession has caused specific "looks" to be adopted by millions—for example, the Madonna, Cool Rap, Heavy Metal, Artistic or Ethnic "look." The tendency toward excessive dependence on the visual scale has contributed to sexual interaction being primarily a matter of visual attraction. Popular polls consistently indicate that men and women prefer mates who have a certain "image." The predominance of visual incitement in the sexual arena has significantly altered not only the way people relate but how they choose partners as well.

SEXUALITY AND THE EROTIC

> There's no such thing as safe sex.
> Barbara Bush (*Newsweek*, January 13, 1991, p. 17)

Because sexuality is such an important facet of sensuality, especially as it relates to the visual modality, it deserves a bit more attention. Sex is a topic that has received ample attention from both the academic and popular press. The recent acquired immune deficiency syndrome (AIDS) crisis has spawned a safe sex campaign previously unheard of in the United States and, for once, people are openly discussing sex. As the need for condoms and "safe sex" becomes an accepted medical and health issue, sexuality can be publicly discussed in respectable clinical terminology. Unfortunately, the thrust of the debate always becomes a one-sided attempt to control, restrict or eliminate sexual behavior. Total abstinence is considered by many to be the only sensible response to the AIDS virus. Magic Johnson, the famous American basketball star who admitted to having the virus, was admonished by numerous groups and politicians for not using his illness as a justification for celibacy.

What always remains noticeably missing from any discussion concerning sex is the role of pleasure. Although people have sex for all sorts of reasons, a principal motivating factor is that it feels good. The fact that sexual intimacy does not feel good for everyone (as in the earlier case study of Lynne) means that many people engage in sex for reasons other than pleasure. Sexual contact is often a compulsion or is initiated for reasons of power, procreation or control. The fact that many people do not experience pleasure in no way negates the fact that pleasure and intimacy are associated with sex.

Under certain conditions sexual encounters can make people feel incredibly close, enabling them to transcend the bonds of customary intimacy. Sexual fusion can unite couples in a way that few physical interactions can. Within the proper context, sexual stimulation acts like a quantum button inducing unpredictable and transcendent experiences. Such experiences have typically been described as feelings of Self-dissipation into a greater whole, a melting or merging into a cosmic oneness, both with one's partner and the universe. Rapture, joy, ecstasy, exhilaration and bliss are adjectives commonly used to describe such an event. Sexual merger of the Self can result in a tremendous interactive effect between different system levels (physical, spiritual, personal, historical, developmental and so forth). There is a special delight in allowing passionate physical sensations to overcome the protective barriers of daily existence. Because the Self willingly abandons control to the Other, sexual union can be not only a release but a joyful encounter, a submission to another realm of primordial, oceanic bliss. Sex can be as complete an act of *physical responsivity* as we are capable of.[3]

But this type of sex is becoming rarer. Too often sex is indulged in mechanically and for the wrong reasons. Ecstatic sexual occurrences are highly dependent on a proper context and must be considered a fortuitous by-product of sexual union rather than an end goal in themselves. Simply put, one cannot achieve mystical transcendence by indulging in sex. A preoccupation with sex as a means to an end is what Ernest Becker referred to as the cult of sex. The optimal proper context would be two whole and integrated Selves willingly choosing to love one another.

Even so, sexual union can be a powerful transformer of reality. The intense passion generated by physical stimulation can dissolve both internal and external psychological barriers, a phenomenon that makes it an anathema to the schizoid personality. In that it induces a fragmentation of an already fragmented self-structure, sexual stimulation tends to release into consciousness parts of the self—memories, feelings, thoughts, images or sensations—that were formally split off and unavailable to consciousness. Because a schizoid structure indicates the presence of an unintegrated Self-system (unconnected multiple selves) the loss of the Self that passionate union with the Other induces is experienced as terrifying. One is, in essence, losing what one never had. The schizoid self does its best, therefore, to avoid such experiences. In order to maintain its familiar schizoid organization, the self system must continue to control itself. If the cultural ethos also emphasizes control and restraint, a synergistic effect ensues in which the self and the culture mutually reinforce each other's terror over affect, in this case, sexual passion.

This augmentive effect between the macro and micro schizoid levels contributes to the general contemporary disapproval and dissatisfaction over sexual intimacy. This interactive effect is *one* of the reasons initial sexual passion wanes so rapidly during extended periods of intimacy such as marriage. Because frankness regarding sexual enjoyment is discouraged, most people do not usually discuss their sexual disillusionment. What is discussed, quite openly on most television talk shows, are stories of sexual abuse, harassment or anything that can discredit what should be a natural physical act. But, part of the problem is that sex for the postmodern self is no longer a natural act. Like the alienated and schizoid pastiche personality that depends on image and appearance, sex too has assumed a primarily visual and abstract nature.

Pornography, a sexual perversion highly dependent on visual stimulation has, despite demands to restrict it, expanded into a legitimate international affair. The new multibillion dollar industry of the 1990s is the phone sex business and the virtual reality of computer sex is not far behind. Sex is becoming increasingly associated with media presentations and thus, as in the accepted and popular display of revealing lingerie, is becoming a primarily visual commodity. As a visual entity, sex becomes a product not associated with love as much as with possession. The "sexual object" becomes something or someone to be possessed and, in a sense, is related to owning the other, holding the power of the other, or having power over the other.

A pornographic approach does not measure sex in terms of love or intimacy but in terms of utilization and efficiency, both of which are directly related to money. The value of pleasure does not even enter the equation. Furthermore, the commercialization of human experience, as in pornography, transforms the practice from an act of pleasure to an act of profit. A culturally conditioned, cosmetically uniform appearance that relies almost totally on vision—what a man or a woman looks like—becomes the desired and coveted norm. Postmodern sexual impulses have become deeply entwined with issues of power and control. The easiest way to have ample sexual opportunities is to become a celebrity, especially a rock star or sports hero. People sleep with such luminaries because in a primitive and almost magical way, they expect to be enhanced by the act. If not to become like the person, then to at least say, "I slept with them," has become a postmodern act of survival, an attempt to fill personal emptiness with the magic elixir of fame. The symbiotic bliss possible from sexual encounters makes the feelings and the act a powerful and addictive drug. People believe it and, like the proverbial Holy Grail, seek elusively after it. Thus, sex becomes transformed from an act of pleasure to an acquisition performance.

What is lost in this transformation is, of course, the truly human sensual, loving and erotic components of a sexual relationship. The fact that the term erotic stems from the word *Eros*, the Greek God of love, is an association that is fast becoming forgotten. The romantic notion of sexual union being the merging of souls is being replaced by anatomically perfect, scantily clad, cosmetically correct bodies having technically precise (and safe) intercourse. The quantum, transcendent possibilities of a sexual encounter are dependent on the full expression and sharing of all aspects of sensuality and consciousness. Smell, taste, touch, sound—the physical—in combination with the ethereal—all of one Self meeting and for a magical moment merging with a complete Other—is what sexual union could be.

But, as Ernest Becker and countless others have pointed out, sex has become both a cult and a means to an end. Pleasure and love are less an issue than the very act of doing it, or doing it with that prized someone. Now, however, sex has gone beyond culthood to become a commodity, a product that can be purchased and utilized. Sex has become a means of acquiring what one does not have—fame, a family, control, power, recognition, acceptance—and is seldom valued for the potential richness of the act itself, a classic case of "being" reduced to "having." Less powerful members of our culture, such as teenagers, are especially vulnerable to the power seduction of sex. As a young adolescent patient told me, "Sure I'm going to sleep with him. He's gonna give me a baby . . . maybe then he'll stay with me and even if he don't love me, I'll have someone who will always love me and be with me and I can always love."

As a culture, our confusion regarding sexual issues extends well beyond the boundaries of adult sexual contact and affects all types of family relationships. Under the microscope of misplaced moral scrutiny and psychological misinformation, parents have become uncomfortable and awkward concerning sexual matters. Concern over sexually traumatizing children has caused affection to be meted out in controlled doses. Few people are comfortable with issues of nudity, joint sleeping arrangements, homosexual families, visible family affection and other matters concerning natural bodily processes. How much is enough? Am I doing the right thing? I don't want (or want anyone to think) that I am damaging my child. These are examples of questions and comments often heard in clinical practice.

I have parents in psychotherapy who were chastised by other therapists or agencies for what was considered inappropriate sexual behavior. Since childhood sexual trauma has gone public and become a media issue, misguided clinicians and overzealous agencies take careful pains to "look for it." This sexual paranoia extends beyond families to schools where teachers are afraid to have needy children sit on their laps or engage in excessive hugging (an oxymoron?).

America's preoccupation with sex is a lot like the academic obsession with political correctness and the literary cannon. It is a fixation of a minority that through media attention has become a popular concern. Like reading, sex is not what it used to be. Obsessive sex, copulation, masturbation and perverse voyeurism do exist, but sexual intimacy, sensuality and genuine eroticism, like immersion in a good book, are becoming vanishing experiences.

THE IRRATIONAL

Rationalism is comfortable only in the presence of abstractions.

William James

The irrational dimension of consciousness is best exemplified by the emotional system. Emotions do not necessarily (nor should they) follow linear rules of logic. As anyone who has ever been in love can attest to, feelings follow their own path. The nature of emotions, as William James alludes to in his comment on rationalism, is that they do not represent the abstract meta-world of ideas but rather the irrational, very immediate "punch you in the face" reality of everyday life. As pointed out in the preceding section, emotions and thought are complementary aspects of reality processing. Thought follows the deliberate and linear, linguistic rules of logic, whereas emotions proceed in a kind of global, non-linear fashion.

The principal thrust of this section has already been covered in the earlier section on emotions and the integration of experience. The basic point to remember is that the emotional subsystem represents a necessary and valid mode of understanding the world. In fact, as Victor Guidano points out, as a way of processing reality, emotions preceded thought.

Assuming that tacit, analogical processes play a crucial role in the scaffolding of the order and regularities with which we are acquainted, it follows that feelings and emotions are primary in personal knowing. When considered within an evolutionary perspective the primacy of affect becomes explicit. While cognitive abilities represent one of the final products to emerge from a long evolutionary process, feelings and emotions were probably the first organized knowing system to actively scaffold environmental regularities. (1987, p. 25)

In training, new therapists constantly hear the admonishment "what are you feeling . . . be in touch with your feelings . . . what is the patient feeling." Therapists and actors, and I use the terms interchangeably because often they are, are probably the only professionals in which emotional awareness is encouraged. For most people and for the majority of professions, acceptance of emotions and their irrational quality is discouraged. It is ironic that acting and psychotherapy represent the principal domains in which irrational experiences like emotional outbursts are encouraged. And yet, oddly enough, the admission of having been in psychotherapy becomes the death blow for many professionals, especially politicians, an irony compounded by the fact that numerous office holders now come from show business.

As a species, we are in desperate need of relearning how to process, understand and integrate the irrational. The danger of not doing so can be found in the cold, sterile behaviors of modern political administrators who can efficiently calculate the destruction of an entire nation. It can be discerned in the prevalence of "value free" legal maneuvers that obstruct freedom and perpetuate injustice. The use of rational discourse and abstract euphemisms allows the most terrifying of events—nuclear war, ecological destruction or racial genocide—to be discussed in extremely impersonal ways. The admonishments, "Don't take it so personally, be rational" or "Don't get so emotional about it" have become commonplace. The point is that we desperately need to emotionally react to events we have become affectively anesthetized to.

Perhaps most of all, the tragedy of the loss of affective awareness can be seen in the very real confusion that most people do not admit to, but becomes more than apparent in psychotherapy. Historically, most practitioners of psychotherapy report a noticeable change in the types of patients coming for treatment. This shift has been described as a migration from neuroses to personality/character disorders, especially of the borderline/narcissistic variety. Over the past 10 years, I have noticed a further change in the type of so-called personality disorders that come for consultation. Increasingly, people are coming in with what I perceive as very basic dilemmas of everyday life. "My children stay out too late, I eat the wrong foods, I don't know how to deal with my wife, my job depresses me" and so on. Complaints have shifted from specific symptoms to a vague confusion and uncertainty concerning the management of ordinary affairs. Now, I am not at all certain that consultation with a psychotherapist is the best remedy for this affair, and my basic instinct tells me that *it is not*. My point is, however, that when I inquire as to what many of these patients are feeling I get very confused and conflicted answers.

The problem *I* experience with this is that the situations I ask about represent circumstances where the emotional response, again to *me*, seems quite obvious. As in, for example, "Yes, I am angry at my son for ignoring me" or "No, I do not feel love toward my wife because she is neglecting me" or "Yes, I feel sad because my mother is ill" or "Yes, my colleague does arouse me and I would like to sleep with her." When I place myself in the situations many patients describe, it seems fairly obvious to me how I, or any other sentient being, might feel. Not, necessarily, that we would all feel alike; the point is simply that we would *feel* something. Any kind of feeling is better than no feeling at all. Why then, when I inquire as to what a patient might be feeling do I never seem to get an emotional admission? What I usually hear is "O.K. . . . I feel alright" or, even worse, "I don't feel anything."

The explanation, I believe, is that *most people confuse what they are feeling with what they think they should be feeling.* The feeling one thinks one should have is not always the feeling one is having. What one imagines one's feelings should be represents culturally conditioned behaviors that, often, are not in accord with what one is feeling. Once again, the proverbial conflict between emotions and ideas arises. In the words of Miguel De Unamuno, "For living is one thing and knowing is another . . . perhaps there is such an opposition between the two that we may say that everything vital is anti-rational, not merely irrational, and that everything rational is anti-vital. And this is the basis of the tragic sense of life" (1913/1985, p. 426).

The fact that I may have an idea about how I should be feeling in no way implies that idea will be what I am feeling. Yet, increasingly, the idea is opted for over the feeling. More bad faith, more inauthenticity and, alas, a further spin into schizoid operations. Inevitably, when real feelings are confronted, guilt and anxiety accompany them and such emotions, admittedly, are difficult to confront. But guilt and anxiety, as innumerable philosophers have pointed out, are part of the territory, an integral part of life. Such feelings, like all affect, have an irrational and a rational component. Unless one experiences what one is actually feeling, it will be impossible to sort out the rational component, and the irrational, like an untamed demon, will be fled from. Perhaps the following clinical vignette will best illustrate my point.

Jim is a 16-year-old male high school student in therapy because of depression and poor school work. Jim's depression is directly related to an extremely conflictual relationship with his father. Through his description, Jim's father sounded aloof, obsessive, cold, controlling, authoritarian and overly intellectual. I asked Jim if he and his dad ever sat down and talked about his problems or their father/son difficulties. Jim acknowledged that they often talked, but, that the conversations were frustrating and usually ended in mutual silence. Part of the problem was that Jim's father usually approached these discussions with a prepared, written set of "points to be made," accompanied by a host of fixed resolutions and a priori assumptions.

Knowing this, I suggested that they come together for a session and suggested that his Dad leave all notebooks behind. The session, which lasted an hour and a half was a gut-wrenching, screaming, sobbing, emotional battle in which the two "erupted" with what seemed to me to be years of accumulated unresolved issues (innumerable quantum buttons were pushed). As they were leaving, the father turned to me and said, "Well, I guess that was a tremendous waste of time, nothing was settled."

As agreed, that week we had two more family sessions. By the third session Jim's father was saying that for the first time in their relationship he and his son were really talking. He admitted to believing that a good father meant acting controlled, organized and 100 percent positive. He began to talk about how his own father was emotionally distant and was becoming aware that he was treating Jim the same way.

Following several additional sessions, both the relationship between these two people and Jim's depression had dramatically improved.

This healing would not have occurred without the initial emotional catharsis. The first session, the emotional "eruption" was chaotic and irrational but, by nature, it was supposed to be. *In relation to affective awareness and emotional eruption, the goal is not resolution but release and integration so that the road to complete resolution can begin.* Affective awareness is the essential first step on the road to healing. Once feelings are released, they can be placed within an historical and rational context that can make sense and authentic progress can be made.

Too often this catharsis of the irrational is avoided. People either try to short circuit the release of emotion or *constantly seek to rationally comprehend their emotions.* Although there are times when emotions can be rationally understood, there are also situations where the sheer intensity of affect precludes rational comprehension. When emotions exist within a schizoid organization, this is almost always the case. The reintegration of affect is usually a passionate and dramatic process and emotional outbursts are common and represent quintessential examples of quantum buttons and quantum effects. One emotion triggers another, which connects to another, which detonates another, none of which might logically be related and eventually, like uranium attaining a critical mass, an emotional explosion results. Explosions are not supposed to make sense, rather their purpose is to clear obstructions so that authentic dialogue can occur.

Peak Experiences

This term was first introduced by Abraham Maslow (1962) who employed it to describe "moments of highest happiness and fulfillment." According to Maslow, such experiences vary in intensity and originate from intense immersion in activities such as sexual, spiritual or parental love; creative work; athletic participation or playful abandonment. The Zen concept of being totally immersed in either the moment or a specific activity represents a similar way of thinking. Peak experiences reflect an integrated consciousness capable of enjoying and being aware of the fullness of life. Agape, an emotional experience described by the ancient Greeks, reflects a similar idea. Agape means a sensation of altruistic love so intense and wondrous that one's mouth, literally, is left hanging open. Agape, like peak experiences, implies a *passionate involvement* in life.

A competitive and materialistic culture places little value on peak experiences. The cultural ethos of the United States places undo emphasis on ends—achievements and acquisitions—over means. Value is placed not on enjoying the *process* of one's endeavors but rather on the end goal—the diploma, the house, marriage to the right person, the large salary. The market ethos of unrestrained capitalism transforms an individual's behavior and relationships into a commodity, a product to be acquired and possessed.

Drugs, especially marihuana and the hallucinogens, are another area often associated with peak experiences. Certain drugs when employed within a meditational or religious context for ritualistic purposes are definitely a possible route to peak experiences or, as the worn-out phrase contends, expanded consciousness. A significant problem, however, is that because our culture discourages the controlled and ritualistic ingestion of drugs, the same drugs are then informally employed to constrict consciousness. Furthermore, drugs that are culturally sanctioned, like alcohol and minor tranquilizers, are substances that *can* seriously clog consciousness and reduce the possibility of peak experiences. Marihuana and the hallucinogens represent highly "politicized" drugs whose restriction exists for reasons more relevant to perpetuation of the existing system structure than for any reasonable clinical evidence. When used correctly, these substances can have a mind enhancing quality that can increase creativity and allow other system perspectives to become more obvious. As a general system strives to maintain its continuous operation, any medium that can alter perception and increase system variability is discouraged.

The dilemma with the cultural lack of venues for peak experiences is further exacerbated by the government's misplaced "supply" side approach to drug control in which the majority of funds are diverted away from education into law enforcement.[4] The lack of education is compounded further by an overly moralistic and decidedly unscientific perspective that perpetuates the grouping of all drugs into a single negative category. Because little distinction is made between heroin and crack and mescaline and marihuana, the average person receives erroneous information and is trapped in a perpetual state of fear and confusion. People have constantly used drugs, like sex, because of the association with pleasure. Unless the "demand" side of the drug equation is addressed, people, especially adolescents, will continue to use drugs for the wrong reasons—to narcotize themselves.

THE COMMUNAL

> Aloneness is man's real condition. . . . We must love one another or die.
>   W. H. Auden

Communal experiences can be one of the most powerful antidotes to the schizoid condition and the aloneness that Auden refers to. Like the traditional concept of community, the term communal denotes active and mutual involvement in the living affairs of others. This type of community interaction can occur only when the total number of people is relatively small, as is customary with the now vanishing *tribal* fashion of living. In relation to quantum psychology, number and size is an extremely critical issue that will be addressed again in the final summary. In terms of the communal experience, at least one that is not mediated by electronic technology, for example, Marshal McLuhan's (1964) concept of the global village, a small number of people is a crucial element.

Although I am uncertain as to exactly what number boundary separates manageable and unmanageable community experiences, I am convinced that an approximate point exists where the sheer volume of people eliminates, on the macro level, any possibility of communal involvement—as in large urban areas. This, of course, does not eliminate the possibility of community on a micro level and, in fact, the nation is cross-saturated with numerous such communities; the newborn and tiny trend toward cohousing communities is one example.[5] My point, however, is that there are not enough such communities and that their existence does little to offset the pervasive schizoid condition and externalization of consciousness that saturates the general culture and affects a large portion of the population. Within the communal context, Self and Other become integrated parts of a greater whole—the community. Because what enhances the individual reinforces the community, a positive synergistic effect develops, a process that allows for the amplification of both the community ethos and individual consciousness.

The process of communal or group enhancement is a well-documented fact of anthropological and social psychology that has also been labeled group contagion. Contagion refers to the magnification of individual consciousness—emotions, sensations, thought and images become intensified and combine with the common group purpose to motivate the group to act in a manner well beyond the potential of any one member. Anyone who has had the opportunity of being involved in a group experience is well aware of how startlingly powerful it can be. References have been made to the "group mind or group consciousness" that supersedes individual consciousness and induces people in groups to act in ways never even contemplated on an individual level.

Because of the contagion effect, the matter of communal ethos or identity becomes a critical issue. In essence, a group can be influenced to rally for reasons ranging from the inhuman, as in racial or ethnic genocide, to the superhuman, as in the heroic acts often witnessed during tragedy, war and disaster. In order for the communal process to have an ameliorative effect on schizoid detachment, the community must band together under a humanistic ethos specifically designed to reconstruct consciousness, that is, human life in a healthier way. The communal ethos must, therefore, transmit standards that value and promote true responsivity.

JOY

The experience of joy should be a passionate one. Like peak experiences, joy can be achieved from involvement in almost any activity. It is not the enterprise, but rather one's approach to the particular endeavor that elicits joy. Tranquil meditational joys along with more rambunctious and physical delights should be available within healthy cultures. Unfortunately, unless one is dealing with infants and children, joy is noticed only by its absence. Julian, for example, is currently fascinated by "The Moon" and has a strikingly delightful way of looking at it. The moon definitely seems to elicit joy in Julian. Yet, too often, the experience of joy ends after childhood.

In children, the innocence of joy is tolerated, encouraged and even admired, but only up to a point. This point ensues at approximately 5 or 6 years of age when formal academic training begins. At this juncture, when linguistic skills are achieving dominance, a great cultural effort is put into making the child function responsibly. Play is tolerated but only in controlled doses and organized settings and as the child gets older the admonishment to act one's age becomes a cultural anthem. Work and play are inculcated as quite separate dimensions of existence and great efforts are made to keep them as such, thus, further perpetuating the schizoid condition. Seriousness, responsibility, diligence and a strong future orientation are stressed as essential for *survival and functioning*. Eventually, *functioning* becomes the raison d'être of living.

Although the concept of functioning is well applied to the physical or medical aspect of a problem, I find it especially distressing that functioning is now being used as a principal criterion of psychological health. "Is the patient functioning" has become a key concern of clinical rounds and treatment assessments. Although I would agree that my liver can be considered a functional organ, an organ that I earnestly hope continues to function, I have strong objections to *exclusively applying the concept of functioning* to the suprasystem level of Self. My intent in life is not simply to function but to be happy about it—to achieve my share of joy. Something is seriously askew with a clinical approach that only measures, for example, the improvement of depression, with the predominant consideration of whether or not the patient is functioning. Yet, I hear this all the time.

Machines and humans both function, but the question of joy is far less relevant for my Honda than it is for myself or the reader. Joy, although not essential for existence, is nevertheless fundamental for a complete sense of being alive, unless, of course, one chooses to simply exist. Here, we again return to a central premise of the text—that because many people are oblivious to the conditions of ordinary consciousness they are equally unaware that better alternatives are possible. Although numerous people will fantasize about improving their state of being, very few will actually do something about it. The "quiet lives of desperation" that Thoreau alluded to are simply accepted as the way things are. I have often wondered, for example, why work and school could not be emphasized as more joyful experiences.

Dancing and Singing

Two decidedly "normal" and universally joyful experiences notably restricted in mainstream U.S. culture are singing and dancing. Both singing and dancing are essential human activities that fall somewhere on the continuum from singular meditation to tumultuous frolicking. All children who are physically capable enjoy dancing and singing. At the point where general cultural conditioning begins and the market ethos predominates, spontaneous singing and dancing is discouraged (when was the last time you could sing or dance at work without people thinking you were psychotic or on drugs?). By the time "adult" behavior sets in, singing is restricted to isolated spots like the car and shower, whereas dancing becomes a province of specialized clubs. Singing and dancing for career reasons or to make money is an entirely different matter. Not only have we become a nation of observers, but of critics as well, who believe that only professional entertainment is acceptable. An intense self-consciousness now exists concerning the public or spontaneous expression of these activities.

Singing and dancing are now considered "professions" and, as such, should be participated in by professionals and observed by the rest of us. However, it is a definite postmodern, electronic-media-influenced phenomenon that makes many people assume a passive "couch potato" approach to life. Prior to the ascendance of visual technology and the age of the specialist, singing and dancing were a routine part of social gatherings. With the exception of teenagers and certain ethnic groups (especially Latinos and Blacks), these activities, as part of the public domain, are vanishing. Dancing and singing might seem like an odd gesture today but, only 40 or 50 years ago, in the United States they were a normal part of social gatherings. The German jazz writer Joachim-Ernst Berendt states that

The basic situation of modern man is being separated from nature, from the universe, from other people. And there are just a few media to overcome this separation. Meditation and love are two; the other is singing. That's why people love to sing in choirs, the feeling of unity, of oneness . . . is a spiritual experience usually you only have in love. (1991, p. 47)

The predominant cultural ethos contributes to the extreme self-consciousness most people have concerning the display of spontaneous joy, and singing and dancing are just two examples. The loss of these five realms of experience represents a serious deficiency in the human ecological balance. Their absence further precludes opportunities for responsivity and resonance and makes authentic dialogue more difficult to achieve.

DIALOGUE

No one is interested in each other's story any longer.

S. M. Christie

Dialogue is the linguistic staple of responsivity. Authentic dialogue represents a verbal interchange in which at least two people *talk*, *listen* and *respond* to each other. Dialogue is a form of communication in which, through language, all subsystems of the Self become available and open for understanding, elaboration and development. By revealing one's ideas to an accepting other who listens and responds, formerly isolated self-systems become less fragmented and more available to consciousness and the overall Self.

Furthermore, the process of "feeling understood" generates a tremendous arena for intimacy. The personal validation and reduction of disconnected confusion that stems from being heard is a powerfully therapeutic medium. Part of our contemporary dilemma is that such expansive exchange is becoming limited to professional "experts" who under the rubric of "the psychotherapy process" employ dialogue as a specialized tool. Dialogue is no longer a thread in the fabric of everyday life; like so much of what should be "ordinary," dialogue is now the province of communication specialists. Once again, we are confronted with the dilemma that it is not the system itself that is the problem but rather the manner in which the system (in this case language) is utilized.

Postmodern communication essentially consists of restricted monologue in which verbal exchanges are utilized for gaining information, conducting business, self-aggrandizement, narcissistic indulgence or, power and control. The following, rather typical clinical anecdote exemplifies this unfortunate phenomenon.

Carol is a bright, attractive, articulate 26-year-old graduate student, in therapy for depression related to relationship problems. At school and work, Carol reports that almost all conversation revolves around the exchange of information and administration of responsibilities. Carol describes this is a "devastating and depressing experience" and claims that by the weekend, she "hungers" for being and talking with someone really interested in her.

Her experience, however, has been that such contact is rarely available. Her female friends usually want to talk about themselves, whereas the males she meets, when they too are not discussing themselves, falsely employ words to get her into bed. For Carol, consulting a psychotherapist has become the only way for her to tell her story and be heard.

The alienation and estrangement induced by limited discourse is gender neutral and quite impartial; Carol could have just as easily been Bob. The lack of authentic dialogue that my patients complain about parallels my own experience. I have noticed that interpersonal exchanges have become restricted, time limited and specific. People talk, not because they want to "hear" another person's story but, only either to tell their own or acquire information. If my conversation is too lengthy, I have the recurrent experience of people impatiently waiting for me to finish so they can begin to talk. Whatever I might have said, except as an excuse for the other person to talk, becomes irrelevant. A rather aware "designated patient" describes her "normal" family dinner experience as follows:

My Dad sits down and asks me how I'm doing. I start to tell him but, without acknowledging me, he starts talking to my mother about his job. My mother is nodding but I know she's not really listening because she's talking to my brother about his girlfriend. Meanwhile my brother is trying to tell my father something but my father is asking me to pass the pasta. By now, my mom is talking about what her day was like, but I know no one is listening because they're all reading something. At this point I usually throw my plate on the table and scream, "Does anybody care about how I'm doing?" They look at each other, laugh, tell me I'm crazy and to "go to my room until I learn how to act like I'm in the family."

Almost everyone in psychotherapy complains of being ignored. We are like lonely script writers, ensconced in schizoid bubbles, each producing eloquent monologues that are never heard. Words are used as commodities of self-fulfillment and listening becomes but an appendix, a vestigial and forgotten process.

I-Thou Communication

The type of dialogue essential for an optimal human ecology is reflected in the writing of the theologian Martin Buber (1970). Buber presented three forms of possible discourse: I-Thou, I-It and It-It. In the *Externalization of Consciousness* (DeBerry, 1991), I pointed out that although Buber intended his schemata to be applied to a relationship with God, it also pertains to relationships between people.

I-Thou communication represents a relationship between Selves. It assumes a complete integration of consciousness so that all subsystems of the Self are available for discourse. I-Thou encounters presume a minimal schizoid condition. Again, it must be noted that although all aspects of the Self are available for sharing, not all aspects have to be shared. That is, I-Thou communication is conditional, dependent on situation and context. *A reciprocal and symbiotic relationship exists between context and consciousness, and awareness and expression represent an interaction between the two.* See "Awareness, Consciousness and General Systems Theory" in Chapter 4. Therefore, not all encounters can, or need to be, I-Thou encounters; at times, interactions result in I-It or It-It relationships.

The I-It connection is a rather skewed affair in which a primarily integrated Self interacts with a predominantly schizoid other. In I-It or It-It relationships, people relate as part objects, that is, objectified others that exist for socially defined roles. The essential element of I-It encounters is that only *parts* of the consciousness system interact. Certain subsystems of the person are split off and unavailable for interpersonal communication. The I-It relationship reflects an association in which one member is objectified and related to along a singular dimension (wife, husband, employer, doctor, merchant). This dimension represents the particular self manifested within that particular relational context and is typical of the postmodern, interactive self described throughout the text. Because a completely integrated Self does not exist, the schizoid nature of I-It involvement is the result of developmental defects in both self and other. Essentially, both people are acting in bad faith.

Bad faith and inauthenticity reach their zenith in the It-It relationship. It-It represents the ultimate schizoid encounter and, unfortunately, the predominant expression of postmodern intimacy. It-It reflects a relationship in which both people relate as fragmented, schizoid selves in limited transactions of intimacy. This is the intimacy encouraged by the market ethos and typified by people doing business with each other. In It-It, the person becomes a means to an end, an objectified commodity of exchange. Not only does It-It represent the way we do business, it reflects the way we live, which increasingly is becoming business, as in the contemporary aphorism "Hey, nothing personal, it's only business." The I-Thou-It dimension is not a discreet entity, but represents a continuum or range in which different permutations and combinations of relationships exist. State University of New York philosopher Marjorie Miller has correctly pointed out that in daily life only *approximations* of I-Thou are possible. Therefore, all that is really available, even to the most integrated of personalities, are fleeting moments of I-Thou wholeness. Such instances, nevertheless, are pivotal moments in which the Self is validated, understood and responded to. The rich feeling of responsivity and resonance are an earmark of such encounters. Ideally, social discourse should contain a balance of I-Thou, I-It and It-It relationships. The problem, however, is that the socially constructed conditions under which the postmodern self operates is characterized by a notable absence of I-Thou encounters. A balanced ecology of "being" depends on I-Thou relationships, not only with an invisible God but in the daily transactions of everyday life.

SUMMARY

The elements necessary for a balanced ecology of *being* were described as experience and dialogue. Experience, connected with the concepts of aliveness and animation, was characterized as a process of full and immediate sensory awareness. Postmodern culture was depicted as limiting at least five key levels of experience—sensual, irrational, peak, communal and joyful. Loss of these system levels further impedes both responsivity and the organic encounter of resonance.

In the linguistic dimension, authentic dialogue was portrayed as the principal vehicle of verbal responsivity, with the I-Thou model representing *one prototype* of responsivity and resonant communication. As the text is drawing to an end, chapter 8 focuses on the implications of postmodern conditions for a quantum psychology and provides suggestions and speculations for future developments.

NOTES

1. See G. Bateson (1972).

2. Within the quantum model, I believe sufficient reason exists to classify emotion and cognition as senses.

3. See M. Armand (1990).

4. For a timely review of this situation, see "The New War," *Newsweek*, January 6, 1992, pp. 18–23.

5. Although in its infancy in the United States, the trend toward cohousing (Bofoellesskaber) is well established in Northern Europe, especially in Scandanavian countries such as Denmark where it originated.

Eight

An Introduction to Quantum Diagnosis: Suggestions for the Future

This is the way the world ends, Not with a bang but a whimper.
T. S. Eliot

A quantum diagnosis represents a thorough and exhaustive analysis of all system level attributes and interactions. Such an approach embodies both *established and original* practices of understanding psychological issues. Because quantum psychology is essentially a *general systems* method of analysis, procedural precedents have already been validated. The consideration then becomes, what exactly distinguishes quantum diagnosis from a systems analysis. Again, it must be stressed that a quantum approach does not replace but rather *augments* traditional methods. The expansion, however, is radical and permanently alters the entire picture, but it is the entire picture that quantum psychology attempts to analyze. The following recapitulation provides a comparison between a traditional and quantum approach.

Quantum model:—non-linear, holistic, normal, dynamic, non-local, synergistic, irrational.

Traditional model:—linear, reductionistic, abnormal, fixed, local, mechanistic, rational.

Quantum diagnosis:—emphasizes a systems analysis that focuses on a personal/community narrative and theme that includes the *future*, and is thus *teleological* in nature. A quantum analysis accepts the premise that schizoid phenomena are an integral part of the diagnostic process and examines the *relationship* between people and events. This combination forces all relevant system levels (historical, community, environmental, political, cultural and economic) to be taken into account.

Traditional diagnosis:—examines personal problems in terms of discreet symptoms and syndromes, maintains a "fix-it" mentality that concentrates on improved "functioning," ignores the issue of personal narrative and disregards the influence of "macro" system factors such as history, politics, culture, environment and money. Rather than concentrate on the relationship between things such as the Self and Community, traditional diagnosis concentrates on the extraction of elements from the total field and their subsequent analysis as isolated elements.

Let us suppose that an individual presents with the problem of clinical depression. The following depicts a *sample* of issues that could be considered from a quantum perspective:

Self-system—exploration of schizoid structure (split-off parts of the Self-system), examines interaction between different parts, including overall consciousness, quantum buttons and quantum effects.

Cultural system—analyzes values and reality assumptions that would lead to the appraisal of key subsystems:

• political—access to power, chance of advancement and education
• economic—availability of money, jobs, education and financial survival and success.

These factors would inevitably address issues of race, ethnicity, religion, gender, geography, community, history and so on. Each of these system levels represents intertwined cultural levels that affect individual consciousness. Established diagnostic practices ignore the implications of many of these system levels, especially the more inclusive political/economic level. The reasons for this neglect will be discussed, but presently, I would like to return to the quantum diagnostic process.

In order for quantum diagnosis to be properly addressed, briefly, we will again examine what happens to new methodologies and theories. In that it attempts to integrate neglected, ignored or unrecognized system elements, a quantum approach echoes the intention of any new psychological doctrine. New theories, especially ones that contribute to the development of paradigm shifts, strive to describe behavior in heuristic and innovative ways. Essentially, this means allowing the scientist to *observe* behavior through fresh and untested epistemological and methodological lenses that, hopefully, represent an improvement over their predecessors.

Unfortunately, what begins to occur over time, as discussed in detail in chapters 1 and 2 is the following: First, the new theory cannot possibly explain all phenomena, especially new events that have arisen after the theory was formulated. *This is a natural and understandable process.* What happens next, is, I suggest, where most social and psychological theories go astray—reality is modified to fit the theory, that is, new observations are either ignored, distorted to fit the theory or incorporated into a modified version of the original theory. The old theory remains essentially unchanged, an epistemological wolf in theoretical sheep's clothing.

What then occurs is what philosopher-psychiatrist Richard Chessick (1985) terms a process of "bad faith and inauthenticity" in which "lip-service" is paid to new elements, which are then appended on to the preexisting theoretical structure, and like magic, a seemingly new theory is created. Ego-psychology, self-psychology, the biopsychosocial model, community psychiatry, community psychology and cognitive/behavioral psychology are all specimens of this hyphenation subterfuge. The recent emphasis on dual diagnoses is an excellent example of this diagnostic fragmentation. The concept of "dual diagnosis" was designed to decide *which* drug abusers also suffered from standard psychiatric diagnoses (depression, mania, schizophrenia or personality disorder). Drug addiction and psychological problems are now separated and, for treatment purposes, considered distinct entities. An additional problem is that increasingly, traditional diagnostic methods are normative in nature. The frequency and intensity of symptoms are counted, tests are given, traits are measured and family histories recorded; results are then compared with normative "pools" of collected data and a diagnostic summary is dispensed. The absurdity of this approach is that it tells nothing about the individual per se but only how the individual "fits in" with normative curves. A classic example of this diagnostic style concerns the accident (discussed in chapter 6) the author was involved in. As part of the legal proceedings, my wife and I were instructed to obtain psychiatric evaluations, which entailed psychological tests, including the Minnesota Multiphasic Personality Inventory (MMPI–2), all of which were given, naturally, by a psychiatrist representing the defendant's lawyers and insurance company. Following is an excerpt from my evaluation.

In general, the family backgrounds of *these* patients have been characterized by poor and very distorted communications of feelings. This pattern has mainly been associated with schizoaffective disorders, although in some cases it has been associated with atypical anxiety reactions, schizoid personalities and schizoaffective trends without psychosis.[1]

Although I readily admit to the reader my share of psychological problems, I likewise have a difficult time finding myself in this statement. This is because the diagnostic summary has little to do with me; essentially it is concerned with *these patients*. But, just who are *these patients*? The answer is that they are a collection of test scores that describe only how an individual *functions in comparison to others* (see chapter 1). Diagnosis by normative test data represents an insidious and reductionistic form of evaluation that totally ignores the rich diversity of remaining system levels. For example, the evaluating psychiatrist and I were from different cultural, religious, ethnic, political and economic backgrounds. Not only were none of these system factors taken into account, the methodology itself denies their importance. Once again, we confront the classic myth that psychiatric diagnosis is a scientific, value-free, objective method.

Perhaps, one of the more disturbing elements is that the political/economic system level was considered irrelevant to my diagnoses. Although this is common practice, in the present case the omission of political/economic considerations was blatantly transparent. Disregard for system factors as painfully obvious as evidenced in the present example is, I believe, cause for alarm. The doctor who interviewed me worked for lawyers representing the defendant's insurance company. (At this point of the process, plaintiff and defendant are completely uninvolved, everything is handled by professionals and lawyers.) Basically, the insurance company is paying the psychiatrist to make a diagnosis that reduces their litigious financial obligation. However, none of this is directly acknowledged—no one admits that financial factors influence the final outcome. What is perceived is that a value-free, objective, "scientific" process is unfolding, when in reality, a textbook example of "bad faith," a deformed hydra appears before us.

Yet no one claims to see the creature. My lawyer's response to my objections to this hypocrisy was that "we" could do the same thing—hire another doctor who would arrive at a diagnosis more favorable to my case. Thus, the game goes on and on; a game that no one admits is a game. This schizoid duplicity transforms daily events into a twilight zone reality where what one *knows* one perceives is denied. Truly, these are the conditions of madness.

In chapter 6, the text explored the spiraling relationship between law, money and daily life. Insertion of the legal profession into market affairs did not begin for reasons of justice and fairness; although, at times, such virtues are welcome by-products, they are nonetheless artifacts. The predominant reason law and economics have become entwined is for the promotion of individual profit. After all, the bottom line is the bottom line. The preceding personal example demonstrates how this relationship accelerates the transformation of things and actions into commodities. Knowledge becomes business. All things, from medical wisdom to philosophy and religion, become saleable items.

This case illustrates another unwholesome factor that affects scientific and clinical progress. Historically, although always present because of postmodern acceleration, this influence has now become a behemoth of potentially ponderous proportions. The influence is money and the creature is the political/economic system level, as reflected by the postmodern market ethos. Increasingly, research and psychiatric treatment are dictated to by financial concerns (grants, funding, loans, third-party insurance reimbursement and direct government funding). Barry Schwartz calls this commercialization phenomenon *economic imperialism*, a process he describes as

The spread of economic calculations of "interest" to domains that were once regarded as noneconomic. It is the infusion of a practice with the pursuit of external goods. This pursuit pushes a practice in directions it would not otherwise take and in doing so undercuts the traditions that comprise it . . . it is not good science to decide what to study on the basis of what people are willing to pay for. Yet government agencies are able to manipulate fields of inquiry by shifting funds from one domain to another. (1990, p. 13)

Doctor Schwartz's statement is exactly to the point. Politics and money, two powerful cultural systems that contribute to both individual and community psychopathology now augment the elimination of these systems from diagnostic consideration. The "bad faith" involved in their denial excludes a part of the Self and thus exacerbates the schizoid condition. Therefore, in addition to recognized impediments to theoretical and clinical advancement, a distorted market ethos creates further and, perhaps, more destructive distortion.

THE OBSTRUCTED CURE

The only antidote to this process is to maintain a systems perspective, a perspective that holistically observes all behavior as part of a greater field of interaction. Thus, any particular event becomes not only a system within itself but part of a greater system as well. Because new properties are constantly emerging, emergent interactionism becomes both a top-down and bottom-up, hierarchical method of understanding system events, requiring both experiential and experimental proofs (Bateson, 1972; Bohm, 1980; Davies, 1983; DeBerry, 1989, 1991; Koestler, 1967, 1978; Lockwood, 1989; Pagels, 1989; Penrose, 1989; Pribram, 1986).

But a rather critical question arises now: Why, at least from the perspective of clinical psychology and psychiatry, has a systems approach never caught on? General systems theory is not part of graduate training in clinical psychology, nor is it required within psychiatric residency programs. As far as I can tell, ever since Ludwig Von Bertalanaffy conceptualized it as a way of describing the interdependence of biological processes, general systems theory has *formally* been in existence for over 50 years. I propose that the answer, partially, has to do with what a quantum psychological approach entails.

Quantum psychology was conceptualized to reintegrate systems analysis into mainstream psychology. The essential differences between general systems theory in 1992 and when Von Bertalanaffy first developed it are the crucial matters of *frequency and acceleration.* These are the postmodern hallmarks of contemporary existence. Simply put, not only are more "events" occurring, they are also happening faster than anyone could have imagined; all of which affects consciousness on both individual and community levels. Interactions, events and relationships, never dreamed of 50 years ago, are now commonplace. As a means of understanding these changes, quantum psychology utilizes the principles of complementarity, the influence of consciousness, system interaction and non-local/non-linear phenomena. In terms of understanding and working with psychological distress, this approach definitely modifies the rules of the game, necessitating the inclusion of previously disparate systems as standard diagnostic practice. This approach inevitably incorporates the total political/economic system within the analysis and, thus, modifies and enlarges not only the parameters of diagnosis but *the political economic system as well*; clinical activism becomes political activism.

Once one truly accepts the quantum premise that separate system levels are correlated, it becomes impossible (except for selfish reasons) to maintain a singular perspective. To focus on any one part or system, such as the individual, while neglecting the political/economic level, constitutes an immoral stance that fosters the schizoid condition. Yet to assume such a holistic approach is extremely painful because it places the entire system in judgment and essentially says, "everything must change." This is anathema, not only to the postmodern self but to the general system as well. All systems strive to maintain their identity and boundaries and will, by nature, struggle against forces that attempt to modify them. Parts may change quickly, but the general structure and purpose of the system transform very slowly.

THE QUANTUM DIAGNOSTIC PROCESS

In clinical terms, what this means is that all system levels and interactions should be examined in a new light. Ordinary human relationships along with their combinations, permutations, associations and emergent interactions, need to be understood within a more holistic paradigm. If the social sciences do not accomplish this, charlatans, celebrities and business people surely will. As Kenneth J. Gergen states,

Traditional practices of therapy, guided by both romanticism and modernism, place the therapist in the role of the expert who goes about assessing the problem of the individual mind, locating repressions, conflicts, misconceptions, or cognitive aberrations, and correcting such deficits through therapy. Under postmodernism, not only is the therapist's expertise in mental matters thrown into jeopardy, but the very reality of a "patient" with a "mind to be known and corrected" loses credibility. (1991, p. 251)

One way to examine the quantum diagnostic process is to explore two system levels that have been notably affected by the postmodern acceleration process—the family system and the political/economic system.

THE POSTMODERN FAMILY

The nature of families and family interaction is definitely changing. The traditional genotypical definition of family has shifted to include non-blood relationships living together under a common bond. A common bond, along with proximity and frequency of daily contact constitute criteria for the description of a postmodern family. The case of Robert, described in chapter 5, is an example of what I am referring to. As our culture changes and events accelerate, people find themselves in totally new relational situations.

By what method do we explain the intense interactions, attractions and family bonding that inevitably occurs when people live in familial situations? What about the return of a gay sibling, the transformation of a heterosexual parent into a homosexual one or the increasingly occurring transsexual metamorphosis? The acceleration of postmodern interactions creates cross-racial, ethnic, professional, national and religious combinations that represent novel emergents. Each of these interactions is going to have to be understood within an alternative paradigm.

How, for example, is a middle-aged man, twice divorced, married to a younger woman and starting another family, supposed to handle the return of grown children from previous marriages? Quantum buttons and quantum effects are bound to unfold. Novel patterns of personal and familial interaction place both psychodynamics and psychotherapy in unfamiliar territory. Quantum buttons—the activation of split-off developmental conflicts by new system interactions—produce quantum effects—unexpected and unexplainable local and non-local Self-system responses. As one patient put it, "At this point in my life I never expected to feel this way."

Quantum buttons are activated by the emergence of unexpectedly novel situations. The case of Helen provides illustration.

Helen is an educated, divorced, attractive and established business executive who, essentially, came into therapy for "confusion" and depression. Helen's symptoms were related to changes in the full spectrum of Self—thoughts, feelings, sensations, images and behaviors. Helen found these changes extremely disruptive. "I am not myself, I am out of control . . . I feel like I am having a nervous breakdown," are samples of Helen's statements. The alteration in Helen's Self came as the result of her 17-year-old daughter returning home. The child, who returned with a 22-year-old girlfriend, had been living 1,800 miles away with her father for the past 5 years. At first, everything seemed fine. Helen was glad to have her daughter home and the friend seemed to be a friendly and cooperative person. As time progressed, Helen and her daughter's friend began to develop an intense attachment. They began, as Helen put it, "falling in love like long lost sisters." Helen began experiencing herself in ways she never thought possible. In addition to acting differently, old and forgotten memories were returning. A tremendous conflict began to develop in her relationship with her daughter and the daughter's relationship with her friend. The situation at home was becoming "explosive." One night, Helen, who detests violence, found herself wildly punching her daughter, while concurrently having images and thoughts about her own mother. It was at this point that Helen came in for therapy.

New relationships and situations have to be understood within a larger perspective that allows for the construction of new explanations. What appears to be the "obvious" conflict may not be the problem at all. Quantum effects connect past, present and *future* events in ways demanding of new interpretations. The essential elements that need to be evaluated are the narrative, theme and projected direction of the situation.

The narrative represents the story the individual is constructing. One of the hallmarks of contemporary existence is that everyone has a story to tell (Howard, 1991). Current diagnostic wisdom ignores the personal narrative, concentrating instead on symptoms, thoughts, family history and biologic markers. In hearing a person's story, crucial system level factors are brought to light. As the narrative unfolds, values and reality assumptions that need to be addressed become more evident. Within contemporary reductionistic interviewing, such system elements are considered tangential or irrelevant to the diagnostic process. This type of thinking ignores the fact that for non-biologic problems there is a minimal if often negative correlation between diagnosis and treatment.

The theme represents the common factors that bind the disparate story elements together. An old supervisor of mine used to describe the theme as "a red thread" that can be found continuously running through the narrative. Postmodern conditions often result in the startling discovery that either no theme is present or, based on personal history, what one would expect to be the logical or historically appropriate theme is absent. Often, because of the quantum effects induced by postmodern conditions, *a new theme is being generated*. Typically postmodern in nature, the new theme is derived from past experiences but is basically original in nature. The identification and understanding of new themes should be an essential part of psychological work.

The projected direction is concerned with where the new theme is taking the person. This is a critical element of quantum diagnosis because it alters psychotherapy from a *focus on the past to an emphasis on the future*, with *consequences* becoming an integral part of the therapeutic process. Although past and present remain important, psychological work assumes more of a teleological nature. Inevitably, addressing the future draws in questions of values, reality assumptions and goals, areas usually neglected in reductionistic diagnosis. The person is forced to examine not only the supposed "causes" of behaviors but the consequences and probable outcomes as well. In addition, because a teleological approach addresses issues of design, intent and purpose, a holistic "grand scheme" orientation unfolds in which other critical factors, for example, historical, political and economic, are added to the intrapsychic or personal equation analysis. A more community oriented or civic approach ensues, a transformation that shifts emphasis away from exclusively intrapsychic concerns to more collective ones.[2]

POLITICAL/ECONOMIC FACTORS

One of the most significant changes that has occurred is the postmodern correlation of the cultural system level, especially as manifested by the political/economic system level, to individual and community consciousness (remember, within quantum psychology once systems interact they become correlated with one another). In terms of the diagnostic process in the United States, the political/economic system is correlated with individual and community consciousness to the point where the market ethos affects both consciousness and clinical decisions. As a culture, we are shifting from an emphasis on process and development to a focus on conformity and productivity—*functioning*. The concept of disfunction has been expanded to include anyone who is not a productive part of the system.

In numerous clinical rounds, consistently, in terms of diagnosis and prognosis I have noted the following issues gaining in prominence: Is the patient working . . . paying his bills, does she have a job, is he going to school, does she have an education, is he getting job training? Questions of happiness, creativity, joy, community involvement or spirituality never enter the picture. No one has ever asked, "Does the patient like to dance?" An increasing number of people in the United States are identified as dysfunctional. Contemporary nomenclature identifies them as the *underclass*, a caste of people that prior to approximately 10 years ago did not exist. Their abundance and proliferation are classic examples of both postmodern acceleration and emergent interactionism.

There is no doubt that it is getting more difficult to function in postmodern society. The negotiation of complex new technologies requires both higher intelligence and more comprehensive education and yet, increasingly, a larger percentage of the population is losing access not only to the favorable developmental conditions that can elevate hereditary intellectual potential, but to quality education and training opportunities as well. A sense of obligation to public education has decidedly been abandoned by the upper and upper-middle class. The wealthy do not send their children to "public" institutions and the middle class is definitely not far behind. Thus, the trend away from civic and community responsibility mushrooms.

As the wealthier segment of the population secedes from civic participation, schizoid fragmentation spreads from the individual to the community through the entire culture. The United States is witnessing the construction of a *postmodern capitalistic caste society* in which the privileged are allowed to devote time to personal change and development (the men's movement, feminism, psychotherapy, channelling, green movements, transpersonal psychology), while the less fortunate are relegated to *functioning*, an existential banishment that means doing work that nobody wants to do. More and more people, willingly or unwillingly "drop out" of society, join the underclass and become part of the demoralized welfare state. As one astute patient put it, "My choice is between feeling shitty about myself for working at McDonald's or getting money from the state for just feeling shitty about myself."

The problem is that an ecological or general systems approach reveals we are all in the same boat. What happens within one part of the system affects the entire system. Being able to insulate oneself with money in no way precludes unhappiness, alienation despair and the augmentation of the schizoid condition. We may be becoming wealthier but, unless something changes quickly, we are also becoming more schizoid and, in the end, we shall lose ourselves and each other. There are, however, possibilities. As the book draws to its end, let us explore them briefly.

CONCLUSIONS AND SPECULATIONS

Ending a book is sometimes more difficult than beginning one. In the present instance, I definitely find this to be true. The preceding pages introduced a number of ideas and general concepts that deserve further elaboration. Ideally, such explication should take two forms: (1) the presentation of additional observations from ordinary life that would further connect conditions of mainstream culture with community and individual malaise and (2) the establishment of a scientific paradigm in which these ideas can be comparatively tested.

The pragmatic reality of space limitations prevents expansion of the first point. The second point is, however, crucial and deserves some attention, or at the very least, a clarification. A principal ambition of the text was to provide a perspective that would encourage social scientists to establish a cultural methodology that could measure and compare different ways of being. Basically, I have been suggesting at least the following postulates:

1. The social sciences, especially psychology, are too fragmented, reductionistic and linear and have now reached a point where, in pragmatic terms, they have become politicized—in order to ensure funding and jobs, social scientists "produce," as a commodity, narrow and culturally acceptable "research."

2. The distortion of the sciences is reflective of a general schizoid fragmentation of the individual, the community and the mainstream culture.

3. This fragmentation represents an inauthentic state of being, essentially selfish and manipulative in nature, that is becoming an ingrained feature of the evolving postmodern self.

4. Postmodern conditions produce an exponentially accelerated number of interactions and *emergents* that need to be understood within a new paradigm—a quantum paradigm.

5. A quantum psychological approach maintains an ecological position: a holistic systems perspective that attempts to explain new interactions and relationships

that the electronic, postmodern culture constructs. This perspective necessitates the inclusion of neglected system factors (politics, economics, history, culture).

6. Through *experience and dialogue*, a quantum approach advocates the reintegration of split-off subsystems of consciousness. This process is *one* way to modify schizoid development and focus human evolution in a preferable direction.

7. The hypothesis of an alternate and preferable direction for evolution could be empirically and experimentally tested.

Such methodology could take the form of constructing communities in which different "interactional styles" are comparatively studied. An operational empiricism in which observations, connected with procedural norms are placed within a greater ecological context, could be a step in this direction. For example, the larger context would be the understanding that the individual and community are mutually connected by cultural conditions that should be of optimal benefit to both. In order to make a distinction be een what can be true in principle and in practice—what can be achieved—the principle of epistemic dualism could be kept in mind.[3] Within this context, interactional styles that inhibit the integration of the Self could be observed and compared with relational styles that encourage the integration of the Self and expansion of awareness. Operationally defined patterns of interaction could then be correlated with specific psychological and physical measures, such as, happiness, creativity, the ability to work and play or organic illness. These factors could then be associated with larger community variables, such as, racial, ethnic, political, economic and sexual equality.

At least four factors are necessary for the development of such communities. First, the size of the community must be limited. Second, the racial and ethnic composition must be heterogeneous. Third, the population must agree on a common cultural ethos. The manner in which the ethos is expressed, that is, the customs of daily life, would essentially be one of the community's developmental tasks. This would require the fourth factor, a commitment to continuously engage in dialogue. The sustained presence of authentic communication would be the one absolute process factor. All we have to do is be able to talk.

To prevent the dominance of any one methodology, the development of dogma or the myopia that comes from a singular approach, the integration of presently fragmented disciplines, for example, anthropology, sociology, medicine, architecture, psychology, literature and theatre, to name but a few, would likewise be necessary.[4] One way of implementing this type of project would be to get existing grant agencies such as the National Endowment for the Humanities, the National Humanities Center or even the National Institute of Mental Health to sponsor a pilot project.

Although I believe that on a limited scale such psychological ecological communities are possible, on a larger level I remain somewhat skeptical.

The schizoid nature of both individual and community, the incredible disparity of wealth and power, the blatant tendency of established educational and government institutions to remain blind, make authentic change a nearly impossible task. As Kenneth Gergen says, "With the conversion of cultures to hierarchies in which upward scrambling becomes the meaning of life, the planet is being laid waste" (1991, p. 237). As an antidote to the fragmentation of the postmodern Self, Kenneth Gergen offers the following suggestions:

The first is to shift the major focus from "principles to participants." It is traditional in Western culture to respond to conflict by locating an abstract system of justification, rules, principles, or laws that can save us from our differences. . . . By resorting to abstract systems of justice, laws and moral codes, we succeed primarily in lending virtue to our own position, fortifying our sense of righteous purpose, and further denigrating the opposition. Postmodernism urges us to abandon such activities *in favor of direct interchange with the other* [my emphasis].

Second, we should recognize that those we call enemies are enemies only by virtue of our own perspectives; were there no systems of belief, there would be no antagonists. . . . *Instead, forms of dialogue should be encouraged that "free the signifiers"— that break down existing structures of language and enable disparate discourses to commingle* [my emphasis].

Finally, the resolution of existing conflicts must "press beyond dialogue." Attention may usefully shift, then, from the linguistic negotiation of reality *to the coordination of actions in everyday life.* [my emphasis] (1991, pp. 257–258)

This passage echoes my sentiments and is in agreement with the text's position. We must cease litigation and begin listening. Perhaps, most of all, as a people we must stop the fragmentation and begin "living together," recognizing in the ordinary activities of daily life our communal interdependence. As a species, humanity is at a juncture where critical choices must be made. Humanity must, to paraphrase singer/songwriter Roberta Flack, kill itself softly through the song of its new knowledge. Not to do so is surely to invite a less than desirable evolution. If we proceed to fragment, if we allow consciousness itself to continue to become a commodity, if we persist, in "bad faith," to care only about individual functioning, profit and survival, my speculation is that indeed, like the dinosaurs, the human race shall not persevere.

As my ideas were partially inspired by physicists, I will conclude with an appropriate passage from one of my favorites, Werner Heisenberg:

It is only within this spiritual pattern, of the ethos prevailing in the community, that man acquires the points of view whereby he can also shape his own conduct wherever it involves more than a mere reaction to external situations; it is here the question of values is first decided. . . . But the decision upon goals cannot be made within science and technology; it is made, if we are not to go wholly astray, at a point where our vision is directed upon the whole man and the whole of his reality, not merely on a small segment of this. But this total reality contains much of which we have not said anything yet. . . . Theoretical deliberations about questions of psychology or social structure will avail us little here, so long as we do not succeed in finding a way back, by *direct action*, to a natural balance between the spiritual and material conditions of life. It will be a matter of reanimating in daily life the values grounded in the spiritual pattern of the community, of endowing them with such brilliance that the life of the individual is again automatically directed toward them. (1984, pp. 41–43)

NOTES

1. This report employs the term schizoid in terms of conventional psychiatric nomenclature and is not representative of the way the text defines it. See S. DeBerry (1989).

2. The anti-democratic basis of psychotherapy is discussed in J. Hillman (1990), while the postmodern distortion of "individual freedom" is examined in O. Patterson (1991).

3. See DeBerry (1991, p. 27).

4. For excellent research into cultural psychology and the value of cooperative societies see E. E. Sampson (1988) and H. C. Triandis et al. (1988).

Glossary of New and Key Concepts

Awareness—the interaction of a culturally induced, situational context with the supraordinate system of consciousness.

Emergent interactionism—a principle of general systems theory stating that the evolution of dynamic and complex systems can lead to new properties and processes that previously did not exist. These novel "emergents" can interact in complex and unpredictable ways and cannot be explained by what was known about the system prior to their emergence.

Operational empiricism—an experiential, pragmatic approach that utilizes observation to describe the behaviors that promote optimal development of the individual and community. This approach eschews references to transpersonal or quasi-mystical domains and concentrates on improving the quality of life in the here and now. Operational empiricism is an essential procedure of both quantum psychology and self ecology.

Postmodern—a term that originated in architecture to describe new styles, subsequently extending to the arts in general and eventually, ordinary language. The term is inclusive and partially denotes the blending of preexisting qualities with novel elements resulting in new, but vaguely familiar emergents. For example, the recycling of 1960s era music in the 1990s results in a recognizable yet distinctly different style. In terms of quantum psychology, postmodernism also refers to an exponential acceleration in the number and frequency of events and interactions affecting the self system. Quantum psychology is a postmodern psychology.

Quantum buttons—sensitive psychological stimuli, especially of an affective nature, that can trigger the release of previously unavailable or undiscovered processes such as thoughts and behaviors.

Quantum effects—the unexpected interactions and emergents that quantum buttons elicit. Quantum effects are non-linear and non-local and may be imagined as a ripple, or wave-like influence that spreads through consciousness.

Quantum factors—postmodern system emergents that conventional clinical psychology ignores but that need to be incorporated within diagnoses and treatment—for example, the postmodern family, the political/economic system, the capacity for joy.

Quantum psychology—a general systems approach to understanding the self that analyzes the acce rating interactions and emergents of postmodern culture.

Resonance—a rare and wonderful experience, similar to the concept of "peak experience," in which the numerous self systems of one person are in conjunction with the identical systems of another.

Responsivity—a process in which the self system is internally aware of its immediate reaction to an interpersonal interaction. The original reaction is not mediated, but the person chooses whether or not the reaction will be expressed. Responsivity is the polar antithesis of schizoid organization.

Schizoid—a continuum designating a structural organization ranging from fragmented and segregated to undivided and integrated. In terms of mental organization, it is analogous to the dissociative state or multiple personality. The schizoid condition reflects a split both within and external to the self—a person "out of touch" with himself and the world.

Self—a general systems concept that signifies a modular subsystem of consciousness that is usually identified with one's identity as a person. Depending on the degree of schizoid organization, the self system may be composed of other less inclusive self systems.

Self-ecology (numanistic)—a discipline that explores the relationship of the self system to the community and larger cultural system. An ecology of the self emphasizes the identification of cultural factors that either promote or inhibit the optimal development and integration of the self and community.

References

Ahlberg, B. (1991, Nov./Dec.). Why Americans hate to vote. *Utne Reader*, p. 81.

Allport, G. (1955). *Becoming: Basic considerations for a science of personality*. New Haven, CT: Yale University Press.

Anderson, W. T. (1990). *Reality isn't what it used to be*. New York: Harper & Row.

Armand, M. (1990). *The art of sexual ecstasy*. New York: Tarcher Books.

Balint, M. (1968). *The basic fault*. London: Tavistock.

Bateson, G. (1972). *Steps towards an ecology of being*. New York: Ballantine Books.

Becker, E. (1973). *The denial of death*. New York: Free Press.

Becker, G. (1976). *An ecological approach to human behavior*. Chicago: University of Chicago Press.

Bellack, L., & Hurvich, M. (1977). Ego functions and their components. *Psychiatric Annals*, p. 62.

Bellah, R. (1987). *Habits of the heart: individualism and commitment*. New York: Harper & Row.

Bellah, R. (1991). *The good society*. New York: A. Knopf.

Benedict, R. (1938). Anthropology and the abnormal. *Journal of General Psychology*, *10*, 59–79.

Berendt, J. E. (1991, Sept./Oct.) In L. Lamb. Where has all the singing gone? *Utne Reader*, p. 47.

Bergin, A. E. (1991). Values and religious issues in psychotherapy and mental health. *American Psychologist*, *46*, 394–403.

Bevan, W. (1991). Contemporary psychology: A tour inside the onion. *American Psychologist*, *46*, 475–484.

Bohm, D. (1980). *Wholeness and the implicit order*. London: Routledge.

Briggs, J. P., & Peat, F. D. (1984). *Looking glass universe*. New York: Simon & Schuster.

Brown, J. (1991, Nov./Dec.). Greenback politics. *Utne Reader*.

Buber, M. (1970). *I and thou* (W. Kaufman, Trans.). New York: Schribner.

Campbell, J. (1988). *The power of myth*. New York: Doubleday.

Camus, A. (1956). *The fall*. New York: Vintage.

Capra, F. (1977). *The tao of physics*. New York: Bantam Books.

Cheever, J. (1991, August 12). The journals of John Cheever. *The New Yorker*, p. 27.

Chessick, R. (1985). The frantic retreat from mind to brain: American psychiatry in a state of mauvaise foi. *Psychoanalytic Inquiry*, *5*, 369–403.

Chomsky, N. (1988). *The Chomsky reader.* New York: Pantheon.

Churchland, P. M., & Churchland, P. S. (1990) Could machines think? *Scientific American, 262*, pp. 32–40.

Coan, R. (1987). *Human consciousness and its evolution.* New York: Greenwood.

Cousins, N. (1992). *Celebration of life* (rev. ed.). New York: Bantam.

Csikszentmihali, M. (1990). *Flow: The psychology of optimal experience.* New York: Harper & Row.

Cushman, P. (1991). Ideology obscured. *American Psychologist, 46*, 206–219.

Davies, P. (1983). *God and the new physics.* New York: Touchstone Books.

DeBerry, S. (1989). Schizoid phenomena, object–relations and psychobiology. *Contemporary Psychotherapy, 19*, 81–109.

DeBerry, S. (1991). *The externalization of consciousness and the psychopathology of everyday life.* Westport: Greenwood Press.

Dennett, D. C. (1991). *Consciousness explained.* Boston: Little Brown.

De Unamuno, N. (1985). In G. Seldes (Ed.), *The great thoughts* (p. 426). New York: Ballantine Books (Original work published 1913).

Dewey, J. (1991). Lectures on ethics. In D. F. Koch (Ed.). *The Lectures of John Dewey* Urbana, Ill: Southern Illinois University Press.

Dionne, E. J. (1991, Nov./Dec.). Why Americans hate politics. *Utne Reader*, pp. 78–91.

Engels, M. (1984). *The language trap.* Englewood Cliffs, NJ: Prentice-Hall.

Erikson, E. (1963). *Childhood and society* (rev. ed.). New York: Norton.

Fairbairn, W.R.D. (1952). *An object-relations theory of personality.* New York: Basic Books.

Feldstein, L. C. (1978). *Homo quaerens.* New York: Fordham Press.

Festinger, L. (1957). *A theory of cognitive dissonance.* Stanford, CA: Stanford University Press.

Foster, L. (1991, Sept./Oct.). Small talk. *Utne Reader*, p. 122.

Fromm, E. (1990). The nature of consciousness, repression and depression. In J. Pickering & M. Skinner (Eds.), *From sentience to symbols: Readings on consciousness* (pp. 261–266). Toronto: Toronto University Press. (Originally published 1960).

Fromm, E. (1968). *The revolution of hope.* New York: Harper & Row.

Fromm, E. (1976). *To have or be.* New York: Bantam Books.

Gazzaniga, M. (1985). *The social brain.* New York: Basic Books.

Gergen, K. (1973). The social   nstructionist movement in modern psychology. *American Psychologist, 40*, 266–275.

Gergen, K. J. (1991). *The saturated self.* New York: Basic Books.

Gleick, J. (1987). *Chaos: The making of a new science.* New York: Viking Press.

Glendon, M. A. (1989). In B. Moyers (Ed.), *A world of ideas* (pp. 470–483). New York: Doubleday.

Goldstein, K. (1939). *The organism.* New York: American Books.

Gould, S. J. (1989). *Wonderful life.* New York: Norton.

Greenfield, M. (1991, July 7). American values. *Newsweek*, p. 42.

Gregory, R. L. (Ed.). (1987). *The oxford companion to the mind*. New York: Oxford University Press.

Griffin, D. R. (1990). The question of animal awareness. In J. Pickering & M. Skinner (Eds.), *From sentience to symbols: readings on consciousness* (pp. 90–100). Toronto: Toronto University Press. (Original work published 1981).

Guidano, V. (1987). *Complexity of the self*. London: Guilford Press.

Guntript, H. S. (1969). *Schizoid phenomena, object-relations and the self*. New York: International Universities Press.

Guttman, S. (1991, January 21). In P. Taylor, Political correctness, *New York*, pp. 31–38.

Hardison, O. B. (1989). *Disappearing through the skylight: Culture and technology in the twentieth century*. New York: Viking.

Harrington, M. (1989). *Socialism past and future*. New York: Arcade Press.

Heisenberg, W. (1984). Scientific and religious truths. In K. Wilber (Ed.), *Quantum questions* (pp. 33–76). Boston: Shambala Press.

Henwood, D. (1992, Jan./Feb.). A caste of millions. *Utne Reader*, 15–16.

Herbert, N. (1987). *Quantum reality*. New York: Doubleday.

Hillman, J. (1990). *Blue fire*. New York: Harper & Row.

Horney, K. (1973). *The neurotic personality of our time*. New York: Norton.

Howard, G. S. (1991). Culture tales. *American Psychologist, 46*, 197–198.

Huxley, A. (1954). *The doors of perception and heaven and hell*. New York: Harper & Row.

Huxley, J. (1990). Evolution in action. In J. Pickering & M. Skinner (Eds.), *From sentience to symbols: readings on consciousness* (pp. 80–90). Toronto: Toronto University Press (Original work published 1953).

James, W. (1890/1950). *The principles of psychology*. Reprint. Dover, England: Constable Press.

Jameson, F. (1991). *Postmodernism or, the cultural logic of late capitalism*. Durham, NC: Duke University Press.

Jankowitz, A. (1987). Whatever became of George Kelly? *American Psychologist, 42*, 481–488.

Jantsch, E. (1980). *The self organizing universe*. Oxford: Pergamon Press.

Jantsch, E., & Waddington, C. H. (1976). *Evolution and consciousness*. Reading, MA: Addison-Wesley.

Jaynes, J. (1976). *The origins of consciousness in the breakdown of the bicameral mind*. Boston: Houghton-Miflin.

Kaufman, W. (Ed.) (1975). *Existentialism from Dostoevsky to Sartre*. New York: New American Library.

Kelly, G. A. (1955). *The psychology of personal constructs*. New York: Norton.

Knowles, R. T. (1986). *Human development and human possibility*. New York: University Press.

Koestler, A. (1978). *Janus*. London: Hutchinson.

———. (1967). *The act of creation*. New York: Basic Books.

Kuhn, T. S. (1970). *The structure of scientific revolutions*. Chicago: University of Chicago Press.

Laing, R. D. (1965a). *The divided self*. Harmondsworth, England: Penguin.

Laing, R. D. (1965b). *Self and other*. Harmondsworth, England: Penguin.

Laing, R. D., Phillipson, H., & Lee, A. R. (1966). *The interpersonal perception method.* London: Tavistock.

Lakatos, I. (1974). Falsification and the methodology of scientific research programs. In I. Lakatos & A. Musgrave (Eds.), *Criticism and the growth of knowledge* (pp. 62–91). London: Cambridge University Press.

Lapham, L. (1992, January). Who and what is American. *Harpers*, pp. 43–49.

Lappe, F. W. (1989). *Rediscovering America's values.* New York: Ballantine Books.

Lasch, C. (1978). *The culture of narcissism.* New York: Norton.

Lerner, A. W. (1990). *The manipulators.* Hillsdale, NJ: L. Erlbaum.

Lewin, K. (1936). *Principles of topological psychology.* New York: McGraw-Hill.

Locke, A. (1990). Universals in human conception. In J. Pickering & M. Skinner (Eds.), *From sentience to symbols: Readings on consciousness.* Toronto: Toronto University Press. (Originally published 1981).

Lockwood, M. (1989). *Mind brain and the quantum.* Cambridge, MA: Basil Blackwell.

Lutz, W. (1989). *Doublespeak.* New York: Harper & Row.

Mahler, M., Pine, F., & Bergman, A. (1975). *The psychological birth of the human infant.* New York: Basic Books.

Marcuse, H. (1955). *Eros and civilization.* New York: Vintage.

Maruyama, M. (1976). Toward cultural symmetry. In E. Jantsch & C. H. Waddington (Eds.), *Evolution and consciousness* (pp. 131–159). Reading, MA: Addison-Wesley.

Maslow, A. H. (1962). *Toward a psychology of being.* Princeton, NJ: Van Nostrand.

May, R. (1953). *Man's search for himself.* New York: Delta Press.

May, R. (1986). *The discovery of being.* New York: Norton Press.

McLuhan, M. (1964). *Understanding media.* New York: McGraw-Hill.

Mendolsohn, R. (1990). Medicine and healing. In *Meetings with remarkable people.* Brookline, MA: East West Books.

Merton, T. (1972). *New seeds of contemplation.* New York: New Directions.

Miller, A. (1984). *Thou shall not be aware.* New York: New American Library.

Moyers, B. (Ed.). (1989). *A world of ideas.* New York: Doubleday.

Moyers, B. (Ed.). (1990). *A world of ideas.* New York: Doubleday.

Murray, C. (1986). *Losing ground: Americas' social policy 1950–1980.* New York: Basic Books.

Murray, C. (1992, Jan./Feb.). In D. Henwood. A caste of millions. *Utne Reader*, 15–16.

Murphy, G. (1947). *Personality: A biosocial approach.* New York: Harper & Row.

Needleman, J. (1990). In B. Moyers (Ed.), *A world of ideas* (Vol. 2). New York: Doubleday.

Ornstein, R. (1987). *Multi-mind.* New York: Houghton-Miflin.

Ornstein, R., & Erlich, P. (1989). *New world-new mind.* New York: Doubleday.

Pagels, H. (1982). *The cosmic code.* New York: Simon & Schuster.

Pagels, H. (1989). *Dreams of reason.* New York: Bantam Books.

Patterson, O. (1991). *Freedom.* New York: Basic Books.

Penfield, W. (1975). *The mysteries of the mind.* Princeton, NJ: Princeton University Press.

Penrose, R. (1989). *The emperor's new mind.* London: Oxford Press.

Phelps, R. (Ed.). (1965). *Twentieth century culture.* New York: Braziller.

Pickering, J. & Skinner, M. (Eds.) (1990). *From sentience to symbols: readings on consciousness*. Toronto: University of Toronto Press.

Popper, K. R. (1959). *The logic of scientific discovery*. London: Oxford University Press.

Popper, K. R. (1972). *Objective knowledge*. London: Oxford University Press.

Popper, K. R. & Eccles, J. C. (1977). *The self and its brain*. New York: Springer.

Pribram, K. H. (1986). The cognitive revolution and the mind/brain issue. *American Psychologist, 41,* 507–520.

Prigogine, I. (1976). Order through fluctuation. In E. Jantsch & C. H. Waddington (Eds.), *Evolution and consciousness*. Reading, MA: Addison-Wesley.

Prigogine, I. (1980). *From being to becoming*. San Francisco: W. H. Freeman Co.

Reich, R. (1987). *Tales of a new America*. New York: Time Books.

Reich, R. (1991). *The work of nations*. New York: A. Knopf.

Reich, R. (1992, Jan./Feb.) in D. Henwood. A caste of millions. *Utne Reader,* 15–16.

Rilke, R. M. (1975). The notes of Malte Laurids Brigge. In W. Kaufman (Ed.), *Existentialism from Dostoevsky to Sartre* (pp. 5–21). NY: The New America Library.

Sampson, E. E. (1988). The debate on individualism. *American Psychologist, 43,* 23–39.

Sampson, E. E. (1989). The challenge of social change for psychology. *American Psychologist, 44,* 862–878.

Schiff, S. (1990, January). Quantum people. *Vanity Fair,* pp. 40–46.

Schwartz, B. (1990). The creation and destruction of values. *American Psychologist, 45,* 7–16.

Schwartz, J., & McGuinness M. (Eds.) (1979). *Einstein for beginners*. New York: Pantheon.

Sinha, C. (1990). A socio-naturalistic approach to human development. In J. Pickering & M. Skinner (Eds.), *From sentience to symbols: readings on consciousness* (pp. 183–184). Toronto: Toronto University Press. (Originally published 1985).

Skinner, B. F. (1986). What is wrong with daily life in the western world? *American Psychologist, 41,* 568–574.

Smedslund, J. (1985). Necessarily true cultural psychologies. In K. Gergen & K. Davis (Eds.), *The social construction of the person* (pp. 119–145). New York: Springer-Verlag.

Sontag, S. (1990). *Illness as metaphor and AIDS and its metaphors*. New York: Doubleday.

Sperry, R. W. (1987). Consciousness. In R. L. Gregory (Ed.), *The Oxford companion to the mind* (pp. 164–166). New York: Oxford University Press.

Stern, D. (1988). Unformulated experience. *Contemporary Psychoanalysis, 19,* 71–99.

Stokols, D. (1992). Establishing and maintaining healthy environments. *American Psychologist, 47,* 6–22.

Szasz, T. (1987). *Insanity*. New York: John Wiley.

Tart, C. T. (1975). *States of consciousness*. New York: E. P. Dutton.

Taylor, P. (1991, January 21). Political correctness, *New York,* pp. 31–38.

Thurow, L. C. (1980). *The zero-sum society*. New York: Penguin.

Toffler, A. (1980). *The third wave*. New York: William Morrow.

Triandis, H. C., Bontempo, R., Villareal, M. J., Asai, M., & Lucca, N. (1988). Individualism and collectivism: Cross-cultural perspectives on self-ingroup relationships. *Journal of Personality and Social Psychology, 54,* 323–338.

Vega, W. A., & Murphy, J. W. (1990). *Culture and the restructuring of community mental health.* Westport, CT: Greenwood Press.

Waldman, P. (1991, May 6). Watering the grass roots: How to buy a spontaneous popular uprising. *Newsweek,* p. 35.

Watts, A. (1972). *The book on the taboo against knowing who you are.* New York: Vintage.

Weimer, W. B. (1982). Hayek's approach to the problems of complex phenomena. In W. B. Weimer & D. S. Palermo (Eds.), *Cognition and the symbolic process* (Vol. 2, pp. 89–117). Hillsdale, NJ: L. Erlbaum.

West, C. (1990). In B. Moyers (Ed.), *A world of ideas* (pp. 102–107). New York: Doubleday.

Whitehead, A. N. (1990). In J. Pickering & M. Skinner (Eds.), *From sentience to symbols: readings on consciousness* (pp. 46–58). Toronto: Toronto University Press. (Originally published 1925).

Whorf, B. F. (1957). *Language thought and reality.* New York: Wiley.

Wigner, E. P. (1972). The place of consciousness in modern physics. In C. Muses & A. M. Young (Eds.), *Consciousness and reality* (pp. 91–135). New York: Dutton.

Wilbur, K. (1984). *Quantum questions.* Boston: Shambala Press.

Will, G. F. (1991, April 9) Editorial. *Newsweek,* p. 59.

Winnicott, D. W. (1965). *The maturation process and the facilitating environment.* London: Hogarth Press.

Winnicutt, D. W. (1988). *Human nature.* New York: Schocken Books.

Wittgenstein, L. (1990). Philosophic investigations. In J. Pickering & M. Skinner (Eds.), *From sentience to symbols: readings on consciousness* (pp. 256–260). Toronto: Toronto University Press. (Originally published 1958).

Wolfe, A. (1991, November). The way we are now. *Harpers, 283,* pp. 34–44.

Wolfe, F. A. (1984). *Starwave.* New York: Macmillan.

Youngdale, J. M. (1988). *Habits of thought.* Minneapolis, MN: CLIO Books.

Index

About the Author

STEPHEN DEBERRY is the Director of Psychology at Broughton State Hospital in Morganton, North Carolina. He is a Board Certified clinical psychologist, and he maintained a private practice for twelve years in New York State. For thirteen years Dr. DeBerry was an Assistant Clinical Professor of Psychiatry at the Albert Einstein College of Medicine. He has published numerous articles in academic journals pertaining to psychotherapy, community and culture.